IN THE NAME OF ISMAT CHUGHTAI

Studies in Comparative Literature
Jadavpur University

Studies in Comparative Literature, Jadavpur University, is founded on the view that the study of literatures and the arts in multilingual and culturally diverse contexts such as India demands a comparative approach. It is informed by an interdisciplinary and intercultural focus on bhasha literatures, translation, orality and performance as well as other arts and digital humanities, in the context of local, national and international literary and cultural transactions. The series is meant for students, scholars, and teachers of comparative literature as well as of single literature and other humanities departments. It brings together the work of faculty members and scholars at the Department of Comparative Literature, Jadavpur University, as well as of national and international visiting scholars who have enriched its research and debates.

Sub-series I: Texts, Contexts, Methods

Ia. Histories and Paradigms
Ib. Approaching New Challenges, Recasting Paradigms

Sub-series II: Indian and Asian Contexts

Sub-series III: Literature and Other Knowledge Systems

IIIa. Literary Studies and Performance
IIIb. Literature and Indigenous Knowledge Systems

Sub-series IV: Lecture Series

Contributions based on talks by visiting scholars

STUDIES IN COMPARATIVE LITERATURE
JADAVPUR UNIVERSITY

SUB-SERIES II: INDIAN AND ASIAN CONTEXTS

IN THE NAME OF ISMAT CHUGHTAI

THE PROGRESSIVE AND THE PLAYFUL

Edited by

Debashree Dattaray
Epsita Halder

Orient BlackSwan

IN THE NAME OF ISMAT CHUGHTAI: THE PROGRESSIVE AND THE PLAYFUL

ORIENT BLACKSWAN PRIVATE LIMITED

Registered Office
3-6-752 Himayatnagar, Hyderabad 500 029, Telangana, India
E-mail: centraloffice@orientblackswan.com

Other Offices
Bengaluru, Chennai, Guwahati, Hyderabad, Kolkata,
Mumbai, New Delhi, Noida, Patna

First published 2026

ISBN 978-93-6973-159-6

042648

Typeset in Adobe Garamond Pro 10.5/13.2 *by*
Shine Graphics, Delhi 110 094

Printed at
Manipal Technologies Limited., Manipal

Published by
Orient Blackswan Private Limited
3-6-752, Himayatnagar, Hyderabad 500 029, Telangana, India
E-mail: info@orientblackswan.com

Contents

Acknowledgements

The pen is my livelihood and my friend, my confidante, a walking talking friend in my hours of loneliness.

—Ismat Chughtai, *Yahaan se Wahaan Tak*

Working within a culture of confinement in the aftermath of COVID 19, Ismat Chughtai has always been a constant source of inspiration and sustenance. We would first like to acknowledge her sterling presence in our lives with such dexterity and creativity.

We are grateful for help received from the Maulana Abul Kalam Azad Institute of Asian Studies (MAKAIAS), Kolkata, and the Centre for Advanced Study (Phase III), Department of Comparative Literature, Jadavpur University, for the initiation of the project.

We thank colleagues, scholars and students in the Department of Comparative Literature, Jadavpur University for their relentless faith in us in the most difficult of times.

We are indebted to the wonderful professionalism of our former students, Sambhabi Ghosh, Rhitama Basak and Anindita Das in the copyediting process of the manuscript.

Finally, our contributors from across the country have been exemplary in their generosity and patience as we tried to bring the project to fruition. We have been enriched by their scholarship.

In the name of Chughtai, we believe. Now and always.

Debashree Dattaray
Epsita Halder
Kolkata 2026

General Introduction

The first full-fledged department of Comparative Literature in India, and the second in Asia, was established in Calcutta at Jadavpur University in 1956. In the late 1980s, the UGC earmarked the department for promotion of teaching and research under its Special Assistance Programme. In the early nineties, the department widened its areas of interest to first introduce courses in the literatures and cultures of Bangladesh, Africa, Canada and Latin America; then it set up centres for the latter three; subsequently, a Centre for Translation of Indian Literatures, and, most recently, a Centre for Studies in Islamicate Asia. During the Tenth Plan, the department was also selected by the UGC to participate in its Assistance for Strengthening of Infrastructure for Humanities and Social Sciences (ASIHSS) programme. In addition to these UGC programmes and these centres, the University with Potential for Excellence (UPE) programme of the UGC also enabled the establishment of research projects in the department. These included translation and intercultural studies under Project Anuvad; documentation and research relating to performers of traditional dramatic forms in different districts of West Bengal under Project Palagaan; and a unique new venture involving an exploration of Kolkata through narratives of sound under the project Soundscapes. The first—and so far the only—UGC Centre of Advanced Study in Comparative Literature in India was also established in this department in 2005, and it continued promoting research into its third phase. This series, Studies in Comparative Literature, Jadavpur University, is rooted in this academic history of over six decades.

When other departments of Comparative Literature finally began to be established in India in the 1990s, a sharing of our research and pedagogic experience became imperative. It was in response to this need that the idea of initiating a series with a reputed mainstream national publisher came about, and we are especially happy about this partnership with Orient BlackSwan, given the important role it has played in the dissemination of scholarship on Indian literatures and cultures. We hold that the study of literatures and the arts in multilingual and culturally diverse countries such as ours demands a comparative approach; hence, Studies in Comparative Literature, Jadavpur University, is a series for students, scholars and teachers of comparative literature as well as of single literature, arts and other humanities departments. It explores a range of histories, theoretical reflections, as well as innovative approaches and concerns relevant to the field of comparative literature. In keeping with the basic imperatives of comparative literature, it is both intercultural and interdisciplinary in that it engages with the trajectories of literatures across cultures as well as with the relations between literatures and other fields of creative expression. It is thus informed by an interdisciplinary and intercultural focus on bhasha literatures, translation, orality and performance, as well as other arts and digital humanities, in the context of local, national and international literary and cultural transactions, and also those of the borderlands.

This series brings together the work of faculty and scholars at the department of Comparative Literature, Jadavpur University, and of national and international visiting scholars. It comprises both edited volumes and authored books, as well as monographs by visiting scholars. The series launches the research carried out under the third phase of the UGC Centre of Advanced Study in Comparative Literature, and the publication of these volumes, we hope, will mark the beginnings of a renewed mapping of comparative literary studies in India.

This series is the collaborative effort of all the faculty members of the Comparative Literature department: Suchorita Chattopadhyay, Kunal Chattopadhyay, Aveek Majumder, Sujit Kumar Mandal, Parthasarathi Bhaumik, Epsita Halder, and Sumit Kumar Barua. They have been working concertedly towards its publication over the last several years; and while the individual volumes will carry their respective names as authors, editors and co-authors, it needs to be put on record that this series saw the light of day through one of the most devastating pandemics in history only because of their determined collective commitment and mutual intellectual inspiration.

We are particularly indebted to the first series editors, Professor Kavita Panjabi (who retired in 2021 from active teaching), and Professor Samantak Das, who left us too soon, for their leadership and untiring effort to make these publications happen.

We also express our grateful thanks to our research fellows—who will be acknowledged individually in the respective volumes—for their selfless and cheerful support. Last but not least, we extend our deep gratitude to Padmaja Anant of Orient BlackSwan for her wisdom and infinite patience—it has indeed been a pleasure working with her.

Sucheta Bhattacharya
Sayantan Dasgupta
Debashree Dattaray
Series editors

Introduction

On a sultry afternoon, Novera Ahmed, the Dhaka-based avant-garde sculptor–painter arrived in Mumbai to meet her favourite author, Ismat Chughtai. It was just after Chughtai's novel *Ajeeb Aadmi* was published in 1972.

It was a tumultuous era when the subcontinent witnessed the bloody birth of Bangladesh (formerly East Pakistan), freed from the clutches of West Pakistan. At a time of intense linguistic nationalism, and new national boundaries, in Novera's multilingual journey across the divided continent, Ismat Chughtai emerges as the symbol of a literary network in Urdu, both cosmopolitan and radical, spread across regions and borders, and connecting Lahore with Dhaka via Aligarh and Lucknow.

The 1970s mark a crucial timeline for Ismat Apa, as Chughtai was fondly called by her admirers. Her audiences started diversifying. Like Novera Ahmed, scholars from the western world started knocking at the door of Chughtai's Bombay apartment for an exchange of ideas, for conversation. Already a remarkable script writer (she wrote twelve scripts with her husband Shaheed Lateef and another five independently) and a literary icon, many of whose stories were adapted by the critically acclaimed film directors of Bombay (now Mumbai), Chughtai entered western academia as a crucial component of New Literature in Urdu. In a few years her work started to be translated into English. Her supra-regional and trans-border journeys have continued to unfold since then via English translations and in other Indian languages like Bangla. Chughtai becomes vital, almost inevitable, to understand the changing ethos of family and society in this subcontinent in the early twentieth century. In her acute depiction of middle-class, Urdu-speaking households of Uttar Pradesh, she offers a close yet objective perspective of unspeakable truths of families, incurable hearts, secrets that men and women carried within for years to be exposed unanticipated, family mythologies, untimely deaths of dreams and then again possible triumphs. She remains historically important as she offers the intimacy of the *zenana*—the arena of complex everyday performance of women—as part of the history of the nation. Even in 2026, Ismat Chughtai remains as relevant as ever.

Chughtai is believed to have said that the first word uttered by her was 'why'. Her lifelong commitment to freedom in all contexts—personal, sexual, economic and intellectual—her involvement with the Progressive Writers' Movement and rebellion against its perceived orthodoxy and rigidity, her fearless and outspoken projection of experiences hitherto unheard of in the world of Urdu letters are stuff that legends are made of. With an abiding belief in *mazhab-e-insaniyat* (religion of humaneness), Chughtai carves a niche for herself among her illustrious contemporaries—Rajinder Singh Bedi, Sa'adat Hasan Manto and Krishan Chander. In the larger context of South Asian women's writing, Chughtai offers unique insights into the issues of identity, violence, belonging and sexuality in predominantly male literary traditions and initiates conversations on gender, work, the family and the question of women's voice and 'agency'.

If we are to remember two iconic moments in her life that determined and influenced her literary career profusely, we have to go back to Lucknow and Lahore. Chughtai attended the first meeting of the Progressive Writers' Association in Lucknow in 1936 that influenced her understanding of human life and its depiction in prose. The progressive circle of Sa'adat Hasan Manto, Rajinder Singh Bedi, Krishen Chander, Sajjad Zaheer, Rashid Jahan and Ahmed Ali did not prefer formalistic innovation to overpower their objective, linear, realistic portrayal of bare human experiences. They adopted the model of European realism, especially French and Russian, to produce a 'Progressive' aesthetics, uncluttered by emotional excess and a fluid subjective treatment. Chughtai joined the three pillars—of Manto, Bedi and Chander—as the fourth to bolster the glorious architecture of the 'new wave' of Urdu *afsane* (short stories) that had started appearing since the 1930s. Her intellectual companionship with Manto is endearingly and strikingly depicted in Manto's contribution to a series on modern Urdu authors and Chughtai's much discussed piece on Manto, '*Mera Dost, Mera Dushman*' (My Friend, My Enemy). But there are stark dissimilarities between the oeuvres of these two comrades. Beside Manto's cold-blooded description of psychic and corporeal violence during the Partition at the time of India's Independence in 1947, Chughtai's intimate realism renders the insignificant yet familiar familial details significant, peppered with wit and an ambivalent voice of the narrator who enters the household as a member then retreats further away to observe from a distance.

Chughtai was most productive between 1935 and 1955. The other moment came when, just two months before her marriage in 1942, she wrote *Lihaaf* (The Quilt). Its publication in the journal *Adab-i-Latif* unleashed a tremendous uproar, finally culminating in her being summoned to the Lahore Court over charges of obscenity and immorality. As the Lahore Court trial of Chughtai becomes the most referred to legal case on the charge of obscenity in literature in any Indian language, Chughtai is celebrated as a fierce and fearless literary force, a precursor to the feminist struggle in the later decades, unabashed in her dealings of female desire and its untamed expressions.

But Ismat Apa beguilingly and playfully offers in her literary oeuvre more than the essences of the Progressive. Defying any box that tried to comfortably pack her in, she offers in her prose more than one singular form of protest against patriarchy arranging kaleidoscopic layers around human relationships that she saw in the inner courtyard of the Muslim households in north India.

The *zenana*, rather than becoming myopic, as the critics of Chughtai have marked her investment in the inner chambers of the Muslim middle-class households, became a multi-angular space. Chughtai's *zenana* doesn't become a confined, private compartment for the presence and in fact is the setting for the in and out flow of close male relatives, attendants, cooks and service women from other classes and religion. Though the primary arena of performance is the inner familial space, Chughtai follows her female protagonists as they go outside of the household too. The middle-class household, oscillating between the sacred Qur'anic chants and the cacophony of the everyday, between faith and newfound joys of transgression, showcases a very unique picture of the generational mobility that tells the story of the nation from the inner courtyards. A narrative that has never found a place in the big histories of the nation, now exposes the small histories of everyday speech and insignificant domestic action. In her oscillating moves, Chughtai also changes her position from being an insider to an outsider and vice-versa, investing to read things around her both sympathetically and critically. These mortal, insignificant female characters, in Chughtai's renditions, become artifacts of history.

This history is intimate for the chronicler's close proximity with her people. She takes no time to turn brutal to depict exactly what she sees. What she sees is far from ideal. That's why Chughtai looks unafraid and unabashed as a storyteller. The scorpion aunties, widows still blossoming like a *gainda* (marigold), a woman amidst the flowering *champaka* trees posing like Radha, grannies reciting from the Qur'an, mothers buying embroidered cushions from the fair of the Ghazi, the abandoned widows, flocks of children fearing the creatures of the dark and telling the readers their versions of things around them, service men and women coming in and going out, all populate Chughtai's *zenana mehfil* (venue for indoor recreational activities for women), punctuated occasionally by the presence of the male figures in authority. The male figures do not always remain in authority as their hearts melt in love for inappropriate women. There are women who fail to empathise with their lot as they ruthlessly or insensitively corner other women more vulnerable than them. Chughtai brings out a far more complex scenario of freedom contrary to what she stands for in popular criticism, and shows emotional treachery, psychic conflict in the utterly mundane, the everyday, where defiance may not always find voice to claim freedom. Perhaps dissent and defiance have not been realised by these women as their path to freedom. Chughtai remains witness to these women's subjugation and incapacity to understand possibilities that life offers. Then she maps the terrain of transgression as someone's abandoned wife elopes with a distant relative. Their escap(ad)e is turned into a mythological tell to nullify its transgressive charge. Chughtai doesn't care to explain.

And therein lies her masterstroke. Chughtai has an apparent neutrality in her voice, when it's an anonymous first- or third-person narrator. If she is a child protagonist—a recurrent feature in Chughtai's stories—it's a half-veiled truth as she doesn't grasp what's happening in the adult world. Gaps and cracks appear between the reader and the narrative. Thus, as a Progressive, very playfully Chughtai takes her readers on a journey which cannot be completely subsumed in a Progressive framework. She seldom places the working class at the centre of her tales. She only brings multitude in the way we should understand the Progressive, as a creative-political literary tool. The Progressive in the Indian regional context now becomes multiple in its implementation, textured with gradations and variations; Chughtai remains one such distinct texture in the fabric.

The essays in this volume revisit the 'Indian' author whose view of life, sense of history and progress, ideas on social justice, religious tolerance, paradigms of human relationship and power structures have undergone continuous transformations since the twentieth century till the present day. The 'author' Chughtai finds herself caught in the crosshairs of political tensions and social upheavals, and engages in debates between literary styles and diction, possibilities of new forms of expressions, narrative structures, diverse registers of different language systems, dramatic modes and performative gestures. How the works of Chughtai have adhered to or resisted systems that belong spatially, historically, or culturally to defined categories, and have consequently led to the transmutation of 'traditional' approaches and formations of stylistic invocations within the Indian subcontinent is a journey of discovery for every reader.

In 'The Unyielding Yen: Chughtai, Kaushal, Sehgal, and All that which Drove Indian Cinema of 1940s–50s' **Madhuja Mukherjee** places Chughtai as a part of the Left imagination within the larger context of the Bombay film industry. She critically locates the cultural and political negotiations of the 'Progressives' with the mainstream forces by engaging with the vibrant presence of Chughtai, actresses Kamini Kaushal and Zohra Sehgal in the films Chughtai was directly associated with—either as the author of the story that the film was adapted from (*Ziddi*, 1948), or as scriptwriter (*Arzoo*, 1950)—and also in the context of the industry she worked in. With a reading of films related to Chughtai and the reflections of her times, Mukherjee explores in her essay the polemic in the film industry where the 'Liberal worldview to radical Left ideologies' together with non-leftist views produced a trope where class and woman's issues, including their everyday experiences, conflicts, bodily sufferings and sexuality, get articulated.

Manas Ghosh, in 'In Search of No Man's Land: Chughtai, Manto and Ghatak', an analysis of Chughtai's story '*Jadein*' (Roots, 1952), Sa'adat Hasan Manto's story '*Toba Tek Singh*' (1955) and Ritwik Ghatak's film *Subarnarekha* (The Golden Line, 1962)—arguably three of the most powerful cultural pieces to reflect the magnitude of the post-Partition trauma—discusses how the Progressive orientation of the authors added to the understanding of decolonisation in the subcontinent. Ghosh focuses on the authors' nuanced reading of the experience of Partition not merely as a tragic incident but as an epic failure of the ruling class of the subcontinent in terms of decolonisation. Ghosh locates a *third* space as a critique of the stable idea of national borders which, he avers, is the main trope in the works of Chughtai, Manto and Ghatak. However, he also differentiates between the terse realism of Chughtai and Manto and the melodramatic mode of Ghatak's representation.

Fatima Rizvi and **Kakul Hai**, in their essay, 'Casements of Selfhood: *Khakas* (Pen-portraits) by/of Ismat Chughtai', bring in a psychoanalytic approach to explore Chughtai's persona, her art and interpersonal relationships as they unfolded in her own writings and in the testimonials of her compatriots. What Chughtai, the individual author, chooses in her pen-portraits to disclose about herself and her objects and what her contemporaries like Patras Bokhari ('*Kuch Meri Yādein*'), Qurratulain Hyder ('*Pompom Darling*'), and Sa'adat Hasan Manto ('*Merā Dost, Merā Dushman*') observe in her persona and her writings disclose the nuanced relationship between selfhood and representation. The personal narratives become a history of the times and literary criticism. The authors situate the whole discourse in the context of the generic possibilities of the *khaka* as a prose genre that emerged during the progressive era of Urdu literature to hold the relationship between the author's conscious and unconscious awareness.

Kiran Keshavamurthy explores how in Chughtai's writings the spatial demarcation between the private and the public temporarily breaks down with the overlap of the erotic and the social in his essay 'Between the Erotic and the Social in Ismat Chughtai's Short Stories'. Chughtai marks the potential threat caused by the transgression of sexual norms through the articulation of love/desire across caste and other social hierarchies. The author shows how the attempts to retain sexual norms and social positions within the household are made at the cost of women, leaving them in a disadvantageous position. Chughtai turns the male authorities into satirical figures in the process.

Kunal Chattopadhyay in 'Socialist Realism and the Progressive Movement in Urdu Literature' draws attention to Chughtai's independence of thought through a discussion on literary politics in India. By drawing parallels between the history of Socialist Realism and the Progressive Movement in Urdu literature, Chattopadhyay highlights the role of Chughtai in the latter with her ability to offer sensitive social realism that was thriving in a plurality of ideas and persistent critical thinking.

In her essay titled 'The Fabric of the Story: Chughtai's Craft,' **Sucheta Bhattacharya** extends the discussion by focusing on the crafts(wo)manship, the actual building of the stories that Chughtai creates. Drawing succinct parallels with the works of Manto, Bhattacharya explores the unique voice of Chughtai in a world dominated by male writers, particularly in terms of keen articulation of plot and use of metaphors of clothes in her oeuvre.

Indeed, the mid-twentieth century in India has been informed by the felicity of diverse *bhasa–sahityas* and **Urmi Sengupta's** essay, 'A Changing Mind, a Changing Body: Understanding the Journey into Female Adolescence through *Terhi Lakeer* and *Lal Tin Ki Chhat*' provides a comparative reading between Chughtai's *Tehri Lakeer* and Nirmal Verma's *Laal Tin ki Chhat*. The paper interrogates the thematic and formal representation of the social, cultural and psychosexual determinants that shape the awakening and expression of female sexuality in the two works, which in turn are determined by the ethos of the Progressive and *Nayi Kahani* movements.

The chronotope in the literary traditions of pre-Independence India may also be determined through the category of 'censorship'. **Debjani Chakrabarty** in 'Codes of Censorship in Pre-Independence India: An Analysis of Chughtai and the Progressives' extends the definitions of censorship to emphasise that even though legal actions are the most common tools of censorship, they are but the external manifestation of a hidden yet dynamic and systemic network of multiple forms of deeply entrenched repression. In the historical context of pre-Independence India and the rise of the Progressive Writers' Association, the essay asks whether there can be a productive consequence of an essentially restrictive process such as censorship.

Much of Chughtai's writings also necessitate an understanding of women's life writing which is initiated by **Krishnendu Pal** in 'The Possibilities of a Genre: Reading the Life Writings of Ismat Chughtai and Amrita Pritam', the final essay in this volume. Through a reading of Chughtai's memoir *Kaghazi-Hai Pairahan* (A Life in Words, 1980) along with the autobiographical work of one of her renowned contemporaries—*Raseedi Ticket* (Revenue Stamp/RT, 1977) by Amrita Pritam (1919–2005), Pal seeks to understand how the generic understandings, theoretical premises and limitations concerning autobiographical/life writings emerge in their works. Pal explores the resilient possibilities of the genre of women's life writing in late-twentieth century South Asia through an understanding of different theoretical and literary positions that have dealt with the idea of life writing, women's life writing and women's life circumstances that enable life writing.

Focusing on the pan-Indian literary dialogue initiated by the Progressive Writers' Association, the essays, in their rich interdisciplinarity, thus engage in discussions on the alternative sensibilities of 'national' belonging which emerged from the experimental and iconic works of the PWA. The anthology seeks to interrogate the spatial, temporal, affective, embodied, performative and literary imagination and memory every time one reads, teaches, performs, sees, feels and thinks of Chughtai's oeuvre. The volume explores the ways in which transformed realities have baffled human convictions and mobilised an alternative understanding of the objects of struggle, transgression, and anxiety.

Debashree Dattaray
Epsita Halder
Kolkata 2026

1

The Unyielding Yen

Chughtai, Kaushal, Sehgal, and All that which Drove Indian Cinema of 1940s–50s

MADHUJA MUKHERJEE

There are two points of entry to this paper, and one simple conjecture. First, I address the forceful presence of the 'Progressives' in Bombay (/Mumbai), especially during 1940s and 1950s, and deliberate on the ways in which their creative interventions produced a notable dent in the narratives of popular Hindi films. However, I am particularly concerned about the larger field and the links, which they produced with the mainstream, and eventually, involved influential directors/producers like Chetan Anand, Raj Kapoor and Guru Dutt. In this connection I examine the setting—or the spatial significance of Bombay—which became a pivotal site for cultural and political negotiations, as well as the Left imagination that made such transactions possible. Secondly, I reflect upon the vibrant presence of three women—Ismat Chughtai, Kamini Kaushal, and Zohra Sehgal—whose dynamic association with mainstream Hindi cinema crafted a specific status for vivacious women characters and highlighted subjects of the desirous body, sexuality, pain, and endurance. I specifically focus on *Ziddi* (1948), an adaption of Chughtai's story of the same name, and *Arzoo* (1950), for which Chughtai wrote the screenplay and dialogue, both directed by her husband Shaheed Latif, a filmmaker in his own right.[1] I will use my personal conversations (on 16 November 2016) with the exceptionally spirited ninety-year-old Kamini Kaushal, the female lead of the Latif-Chughtai films, to understand the course of such artistic drives. And, the 'simple conjecture' is, as and when we unravel the textures of the filmic story, that the *process* itself makes visible the manner in which more than one 'author' fabricates a certain kind of cinema. I hence, argue for 'multiple-authorship' vis-à-vis the films analysed below.

The Progressives Land in Bombay

By the 1930s Bombay became a vibrant place for artistic interactions. There were a number of groups and associations such as the Progressive Writers Association (PWA, 1936), Indian People's Theatre Association (IPTA, 1944) and Progressive Artists Group (PAG, 1947), which made Bombay their primary location for political-cultural movements. Furthermore, in 1943 the headquarters of the Communist Party of India (CPI) was moved from Lucknow to Bombay.[2] Thus, one may contend that there was an animated presence of a number of influential figures in Bombay, who eventually contributed to the motivating cultural strife and shaped a range of landmark texts during the period. There were for instance, remarkable writers like Sa'adat Hasan Manto, who arrived in Bombay during 1936, worked in the film industry (primarily with Filmistan studios) and became involved with the making (or writing) of eight or more films.[3] Manto's stories about the film industry in Bombay remain one of the most valuable and caustic comments on the social rubric of film production.[4] In addition, there were other Left writers, namely Krishan Chander, Ali Sardar Jafri, along with performers like Balraj Sahni and Zohra Sehgal, and poets like Sahir Ludhianvi, Majrooh Sultanpuri, Prem Dhawan, Shailendra, Kaifi Azmi, and others, who gradually drifted toward popular cinema. M. F. Hussain, who was associated with the PAG, reportedly painted posters for popular films during the early phase of his career. In point of fact, IPTA had a broad base and a number of artists—eminent musician Ravi Shankar and singer-composer Hemant Mukhopadhyay (nee Kumar) along with Raj Kapoor and director/producer Mehboob Khan—were active members of the group and the movement.

Other than that, there was of course, the incomparable and zestful author, Ismat Chughtai. Kamini Kaushal talking about her director Shaheed Latif, for example, says 'I think his wife [Chughtai] was a bigger contributor. [...] I mean he was good, he was okay; he executed her concepts very well. But she was the one; she was the thinker behind him. It's a fact. There was a warmth about her writing.'[5] And, how do you remember her? I asked. 'Smiling, always smiling,' Kaushal added. Later, Kaushal insisted that, 'she is a very, very lovable person. Very friendly and very warm.' Indeed, Kaushal's association with Chughtai and her films, as well as her memory of the times, highlight a particular kind of camaraderie that was perhaps infectious. Truly, mainstream Hindi cinema of that moment involved many well-known artists and authors, whose ideological standpoints ranged from the liberal worldview to radical Left ideologies. Together they produced a trope that emphasised class and the woman's question. Though, as analysed later, with Chughtai's films the subject of a woman's everyday conflicts, the 'unyielding yen', her bodily suffering and sexuality become apparent with great fervour and spontaneity.

Bombay's urban map and its massive expansion through the last century has been discussed by historians, just as the quick economic development during this time as well as growth of small-scale industries in the suburbs, which caused mass migration towards the city, have been examined in length.[6] In relation to this, it may be stated that, by the 1940s—considering the political unrest in Lahore and Calcutta—Bombay became, figuratively speaking, a place to arrive at.[7] In time, artists, writers, filmmakers, music composers, singers, et al, headed for the city, and in due course generated a formidable environment as well as spaces of artistic dialogue. Gyan Prakash in his book *Mumbai Fables* writes that 'Manto and Chugtai were not the only ones inhabiting and exploring Bombay's modern life. [...] Intellectuals and artists were drawn to Bombay's pulsating modernity, but they also viewed it as deeply contradictory. If the city's promise of progress and freedom attracted them, they were repelled by its depredations and injustices' (2010, 128).

While the city emerged as a picture-perfect place for the *flaneur*, the film industry became a place towards which many artists wandered; cinema became a decisive medium for mass mobilisation as well as a mode through which the darkness of the times could be effectively articulated.[8] By drawing inspiration from French and Spanish Popular Front cinema, IPTA as a matter of fact, stated a pronounced agenda vis-à-vis cinema. IPTA, as specified by Sudhi Pradhan, proposed a movement through 'film shows of progressive films depicting the life of the people like "Grapes of Wrath" [John ford, 1940] or by producing films in consonance with the ideals of the People's theatre' (1979, 248).

However, it must be noted that by the late 1930s, the studios in Bombay, Calcutta and elsewhere, had more or less consolidated their production-distribution-exhibition systems across provinces and had, broadly speaking, amalgamated a specific narrative mode, which has been described as studio 'Socials'. The 'Socials', according to Ravi Vasudevan, dealt with themes of social reform. Broadly, the Social did not always consider social ills; rather, set in the contemporary times, the genre generated social images that delineated ethical problems of 'identity, equality, honesty'. Bombay Talkies (established in 1934), which was one of the most respectable production houses of the epoch (partly because of the reputation its proprietors, Himanshu Rai and Devika Rani, and partly due to the popular social reform films they produced, which were propagated by *Film India* magazine), housed quite a few major directors and writers.[9] Indeed, some of the renowned directors of New Theatres (established in Calcutta in 1931) such as Nitin Bose and Bimal Roy shifted to Bombay in the mid–1940s and started working with Bombay Talkies, as the studio structures (specifically in Calcutta) disintegrated amid the Second World War and riots.[10] Bose later joined Filmistan (established in 1943), which was set up by the well-known actor Ashok Kumar and Bombay Talkies' associate Sashadhar Mukherjee. Furthermore, by this time, one of the most celebrated directors of Indian cinema, Mehboob Khan, had started Mehboob Productions (in 1945), which was preceded by the successes of his social–realist films *Aurat* (1940) and *Roti* (1943). Briefly, the life of the poor, conflicts between tradition and modernity, individual suffering, grief, redemption and social reform were widely accepted themes. Nevertheless, the direct involvement of the Left brigade in film production shifted the focus to specific issues of class, nation, social hierarchies and means of production, and more importantly perhaps, transformed existing narrative styles by bestowing a new direction and flair. *Dharti ke lal* (Dir. K.A. Abbas, 1946), produced by the IPTA collective, for example, is regarded a cinematic milestone, especially because of its mode of narration, staging of situations, mise-en-scene, and performances. While the film did not do well at the box-office and was criticised by *Film India*—a proto-nationalist magazine—nonetheless, both the city and the film industry offered the writers, artists and activists, from the Left, exceptional opportunities and good earnings, which prompted them to explore radical worldviews and reinvent international forms in Indian political contexts. In the process, IPTA and PWA became important constituents of the Bombay film industry.

Just as the Left emerged as a mediator in the movie business through varied ways, one of pioneering the films that emerged out of such intense engagements was Chetan Anand's internationally acclaimed film *Neecha Nagar* (1946). While Chetan Anand was associated with IPTA and his house became a centre for lively deliberations, in actuality, Anand wasn't a communist; however, both the theme and formal experiments of *Neecha Nagar* underline the ways in which filmmakers of the period were speaking to world cinemas. *Neecha Nagar* was loosely adapted from Maxim Gorky's *Lower Depths* (1902), and depicted with great intensity the physical misery of the people living in the slums or ghettos. Kamini Kaushal, who had her debut with *Neecha Nagar*, said,

> *Necha Nagar* was quite literarily thrown into my lap. Chetan [Anand] knew my brother. I use to do a lot of plays [in Lahore]; he knew that. We had our dramatic society. He said "why don't you work in my film?" I said "it's not nice to work in films".... My brother said, "Why don't you work in Chetan's film?" He [Anand] was trying to do something definite, not something vague... He was very motivated, and well read... There is a very dramatic scene in which I am taken to the hospital and I don't want to go. It was very, very dramatic. And, I did the scene... Having done so much radio, you knew how to control your voice... We were all theatre people, not film guys. We were very raw. It came easy... Only I didn't like the smell of makeup... We used to have our rehearsals at Chetan's house in Bandra. I would take the train from my home by myself. (Kaushal, conversation with the author)

Such mode of functioning and the itineraries of actors like Kaushal (or Shaukat Azmi and Zohra Sehgal) were in fact, remarkably different from the descriptions of the film industry in Manto's writings and as is evident from the biographies of the illustrious stars of the period. For instance, Nargis, famous for her role in *Mother India* (Dir. Mehboob Khan, 1957), was the daughter of Jaddan Bai, who was effectively the first 'female' producer of the film industry. Similarly, Meena Kumari, remembered for her performance in *Pakeezah* (Dir. Kamal Amrohi, 1972) was the daughter of Ali Bux, an actor and music composer from the early 'Talkie' period. Contrarily, Madhubala's (recognised for her delicate acting in *Mughal-e-Azam* [Dir. K Asif, 1960]) family were immigrants and cinema, in the long run, became a source of sustenance for them.

The 'Progressives' and their associates were, however, following a different course, both in terms of their backgrounds, training, as well as through their cinematic experiments. Clearly, the film industry became a pulsating melting pot, which involved émigrés, performers from disparate fields, writers, musicians, singers, theatre activists, technicians, university graduates and everyone else who appeared on the scene.

Kamini Kaushal, for example, spoke at length about her life in Lahore, her college days, and how she came from a 'very progressive family'. 'My father [a renowned Botanist], what he stood for was really very special... We were a very open household. Unfortunately, I lost my dad early; it was my brother who brought us up' (Kaushal, conversation with the author). Likewise, Zohra Sehgal was born in a traditional family in Uttar Pradesh and was educated in Lahore. Sehgal was one of the leaders of the Cultural Squad of the Communist Party of India, who not only performed in IPTA's *Dharti Ke Lal* but also acted in *Neecha Nagar*. In the interim, Sehgal was engaged as teacher at the Uday Shankar 'India Cultural Centre' near Almora and had also performed in Shankar's outstanding modernist film *Kalpana* (1948). Uday Shankar famously designed his dance movements and gestures (especially hand movements) by referring to everyday actions, and also by reinventing the 'rhythmic' physical movements of labourers at work. His style of choreography, as evident in *Kalpana*, was a crucial departure from the classical dance films framed by ritualistic *mudras*.[11] Additionally, Guru Dutt (not a celebrated director at that time) was Sehgal's student at Uday Shankar's centre. Therefore, when Navketan (of Anand Brothers) produced *Baazi* (Dir. Guru Dutt, 1951) etc., Sehgal choreographed some of the dance sequences and introduced to Hindi cinema a specific type of performance style that was unique and recognisable.[12] Thus, one may propose that, through such intense linkages with IPTA's formal experiments, Hindi cinema discovered certain radical modes of expression. In point of fact, the Left revolutionary spirit infused a specific kind dynamism into Hindi films, which, in due course, became a telling feature of the moment.

A similar argument may be forged regarding the remarkable writer Sahir Ludhianvi and his involvement with Guru Dutt's films. After his expulsion from the Government College, Ludhiana, in 1943, 'Ludhianvi' shifted to Lahore and began to write purposefully. Thereafter, he became a member of the PWA, and quickly earned the respect of the readers and resentment of the Government of Pakistan following the publication of his idealist writings in *Savera*, a journal. The rift compelled him to immigrate to India in 1949. Then again, his leftist ideology along with his personal anguish produced many of the lyrics, which featured in popular films. For instance, his famous lyrics—'*Zara is mulk ke rahbaro ko bulao/ Ye kuche, ye galiyan, ye mazar dikhao/Jinhe naaz hai hind par unko lao/ Jinhe naaz hai hind par woh kahan hai*' (from *Pyaasa* Dir. Guru Dutt, 1957)—come at the point when Vijay, the protagonist, loses his mother, and thereafter visits a brothel and encounters a courtesan whose child is wailing in the background. Following such fateful happenstances, Vijay (a failed poet, a lover, and a *flaneur* of sorts) rushes out on the streets and sings the song like a lament, mourning the death of this 'mother'(land). The contemptuous words (which were censored), however, not only reflect personal distress, they accentuate the political, the failure of the nation-state as the character/actor/director/author summon the patriot to visit the underbelly of the city. Besides, these lines fabricate a flow of thoughts, which work via multiple registers and films. Therefore, while Gyan Prakash with reference to another legendary song, '*Mera juta hai Japani* (that's harps on inter-nationalism, written by yet another leftist author Shailendra, for the film *Shree 420* [Dir. Raj Kapoor, 1955]), emphasises upon the 'cosmopolitanism' in Hindi films, one may propose that Ludhianvi's song or mourning, '*Chin-o-arab hamara/hindustan hamara/rehne ko ghar nahi hai/saara jahan hamara*' (from the film *Phir Subah Hogi*, Dir. Ramesh Saigal, 1958), is a riposte of sorts. Thus, if Guru Dutt and Raj Kapoor (according to Vasudevan, 1989) were considering 'renunciation' and 'conflict' vis-à-vis the newly formed nation-state by means of films like *Pyaasa* and *Awaara*, then Ludhianvi's derisive lyrics and his authorial contributions, which resound through multiple films, question the very premise and promise of Indian democracy.

In a way, *Mother India* and *Pyaasa*, both produced in 1957, present two incongruent models of Indian cinema, and its many contestations. Indeed, interactions with the Left introduced a rebellious spirit, international styles, and brought forth the question of class mobilisation in films produced by directors, who were in no way active members of the CPI. Contrarily, a comparative study especially with regard to the oeuvre of the pioneering Bengali author Bijon Bhattacharya informs us that Bhattacharya not only co-wrote *Dharti Ke Lal* (which also drew from Krishan Chander's *Annadata*), and had penned the ground-breaking Bengali film *Chhinnamul*

(Dir. Nemai Ghosh, 1950), he was also involved with popular Bengali films like *Sharey Chuattor* (Dir. Nirmal Dey, 1953), and thereby wrestled with and contributed to mainstream cinemas.[13] The wave of radicalism, nonetheless, subsided in the 1960s, especially in the context of the larger national and political crisis, and the divide within the Communist Party; furthermore, the film industry also consolidated around a new type of social melodrama (described as 'feudal family romances' by Madhava Prasad), and witnessed the emergence of big stars and the blockbuster model. As a matter of fact, Bimal Roy, who became IPTA president in 1953, gradually drifted towards nationalist narratives (*Sujata* 1959, *Parakh* 1960), and made films about social development; just as Abbas, the director of *Dharti ke Lal*, as well as of the Indo-Soviet Production *Pardesi* (1957), was later involved with a range of popular films made by Raj Kapoor.

Kamini Kaushal in *Shair* (Dir. Chawla, 1949)

Shair featured on the cover of the famous film magazine *FilmIndia*

All Those Elements that Dissolved into Cinema

In her (quasi) biography *Kaghazi Hai Pairahan* Ismat Chughtai (translation M. Asaduddin) mentions how her life was 'comfortable—income from my career in films was substantial', and that she 'didn't care much about literary death or life' (2012, 40) despite the infamous court-case following the publication of her most famous story *Lihaaf*. In fact, a number of Left-wing 'female' actors and writers (including Saukat Azmi) joined the film industry via radio, and many of them worked in the industry for sustenance. Acting or writing in many instances was a 'job'. While I have discussed the question of gender, work and desire elsewhere, in this paper I wish to deliberate on the ways in which Chughtai's writings for films may also be read as an 'interpolation'.[14] Before her story was adapted into film in 1948 by her husband and filmmaker Shaheed Latif, Chughtai had already borne the court-case vis-à-vis *Lihaaf* (during 1944–46). The comical descriptions of the courtroom situations in Lahore are crucial for us to understand what Chughtai stood for. For instance, she writes,

> The witnesses who had turned up to prove *Lihaaf* obscene were thrown into confusion by my lawyer. They were not able to put their finger on any word in the story that would prove their point. After a good deal of reflection, one of them said: 'This phrase "... collecting lovers" is obscene.'
>
> 'Which word is obscene? —"collect" or "lover"?' the lawyer asked. (2012, 36)

In the same section Chughtai describes her excitement about travelling to Lahore, and how she and Manto (along with Latif) had gone there for their respective cases. 'Lahore was beautiful, lush and lively,' she writes. 'It greeted everyone with open arms. It was a city of people who were amiable and loved life. It was the heart of Punjab.' 'We wandered about the streets of Lahore ...' (ibid., 27). Lahore, where many of the Left authors were educated (though Chughtai herself studied and married in Aligarh), and its progressive milieu are significant in this regard.[15] For instance, when I conversed with Kaushal, who graduated from Kinnaird College for Women University, Lahore, regarding her college life, she said,

> We used to cycle around. But I grew up much later ... I was interested in doing things. Like whether it is drawing or painting or elocution or making films ... we were given complete freedom in our home. That was the most important element I think I imbibed... That was the norm in our home... Let them explore the world, let them discover. My brother would take us with him everywhere. Us, three sisters... I learnt Kathak and Bharat Natyam in Lahore, before Partition.... There were no restrictions as such. I went cycling, I went swimming, I played all the games. But it was not anything that I was doing anything extra special... I did all this without self-consciousness...
>
> And, "boyfriends"? I asked cautiously.
>
> I did not have boyfriends. Right next to us was the FC College (Forman Christian College), I could have *picked up* (italics added) so many. So one day, one did ask me, 'May I cycle down with you?' I said, 'Well the road belongs to you as much it belongs to me'. [Laughs loudly...] I had so many interests that the romantic interest lit up in my life a little late... I was intriguingly preoccupied with so many things. (Kaushal, conversation with the author)

While speaking to Kaushal I was reminded of Chughtai's court case and the debates on the expression 'collect lovers', which in my understanding is described spontaneously by Kaushal as 'picking up boys'. But what is perhaps more critical, is the straightforwardness of their manner of speaking/writing, and the joy they experienced in exploring the world and the process, which to reiterate Kaushal's words, wasn't 'anything extra special', but a 'norm'. Zohra Sehgal for example, travelled to Europe in a car (convertible Dodge) with her Uncle 'Memphis' (maternal Uncle, S. S. Khan) and others, in 1930.[16] As described by Kiran Sehgal, Zohra wore jodhpuris, a cotton top and a Kashmiri jacket. They journeyed from Dehradun to Lahore, and to Multan and Ziarat; from there on they toured to Quetta and Baluchistan, and to Meshad in Iran. Afterwards, they travelled to Tehran, Isfahan and Shiraz. From Shiraz they went to Basra, and to Beirut; thereafter, from Beirut they visited Balbek, Damascus, Jerusalem, and Egypt. Finally, they took a boat down the river Nile, and in due course via some detour reached Dresden. In addition, as described by Kiran Sehgal, after they landed in Ziarat the following incident took place at the house of Sherbat Khan, a political agent of British Government: '[t]he first thing that caught their eye was a table lined with all the sherbets that one could think of! Ammi [Zohra] could not stop giggling and her uncle had a hard time trying to control his laughter. The compensation was Sherbat Khan's very handsome son on whom Ammi developed an immediate crush!' (2012, 55).

The humour, even impishness, and the scathing critique of social life is truly a customary style of Chughtai, Kaushal and Sehgal's narratives. And then, to borrow from Chughtai, 'Lahore! How beautiful the word sounds!'(2012, 27). Truly, the import of places and spaces like Lahore is as imperative as the times they lived in.

It must be, however, noted that amongst these three, Chughtai was a writer, that too a celebrated one. I nevertheless, argue that if Chughtai was the voice of the 'woman's question', then Kaushal rendered a physical form to it and through the specific bodily gestures, she performed the 'unyielding yen' of women. While the Progressive Writers' group delved into the style of the nineteenth-century French and Russian realist writings, it is widely known that by taking up Rashid Jahan's mantle, Chughtai evocatively portrayed the conditions and aspirations of women of middle-class families of Uttar Pradesh. Chughtai is distinguishable for her wit, liveliness, and a language that is characteristic of Begmati Urdu (or idiom of places in which her stories are set). Her cutting-edge ironic tone, playful treatment of themes, descriptions of the passage of time, stories of longing and agony, and detailing of situational 'sound', all present distinctive places, which are locked in a distinctive historical circumstance. Tahira Naqvi in her tribute to Chughtai writes,

> Many of Ismat's critics, past and present, lament her single-minded preoccupation with women's lives, with a middle-class society and its concerns, what they deem to be her myopic view of the world.... And thank God for that! How else could we have had stories like "Chauthi Ka Jora," "Badan Ki Khushboo" and "Do Haath" (to name just a few), and longer works like "Ziddi", "Dil Ki Duniya", and "Terhi Lakir"?[17] (1993, 28)

The cinematic adaptation of a story like '*Ziddi*' (Unyielding) belonged to the all-encompassing Studio Social, albeit with variations. The film, narrates the story of two headstrong lovers, Puran (Dev Anand) and Asha (Kamini Kaushal). Puran's uncle has an unfinished affair with Asha's mother and in his present physically challenged state (caused by age and grief), he relentlessly mourns the loss of his love. The problem of class is key to the story; moreover, the plot line is cyclic. After, Asha (now a 'poor orphan') is brought to Puran's respectable household she is immediately drawn towards the young and dashing man (who rides a horse and sports a gun), and they meet in a clandestine manner. While Puran promises marriage to Asha and they elope to escape the wrath of his elder brother, a chase between the horse-drawn carriage and motorcar ends in an accident, in which Asha falls off the bridge and is apparently drowned. Puran is haunted by her memory and almost loses his mind. However, he soon agrees to marry someone his family chooses. Meanwhile, Asha has been rescued and lives in the house of Shanta, with whom Puran's marriage has been fixed.

Puran's marriage scene is pivotal in this context, especially because of the ways in which the film stages longing and despair of *three* women. First, of course, there is Asha, who secretly watches Puran being married off to Shanta, but then, Shanta weeps too as she realizes that Puran's heart is attached to someone else. The third woman is Chhutki, Puran's housemaid, who has harboured a deep affection for him, for a long time. Chhutki is also a dancer, and thus, performs during the marriage. When asked '*Tu nahi nachegi aaj*?' (will you not dance today?), Chhutki replies, '*Aaj nahin naachungi, to kab naachungi*?' (if not today then, when will I dance). And, as the performance begins Chhutki sets her 'dupatta' (long scarf) on fire, which eventually burns down the whole marquee. The scene mobilises subjects of class, gender and incredible yearnings of the woman in a complicated fashion, and makes each situation a reflective aspect of the other. Furthermore, such fervent expressions of women in love, a rarity in popular films, draw attention to Chughtai's narrative patterns, and in the way her stories fuelled a new kind of cinema. The film however, deviates from Chughtai's original novella. It narrates the tragic love affair between Puran (of princely lineage) and Asha (the 'pauper' or the maid). In this text, Puran is non-conformist, charismatic and wild, and declares his intention to marry Asha. His family, nonetheless, banishes Asha and coaxes him to marry a woman of his own class. After his marriage Puran loses interest in life and finally his marriage fails. When Asha returns to him, he dies tragically in a fire, following which Asha also sets herself on fire. While the 'death by fire' (a recurrent theme) is borne out by Chhutki in the film, it does not simply pave the way for a happy ending; rather, her dialogue, gestures and performance, surreptitiously make the narrative more complex by attaching layers to the unfinished love stories and the main plot. As a matter of fact, one may speculate that, eventually through such manifold additions the film attains a 'quilt' like form, and thereby reveals many layers of the social rubric.

Additionally, in the film, during the fire Puran realises that Asha is alive, and becomes progressively distressed. Since the marriage is never consummated, Shanta gradually becomes anxious and frantic. In one of the scenes towards the climax, Puran thus, prompts his wife to elope with her male friend/admirer. And, although in due course Shanta suffers a predictable ending—and is punished for her transgressive act—the ending by itself is insightful in the way the incapacitated uncle eventually becomes preemptive and prevents Asha's marriage to Ranjit (a very reluctant groom, who is a wrestler). Ranjit is delighted that his would-be-bride has been effectively abducted by the 'Thakur', and is particular happy that his physical prowess would not be wasted on sexual encounters. Hence, Puran's uncle while taking Asha away says somewhat wryly, '*Beta jao dangal karo'* (son, go and wrestle). The film ends on a happy note, and I would like to contend that, in the process, a particular trope emerges which Leslie A. Flemming, with regard to Chughtai's stories, describes as, '[a]nything but narrow. Rather, it provides a unique view of such human universals as the price of social acceptance, the fate of lovers attempting to cross social boundaries, the consequences of selfishness and greed, the tensions between religious credulity and skepticism, and the capacity of human beings for both self-delusion and self-sacrifice' (1995, 201).

In relation to this, I wish emphasise one of the early scenes of the film, in which, after Asha has come to live in Puran's household, she visits the bedridden Uncle. The elderly man, almost immobile, holds her face passionately, and cries, 'The same face!' (of the mother). Asha, terrified by the touch and his action, rushes out. There are many such scenes and song sequences (principally the song '*Chanda re, ja re ja*' shot against a dark, sinister sky), which bring forth the vigour of Chughtai's narratives through movement, gesture, and a compelling audio-visual register. Such stories tackled subjects of bodily desire, the woman's question and sexuality with great intensity.

Several critics and scholars describe Chughtai's work as a play between ethnography and fiction. Geeta Patel also discusses that,

> Krishan Chander points to Ismat Chughtai's *raftar*, the quickness with which her words seem to move across a page, ... The photographs of Chughtai lying across her bed looking up, which one sees scattered over the course of the Katha collection, gives a reader a sense of the movement, of remembering this quality (raftar) of hers over time... photographs of the author's body caught in the act of writing seem suspended in time, ... [Moreover] Speed has to do with the simultaneous evocation of space and time... Ismat Chughtai's dexterity with sensuousness and with temporality are qualities that characterize films... These qualities trigger the illusion of a body (2001, 349–50).

Such cinematic qualities of Chughtai's writings, for instance the sense of 'time', 'space' and the 'body', oftentimes dissolved into her films. Elina Del Rio (2008) writing about cinema, performance, and 'Powers of Affection', circumvents the established feminist theories about gender, visual pleasure, narrative cinema and 'performativity'. Drawing from Deleuze and Guattari's (1989) seminal work, Del Rio discusses in her book length study issues of body, performativity and affection. She elaborates that 'Performance is the actualization of the body's potential through specific thoughts, actions, displacements, combinations, realignments—all of which can be seen as different degrees of intensity, distinct relations of movement and rest. Thus, the body's expressivity coincides dimensions of expression...' (2008, 9–10).

Truly, in relation to cinema, performance and movement (*raftar* and time) emerge as pivotal categories. As highlighted by Del Rio, the moving body in cinema—the movements during the song and dance sequences, for instance—is *not* merely a series of a-priori static poses. Rather, through composition and action, and particularly via the cinematic *event*, a dynamic practice of 'becoming' and 'unbecoming' is at work. 'Through moving and gesturing processes' Del Rio suggests that, 'the body emerges as an assemblage of virtual and actual expressions with the capacity to affect and be affected by other bodies' (2008, 12). Furthermore, Del Rio borrows from Deleuze and Guattari who proposed that the body, 'force[s] us to think what is concealed from thought' (1989, 189). Indeed, especially in Indian popular films of the early Talkie period (prior to 1950s roughly), many a times the movement is not always suave or sleek, or entirely choreographed and controlled; rather, we often encounter unhurried and unformed/incomplete gestures, which (arguably) foreground the very 'process' pertaining to the making; and thereby, inform us about the gamut of possible interpolations. Moreover, in a dance sequence, movements, gestures, speed (*raftar*) and rhythm vary considerably, and thereby produce what Del Rio describes as 'kinetic and gestural interruptions' (2008, 13). To sum up, by referring to Deleuze and Guattari, Del Rio makes a distinction between 'cinema of action' and 'cinema of the body' and focuses on the affective-performative registers of cinema. In fact, one may consider some of the choreographed movements of *Kalpana*, or the recurrence of hand gestures in the dance sequences choreographed by Zohra Sehgal to elucidate the subject of performance, affect, and reflection. Briefly, I propose that the *performing* body of the actor (like Kamini Kaushal) becomes the reflective plane, which provokes us to think through and rethink cinematic narratives.

I am particularly considering some of the opening scenes of *Arzoo* (yen), which was written by Chughtai, and directed by Latif. In the film, Badal (played by Dilip Kumar) and Kammo (Kamini Kaushal) are childhood playmates, and are—at the point the film begins—in an intimate relationship. However, what is crucial for our deliberation are the settings and the manner in which the couple interact, speak, move, assemble, as well as the framing and the lighting, and particularly the performing 'bodies', which portray the forceful yearning. Moreover, there are definite bodily gestures performed by Kaushal (particularly hand actions and the movement of the torso), which draw attention to the idea of a 'desiring' woman. The intense sensuality (sometimes subtle, sometimes brutal) played out by the 'body' becomes evident in a film like *Arzoo*.

The story of *Arzoo* is briefly as follows: as Badal and Kammo romance secretly, the village buffoon often monitors them. Badal, however, is an idler; finally Kammo inspires him to leave for the city to obtain work. On the day of his departure, as Badal is leaving, one of his relatives arrives. Badal asks him to sleep in his room, and then leaves. The room catches fire and his relative is charred to death. Everyone, including Badal's family, Kammo and villagers assume that Badal is dead. A deeply disheartened Kammo is then married off to the 'Thakur' of the village, and is transformed into a fashionable woman. Meanwhile, Badal has joined the Indian army, and returns to discover that Kammo is already married. Rather than leaving Kammo alone, he decides to take revenge, and thus, befriends the Thakur, pretends to be in love with his sister and thus stays close to Kammo. Kammo is not only still very attached to Badal but she also seems to understand that Badal too is still in love with her. In the climax, the Thakur comes to know about Kammo and Badal's past affair and tries to shoot Badal, though in the end Kammo takes the bullet and dies.

Such themes of (women's) pining, transgression and death recur in films like *Andaz* (Dir. Mehboob Khan, 1949), *Mahal* (Dir. Kamal Amrohi, 1949), *Daera* (Dir. Kamal Amrohi, 1953) among several others of that time. However, to use Tahira Naqvi's expression 'The better part of her [Chughtai] writing shows a deep and abiding preoccupation with women's issues, particularly their cultural status and their myriad roles in Indian society. By underscoring women's struggles against the oppressive institutions of her time, she brings to her fiction an understanding of the female psyche that is unique' (1993, 41).

Indeed, one may argue that many of the filmic texts of the period, especially those with which the Left were associated, actually bear deep ruptures. Such breaks are apparent through the dialogues (written by Chughtai), and through the progression of scenes (or screenplay), in the manner in which couples are framed, both in public and private spaces, as well as through the passage of time, and the rhythm of the films. Thus, there is a strong 'stench' of extra-diegetic elements so to speak, which repeatedly disrupts the aspired resolution. Let us, for instance, consider one of the early scenes of *Arzoo* in which Kammo steals the Thakur's cart and drives it away. While the Thakur chases her and scares her off with his hunter, this is followed by a scene with Badal to whom she complains about the incident, and another, in which she encounters the Thakur. In the third scene of the sequence, the Thakur is seen fishing and Kammo enters the scene.

> **Thakur cries**: *Ei Ladki!* (Hey girl!)
>
> **Kammo replies**: *Main eyi ladki nahin, mera naam Kamini hai ji, Kamini.* (I am not 'hey girl'; my name is Kamini).
>
> **Thakur:** *Dekhti nahin hum machliyan pakad rahen hai* (Can't you see that I am fishing?)
>
> **Kammo:** *To main kaab kaheti hoon ki aap jhak maar rahen hai...* (So when did I say that you are idling?).
>
> Then she adds: *Machli to kya, maindak bhi na phasega ... aisa karwa moo bana ke baithenge...* (Neither fish nor frogs will take the bait; you have such an unpleasant face!) And further, after Thakur smiles, she adds, '*Aare aap ko hasna bhi aata hai? Main to samjhi thi sirif ghore mein baith ke... hunter chalana aata hai ... Kahiye aapki gari to razi khusi hai? Kahin hamare baithne se bechari ki kamar to na toot gaayi?* (Oh, you can smile too? I imagined you can only ride the horse, and swing the hunter. So I hope your cart is fine? I hope it's not damaged because I rode it?)
>
> Thereafter, her mood quickly changes as she hears Badal's flute. She makes a typical hand gesture and cries, '*Badal! Badal aa gaaya*' (Badal is here) and exits quickly.

Note, the word 'Badal' denotes clouds and 'Kamini' signifies woman and hence, the Thakur looks up into the sky in bewilderment and notices nothing.

Truly, there is verve and comic interjection (or 'warmth' as Kaushal described it) in such writings, which is typical of Chughtai. More important, nonetheless, is the figure of the vacillating woman, via whose experiences of the multiple layers of conflicts within social and political histories are revealed. Chughtai's films and stories thus, examine her social status, and highlight how women reside in multiple registers. Additionally, I wish to stress that Chughtai's style and her expressions, not simply the themes and plots, become a significant aspect of film narratives and history. Besides, if Chughtai's prose produced a tactile world through words, then this tactility, or the sensory ambience, its intensity, and harshness, are present in 'her' films too, with all its dynamism. Such plots, themes, characters, performance, and storytelling depict the socio-cultural struggles, and the fashion in which the political everyday is, in actuality, disrupted by the woman's pungent need.

Regarding *Arzoo,* Kaushal said the following,

> [...the character Kammo] is very flamboyant and very bubbly.... We had less of artificial exuberance.... I let myself be myself.... You must use all parts of your body [while performing], you must not only use your mouth and spurt out your lines. You must be that person.... our gang—Dilip [Kumar], Raj Kapoor, Dev [Anand]—we all had a spontaneity. We brought naturalness [to acting], that's our main contribution. (Kaushal, conversation with the author)

Kaushal further added, 'She [Chughtai] understood that I understood the characters.... I didn't incorporate any dramatic gestures, molding of your voice.... Your fingertips, your toes are working.... I am such a bouncy girl in *Arzoo*, but it's not that my dialogues are bouncy; my whole personality is bouncy.'

In effect, one may argue that, such 'performativity' became the reflective interface, which both performed and remarked upon the scene. In addition, such bodily gestures generated 'affect', which as suggested earlier, sutured into Chughtai's stories, a quilt-like thickness (and depth).

Kamini Kaushal with Dev Anand in *Shair*

Kamini Kaushal in and as *Rami Dhoban* (Dir. Hiren Bose, 1953)

Rami Dhoban narrated the love story of a widowed Dalit woman and a priest

Kamini Kaushal in a publicity poster (untitled, n.d.)

The Popular and the Political

By way of conclusion, I wish to highlight how the Progressive charge of 1940s–50s was reinvented and channelised into New Indian Cinema of 1970s. For instance, besides the subject of longing—the issue of women's attachment to people and places—becomes apparent in the landmark Hindi-Urdu film *Garam Hawa* (1973) directed by M. S. Sathyu. The film adapted an unpublished story of Chughtai, and recounts the strife of a Muslim family, who are gradually forced to leave India due to the problematic local conditions, marginalisation of the minority community, politicking, as well as lack of opportunities. In the end young Amina (Geeta Siddharth), waiting for her lover's homecoming, commits suicide, and Salim Mirza (Balraj Sahani, also a Communist Party associate), her father, driven by his son's inspiring thoughts, joins (Left) movements for political change, and stays back in India. The desire of the *three* women of the film—Ammi/Dadda, Jamila (Salim's wife), and Amina—nonetheless, leave a stain on the body of the film. While Sathyu weaves an engaging narrative through aural and visual imageries (I am thinking of the screeching sound of a train departing, which is juxtaposed with Amina's extreme close-up in order highlight her sense of desolation as well as the larger theme of separation and Partition), more important, in this context, is Chughtai's story, which underscores the violence triggered by Partition, and the manner in which the divided sub-continent split women's lives and the sense of belonging.[18]

The scars of separation and the trauma of departure—be it in *Ziddi, Arzoo* or in *Garam Hawa*—are borne by the women. In point of fact, if partition created long drawn political and economic crises, its outcome, in the film, is expanded through Amina's anguish. One may consider the first departure indicated in the film, which involves Salim Mirza's brother, Halim. Following Halim's departure, the Mirzas lose their ancestral home, just as the parting results in Amina's separation with Kazim, her lover/fiancé. With regard to this, I propose that, passing through Amina's hopelessness a far more complicated reading of the state of affairs becomes possible. For example, after she gradually accepts another man namely Shamshad, his family too migrates to Pakistan. Wavering between lovers and loneliness as well as between hope and despair Amina kills herself. Yet, Amina had sought love, companionship, and joy. And, her sexual energy is visible in the intimate scenes (shot engagingly around Fatehpur Sikri, Agra) and even in her death, when she wears the red bridal wear, slits her wrists, and bleeds to death.

The duality between 'Desire and Death', as a narrative element, is further developed at the point the elderly grandmother (Dadda) or Salim's Ammi (mother), remembers the long lost winters as well as the state of the house at the time she was married.[19] In the scene in which the grief stricken and frail figure is brought back to the old house in a *palki*, she is engulfed in a reverie, and seems to hear the music of *sehnai*, and the voices of the people who had surrounded her at the time she had entered the *haveli* (house) for the first time. Ammi/Dadda in the first place had fiercely resisted the evacuation. Her (ritualistic and momentary) 'return' thus, underscores the loss of 'home' and the circumstances of 'homelessness' provoked by Partition. The question of 'home' and 'rootlessness', which have been tackled by certain narratives, especially by films of Ritwik Kumar Ghatak, nevertheless, become far more layered—like the structure of the *haveli* as it were—as we revisit it through women's yearnings.[20] Similarly, Jamila (played by another 'comrade' Shuakat Azmi), caught between many deaths and departures, witnesses the brutality of Partition and its aftermath in multiple ways.[21] Certainly, the intensities of Chughtai's (fervent) women, when performed and regenerated through cinematic narratives, produces a sense of 'want', which is not only exceptionally tangible but, surges into diverse streams and directions, and finds a new life in contemporary political conditions.

Acknowledgement

I am grateful to the exceptional actor Kamini Kaushal for speaking to me, and Shivendra Singh Dungarpur for introducing me to her.

The images used are from the following research projects:

- Jadavpur University Research Grant to write on 'Images in the dark: Glass Negatives and Publicity material of Bengali Cinema (1950s–1960s)', 2008–10.
- Sarai, CSDS, Delhi, Independent Research Fellowship to retrieve and study glass negatives, titled 'Looking at the glasses darkly: Revisiting Calcutta Film Studios', 2004.

Notes

1. Latif studied at Aligarh Muslim University; Latif and Chughtai married in 1941. Latif was a writer and director; he started his career with Bombay Talkies. *Ziddi* was his directorial debut. *Baharen Phir Bhi Aayengi* (1966), produced by Guru Dutt, was one of his most successful films.
2. Also see Pradhan's *Marxist Cultural Movement in India.*
3. See Debashree Mukherjee's "Lost films of Manto" http://pharaat.blogspot.in/2012/05/debashree-mukherjee-lost-films-of.html (accessed on 19th February 2017).
4. See Manṭo and K. Ḥasan's *Stars from Another Sky.*
5. The interview was conducted in English, Kaushal's words and expressions have *not* been edited.
6. See Meera Kosambi's *Bombay in transition.*
7. See Gyan Prakash's *Mumbai Fables.*
8. See Madhuja Mukherjee "That figure in the dark" for an extended discussion on film styles of 1950s.
9. For example, Sharadindu Bandyopadhyay, the noted Bengali author, also wrote screenplay for three Bombay Talkies films during 1939.

10. See Madhuja Mukherjee *New Theatres Ltd.*
11. See Prarthana Purkayastha's "Dancing Otherness".
12. Also see "Zohra Segal's Shankar-Style Choreography in *Neecha Nagar* (Hindi, 1946)" on http://cinemanrityagharana.blogspot.in/2014/02/zohra-segals-shankar-style-choreography.html (accessed on 2nd February 2016).
13. For an elaborate discussion on *Chhinnamul* see Moinak Biswas's "The City and the Real."
14. See Madhuja Mukherjee edited *Voices of the Talking Stars.*
15. See Karuna Chanana "Schooling of girls in pre-Partition Punjab".
16. See 'Uncle Memphis' in Kiran Sehgal's *'Fatty'*, 47–62.
17. See Madhuja Mukherjee's "My Gori" http://kindlemag.in/my-gori/ (accessed on 11th January 2017).
18. Also see Urvashi Butalia's *The other side of silence.*
19. Badar Begum played the role of Dadda/Ammi. In *Voices of the Talking Stars* (2017) I have discussed how Sathyu had narrated that he was hunting for a mansion to shoot *Garam Hawa.* One night, he visited an old deserted house in a certain city (Agra) in North India. It was seemingly a 'house of public women'. An elderly, ravaged-looking woman opened the doors and insisted that the house was unmanned. While Sathyu did not like the house he actually loved the woman. He wished to cast her as the old woman/mother in *Garam Hawa.* However, Sathyu was unsure if she would or could act at all. Eventually, not only the woman agreed to act in his film; she disclosed that she always wanted to be an actor. Sometime during the early phase (the twenties) of Indian cinema, Badar Begum had travelled to Bombay/Mumbai to look for work. In the process she was abused and exploited and after such violent encounters with cinema she returned to her city and worked as a 'public woman' of sorts. Yet, at a very late stage in her life, such an opportunity knocked at her door. Later, *Garam Hawa* received national award and produced one of the most remarkable moments in the history of cinema.

    Badar Begum's memorable performance and her own life tell us a very complicated history of the nation and the state of film industry. Moreover, her life is an inspiring story that speaks about the doggedness of dreams and the irony of it.
20. Consider for instance, Ghatak's landmark *Meghe Dhaka Tara* (1960).
21. The film also starred another Left revolutionary A. K. Hangal.

References

Bagchi, J. and S. Dasgupta (eds). 2003. *The Trauma and the Triumph: Gender and Partition in Eastern India*. Calcutta: Stree.

Moinak B. 2007. "The City and the Real: *Chinnamul* and the Left Cultural Movement in the 1940s." In *City Flicks: Indian Cinema and the Urban Experience* edited by Preben Kaarsholm. Calcutta: Seagull Books.

Butalia, U. 1998. *The Other Side of Silence: Voices from the Partition of India*. New Delhi: Penguin Books.

Chanana, K. "Schooling of girls in pre-Partition Punjab." *Indian Journal of Gender Studies* 4(2), (1997):141–66.

Chugtai, I. 2013. *A Life in Words: Memoirs*. Gurgaon: Penguin Books.

Del Rio, E. 2008. *Deleuze and the Cinemas of Performance: Powers of Affection*. Edinburgh: Edinburgh UP.

Flemming, L. A. "Out of the Zenana: New Translations of Ismat Chughtai's Work." *The Annual of Urdu Studies* 10, (1995): 200–07.

Kosambi, M. 1986. *Bombay in transition: the growth and social ecology of a colonial city, 1880–1980*. Stockholm: Almqvist & Wiksell International.

Manṭo, S. Ḥ. and K. Ḥasan. 1998. *Stars from Another Sky: The Bombay Film World in the 1940s*. Delhi: Penguin Books.

Manwani, A. 2013. *Sahir Ludhianvi: The People's Poet*. Harper Collins Publishers India.

Mukherjee, M. 2009. *New Theatres Ltd: The Emblem of Art, the Picture of Success*, Pune: National Film Archive of India.

———. 2016. "That figure in the dark: Of melodrama, noir and multiplicity during 1950s." In *Indian Film Culture/Indian Cinema*, edited by Gautam Kaul, Kolkata: Codex: 116–36.

———. 2017. ed. *Voices of the Talking Stars: The Women of Indian Cinema and Beyond*, Sage/Stree: Delhi/Kolkata.

Naqvi, T. 1990. "Introduction." In *The Quilt and Other Stories*. New Delhi: Kali for Women.

———. "Ismat Chughtai: A Tribute." *The Annual of Urdu Studies* 8, (1993): 37–42.

Patel, G. "An Uncivil Woman: Ismat Chughtai." *Annual of Urdu Studies 16*, (2001): 345–49.

Pradhan, S. 1979. *Marxist Cultural Movement in India, Chronicles and Documents (1936–1947)*. Calcutta: Shanti Pradhan.

———. 1985. *Marxist Cultural Movement in India, Chronicles and Documents (1947–1958). Volume-II*. Calcutta: Navana.

Prakash, G. 2010. *Mumbai fables.* Princeton: Princeton UP.

Prasad, M. M. 1998. *The Ideology of the Hindi Film: A Historical Construction.* Delhi: Oxford UP.

Purkayastha, P. "Dancing Otherness: Nationalism, Transnationalism, and the Work of Uday Shankar." *Dance Research Journal,* 44 (1), (2012): 68–92.

Sehgal, K. 2012. *Zohra Segal, 'Fatty'.* New Delhi: Niyogi Books.

Segal, Z. 2010. *Close-Up: Memoirs of a Life on Stage and Screen.* New Delhi: Women Unlimited.

Varis, A. 2000. "Some Aspects of Ismat's Art." In *Ismat: Her Life, Her Times.* New Delhi: Katha.

Vasudevan, R. "The Melodramatic Mode and the Commercial Hindi Cinema: Notes on Film History, Narrative and performance in the 1950s." *Screen* 30.3, (1989): 29–50.

———. "New Cultural History and Experience of Modernity." *Economic and Political Weekly* 30. 44, (1995): 2809–14.

———. "Addressing the Spectator of a 'Third World' National Cinema: The Bombay 'Social' Film of the 1940s and 1950s." *Screen* 36.4, (1995): 305–24.

2

In Search of No Man's Land

Chughtai, Manto and Ghatak*

Manas Ghosh

'The flood of communal violence came with all its evils and left, but it left a pile of living, dead, and gasping corpses in its wake. It wasn't only that the country was split in two, bodies and minds were also divided. Moral beliefs were tossed aside and humanity was in shreds. Government officers and clerks along with their chairs, pens and inkpots, were distributed like the spoils of war. And whatever remained after this division was laid to waste by the benevolent hands of communal violence. Those whose bodies were whole had hearts that were splintered,' writes Ismat Chughtai in the wake of the partition of India (2000, 445).

Although the blind nationalists and their followers 'danced about and gamboled, clapping their hands like little children the moment they saw the white-skinned pirates leaving Hindustan,' she observes, 'Most of the Progressive Writers in Hindustan and Pakistan turned their attention to this issue and, helped by other *progressive elements*, began their work in earnest. The pen was drafted to check the attacks of the knife and the dagger' (ibid., 448). The resistance was proved meagre compared to the magnitude of the tragedy and loss. But the powerful creations of Ismat Chughtai, Sa'adat Hasan Manto and Ritwik Ghatak in the face of knives and daggers moved the readers and audiences of the subcontinent. In this chapter I would like to discuss Chughtai's story '*Jadein*' (Roots, 1952), Manto's story '*Toba Tek Singh*' (1955) and Ghatak's film *Subarnarekha* (The Golden Line, 1962) in the background of Partition. These masterpieces are arguably the most powerful works in modern Indian creative culture

*I acknowledge my debt to Lacanian psychoanalyst and literary critic Dr Santanu Biswas, Professor, Dept. of English, Jadavpur University.

which are able to reflect the magnitude of the post-Partition trauma caused by the irreversible loss.

Chughtai, Manto and Ghatak belonged to the tradition of the 1940s Progressive Writers' Association (PWA) and Indian People's Theatre Association (IPTA). Partition in their works figured not merely as a tragic incident but also reflected an epic failure of the ruling class of the subcontinent in terms of decolonisation.

The Partition did not merely split undivided India into two sovereign states but it ripped the societies and politics of the subcontinent by yielding the false consciousness of two 'enemy nations'—namely India and Pakistan. The Partition endangered the socio-politics of postcolonial Indian subcontinent by introducing a set of mutually exclusive terms—a set of binaries, for example, Hindu/Muslim; Hindustan/Pakistan; Muslim League/Hindu Mahasabha.

The situation can be explained more effectively if we bring in the psychoanalytic metaphor of a schizophrenic split. The extreme manifestation of this is a mental state where the split is so severe and intense that the psyche is guided by only two master registers—kill or die. Partition imposed such a paranoid and cruel state of mind that no bridge between the binary opposites was possible. The in-between space of the two signifiers of opposite poles withered away from the realm of signification.

Let's just quote a relevant part from Chughtai's short story *Jadein* which is a tale of a Muslim family during Partition. The story is told in first person. Chughtai introduces the reader to the social setting of the story, framed in the politics in pre-Partition colonial India:

> There were those who supported Muslim League, Congress, and Mahasabha in both families and heated debates on the topics of religion and politics frequently took place, but it was all like a game of football or cricket. Abba was a Congressie, Roopchandji and Bare Bhai were Muslim Leagies, Gyanchand was a Mahasabhi, Manjhle Bhai was a communist and Gulabchand was a socialist. And the wives and children were the supporters along the same line. (Chughtai 2010, 189)

The situation was changing very rapidly as Partition approached. Chughtai observes, 'But for some years now the Muslim League and Mahasabha had been gaining strength.' The other opinions were just flushed out by the jingoistic politics of hostile polarisation between the Muslim League and

Hindu Mahasabha. The entire discourse was reeling around the binaries of Hindustan/Pakistan and Hindu/Muslim. The only option left in the realpolitik was: kill/die. There was no space left for a hyphen between the two signifiers. All *third* options, Chughtai indicates, lost their ground as Partition was let loose on the people of India.

The third, which withered away from the domain of rationality in the time of the Partition, is most important in determining the relationship of self and other. Jacques Lacan, inspired by Aristotle, Hegel and Freud, argued in favour of the third. He says that the third is like a hyphen between two borders or two terms which is a separator as well as conjoiner of the two entities or two signifiers. The third subverts the mutually exclusive concepts of inside and outside; sometimes it shows the borders as non-existent and fallacious. Lacan argues that understanding of any of the two signifiers in a couple is only possible if it is mediated by the third. It is understood from Lacan's framework that 'the third' or *la troisieme* plays a very significant role in understanding the dyad of self and other. Fredric Jameson explains the Lacanian third as:

> [T]he binary systems of the Symbolic must now be understood as introducing a third term into the hitherto duplex logic of the Imaginary. . . Imagination and desire are the realities of a finite being which can emerge from the contradiction between self and other only by the genesis of a third term, a mediatory 'concept' which, by determining each term, orders them into reversible and progressive relations. (1977, 337–38)

The third, which withered away from the reality of Partition-inflicted India, returns in Chughtai's narrative in the form of Amma's decision to stay back at her own home. All the other members of her family leave Indian territory and set out for the newly formed country. But Amma denies the rationale of Partition; she only knows her home where she belongs. Amma's home, in Chughtai's narrative, is a radical space because it is the third which subverts the binary of Hindustan/Pakistan. It is neither Hindustan nor Pakistan but a piece of land of her own.

The narrative of Chughtai's story *Jadein* begins from a state of social becoming and ends at a state of denial of the binary by Amma in order to reinstate the third. Manto's *Toba Tek Singh* starts with the complete disavowal of the nationalist rationale as the protagonist of his story is a madman. He survives in a state of severe psychosis; the 'law of the father' which drafts the rule of society vis-a-vis the logic of dominant ideology has been foreclosed in his psyche. He is in a state of complete disavowal. The physical space described in the story is a lunatic asylum situated in Lahore. The time depicted is 'two or three years after the partition'. Among the inmates there was a psychotic person called Bishan Singh who is the protagonist of the story.

The asylum is a place where reason is banished from the sphere of the remanded inmates. Michel Foucault explains 'unreason' in a madhouse as the absence of language. He notes, '[T]here was no longer any common language between madness and reason; the language of delirium [of a madman] can be answered only by an absence of language' (2001, 249). Lacan calls the language of psychosis as *la langue*. As the 'language of reason', which acts as the fundamental structure of the rational of the psyche is absent, the sense of social contract on which the identity of a modern subject is constructed ceases to exist. Consequently, a mad person is excluded from the status of citizen subject. Thus, a madman becomes a 'no-man' from the vantage point of governmentality.

Manto writes,

> For one lunatic, the entire issue of Hindustan-Pakistan and Pakistan-Hindustan resulted in further disorientation. One day, while he was sweeping the floor, he suddenly suspended his task and climbed onto a tree, where he remained for nearly two hours. During that time, he lectured extensively and nonstop on the matter of Pakistan versus Hindustan. When ordered by the guards to come down, he climbed higher still; when threatened with force, he said, "I want to live neither in Pakistan nor in Hindustan—I will live on this tree". (2007, 15)

Bishan Singh had heard about India and Pakistan while he was in the asylum in Lahore. Now he began asking people where Toba Tek Singh was; for that was his hometown. His name was Bishan Singh, but people now started calling him Toba Tek Singh. He frantically asks, 'Where is Toba Tek Singh? It is in Pakistan or in India?' It was his only question. He frequently utters these words 'Toba Tek Singh' which may not be a geographical location existing in reality. It erupts regularly, sometimes in a form of oral hallucination which the Lacanian psychoanalysis marks as 'signature' of a psychotic mind.

At last, the day when the inmates of the asylum are to be exchanged between the two newly formed countries India and Pakistan comes. Manto's story ends with this paragraph:

> Before the sun rose, a piercing cry arose from Bishan Singh, who had been quiet and still all this time. Several officers and the guards ran towards him; they saw that the man who had stood on his legs, day and night for fifteen years now lay on the ground, prostrate. Beyond a wired fence on one side of him was Hindustan, and beyond a wired fence on the other side was Pakistan. In the middle, on a stretch of land that had no name, lay Toba Tek Singh. (ibid.,16)

Finally, Bishan Singh finds his Toba Tek Singh which is situated at the no-man's land between India and Pakistan. He is convinced that the piece of ground or space which is neither India nor Pakistan but a third space is his own land. In Lacanian terms Bishan Singh's conviction is explained as 'psychotic certainty'.

Like Chughtai and Manto, Ghatak invested his creative efforts majorly in reinventing a cultural and ideological space which this chapter is trying to establish as a *third* space that subverts the binary of India and Pakistan. But Ghatak's project is stylistically slightly different from that of Chughtai and Manto. Chughtai and Manto articulated the unspeakable tragedy of Partition through their own uniquely powerful realistic styles while Ghatak's project is remembering Partition in a melodramatic mode. Among his Partition films *Komal Gandhar* is directly political where Ghatak constructs a discursive space for a radical cultural reconciliation between the post-Partition Bengals. Ghatak's other films like *Meghe Dhaka Tara* and *Subarnarekha* struggle to recover the memory of Partition from the noose of amnesia. The tragedy of Partition with which his films begin, like Chughtai and Manto's stories, constructs a strong sense of *disbelief* in the rationale of the two nation theory. Amma in *Jadein*, Bishan Singh in *Toba Tek Singh* and Haraprasad in *Subarnarekha* decline to accept Partition, which most of the people around them, though unwillingly and by compulsion, accept as the only practical solution left.

Subarnarekha tells the story of a group of displaced people who finally try to settle at a place in the outskirts of post-Partition Kolkata. They rename the place as 'Nabajibon Colony'. Two friends, Iswar and Haraprasad, are the ushers of this project. But Iswar leaves Nabajiban Colony in search of a 'new home' at Chhatimpur. He takes his young sister Sita and an orphan boy Abhiram with him. After decades of isolation without contact, one day Haraprasad appears at Iswar's window when lonely Iswar is about to commit suicide. After leaving Nabajiban colony, Iswar makes a success of his life but in order to fulfill his ambition he did injustice to Sita and Abhiram. In protest Sita and Abhiram have abandoned him. Haraprasad on the other hand is almost insane. He declares, 'We are defeated—no matter we ran away or we stood and fought'. As the story moves on, a drunken Iswar, in search of a whore, enters Sita's home. Following this, Sita commits suicide. The last shot of the film shows Iswar along with little Binu, Sita and Abhiram's son, walking through the rocky bank of the Subarnarekha river, towards a indefinite horizon in search of a new home and new neighbourhood.

The characters in Ghatak's *Subarnarekha*, with the progress of the narrative, pass through an epic erudition of bitterness and trauma, and tragic failure to accept the fractured freedom. Like Amma's own room and Bishan Singh's imaginary village 'Toba Tek Singh', Ghatak's film also tells about 'Nabajibon Colony' which is Iswar and Haraprasad's failed project to recover the lost third space. The film mourns the absence of the third space which is lost as a result of Partition.

One very interesting similarity in these three pieces of work is their serious exploration of the notion of neighbour/ neighbourhood. The locus of the narrative of Chughtai's masterpiece is the relationship between the narrator's family and the family of Roopchandji, their most dependable and close neighbour. The writer very lovingly depicts the faces of her neighbours in the village including that of Roopchandji. In Manto's story the protagonist wishes to go back to his imaginary village Toba Tek Singh and to inhabit with his neighbours. He does not care whether it falls under India or Pakistan. Ghatak's film also emphasises Haraprasad and Iswar's attempt to re-construct the pre-Partition lost neighbourhood which finally fails. Chughtai, Manto and Ghatak establish a link between the neighbour/neighbourhood and third space which is lost during the years of othering and violence.

It is interesting to note that the studies by Veena Das (1986), Urvashi Butalia (1998) and Alok Bhalla (2006) on women and other people who survived the Partition violence reveal how Partition transformed a dependable neighbour into a 'demon'. No positive exchange was possible with that demon. The space for dialogue and other social exchanges, which had knitted them for years in a society as neighbours despite their differences in communal belief, suddenly evaporated into thin air. The 'third', the hyphen, the conjoiner is withdrawn from the dyad of

Hindu-Muslim. There were only two options left—falling victim to the demonic violence or smashing the face of the demon. The dependable neighbour all of a sudden becomes an impenetrable other, as Zizek explains, through a process of 'defacement' of the neighbour.

In such situations, the neighbour's face no longer remains a human face; it becomes the incomprehensible 'thing' which is a part of a demonic existence. The civil war in Serbia (1992–95), a tragedy similar to the partition of India, has brought back in recent times these politico-ethical issues. In this context Zizek asks,

> [H]ow does my neighbor whom I face relate to this Third? Is he the Third's friend or his foe or even his victim? Who, of the two, is my true neighbor in the first place? All this compels me to compare the infinites that cannot be compared, to limit the absolute priority of the other, to start to calculate the incalculable. (2007, 148)

Zizek argues that the answer to the questions must be derived neither from the factuality of violence nor from escaping the other but from an absolute ethical responsibility to the other. He agrees with Levinas (1969),

> The key question that poses itself apropos this Levinasian notion of the other's face as the epiphany, as the event that precedes Truth itself, is: how, then, do the laws, courts, judgments, institutions, etc., enter? Levinas's answer is: by way of the presence of the THIRD. When face to face with the other, I am infinitely responsible to him, this is the original ethical constellation. (ibid.)

The 'infinite responsibility' to the other, to the neighbour is echoed in *Subarnarekha*'s concluding scenes as Iswar and Binu move from the finitude of bitterness to infinity as the film echoes Tagore's poem *Sishu-Tirtha* and the Upanishad's mantra of the infinite journey *Charaibeti*. A similar attempt is found in the concluding paragraphs of Chughtai's story. The violence of Partition violence and the communal mistrust have ruined the harmony of society. Their Hindu neighbours, even the family of Roopchand, have cut off decades of social relationship with them. Communal riots break out in every corner of the province. The other members of her family have left for Pakistan; Amma however, has declined to leave her home. She stays back in her empty house. The sun sets; darkness encompasses the empty house. Amma locks herself up in her room, dismayed and traumatised. She passes slowly into a state of delusion. She imagines the violence that hounds, kills, dishonours and dismembers her sons and daughters. Suddenly she hears a sound on her locked door; some people are trying to break in. 'The pounding on the door was getting louder. The angel of death was in a hurry, was he not?' Amma realises. She shuts her eyes. But it seems that she senses a familiar touch on her hand. She opens her eyes and finds Roopchandji as usual speaking from behind a curtain; he says, '*Arey* Bhabi, I will come if you send for me. Why do you have to undertake this charade?'

Does her neighbour (Roopchandji) really come to see her as he would do in the past? Or it is a part of Amma's hallucination? There is doubt; we are not very sure. Perhaps it is not Roopchandji; it is a group of rioters who have broken in, who will slit Amma's throat, will smash her face. It might be merely Amma's imagination that her old neighbour has come to comfort her. But real or unreal, the moment is necessary; because it is the moment which prepares the condition of possibility, of infinite responsibility to the other. The third, the hyphen which was lost, is retrieved for a moment. It is the moment when the defaced other is given his face back. Thy neighbours stand before you—Levinas suggests (1979)—you are 'infinitely responsible to them since this is the only original ethical constellation'.

References

Bhalla, Alok. 2006. *Partition Dialogues: Memories of a Lost Home*, London: Oxford UP.

Bhutalia, Urvashi. 1998. *The Other Side of Silence: Voices from the Partition of India*, New Delhi: Penguin Books.

Chughtai, Ismat. 'Communal Violence and Literature'. Translated by Tahira Naqvi and Muhammad Umar Memon. *The Annual of Urdu Studies* Vol. 15, (2000): 445–56.

———. 2010. 'Roots'. Translated by Tahira Naqvi. In Muhammad Umar Memon (edited and translated) *An Epic Unwritten*. India: Penguin.

Das, Veena. 1986. *The Word and the World: Fantasy, Symbol and Record*, New Delhi: Sage.

Fredric, Jameson. "Imaginary and Symbolic in Lacan: Marxism, Psychoanalytic Criticism, and the Problem of the Subject". *Yale French Studies*, 55/56, (1977): 338–95.

Foucault, Michel and Richard Howard. 2001. *Madness and Civilization: A History of Insanity in the Age of Reason*. London; New York: Routledge.

Ghatak, Ritwik. "Subarnarekha Prasange." *Chitrabhas* Vol. 39, (2005): 1–4.

Hasan, Mushirul. "Partition Narratives.". *Social Scientist*, Vol. 30 (7/8), (2002) 24–53.

Lacan, Jacques. *La troisieme*. Translated by Ellie-Ragland, *Lettres de l'école freudienne*, no. 16, (1975): 178–203.

Lavinas, Immanuel. 1979. *Totality and Infinity: An Essay on Exteriority*, translated by Alphonso Lingis. Hingham MA: Martinus Nijhoff Publishers and Duquesne UP.

Manto, Sa'adat Hasan. 'Toba Tek Singh'. Translated by Tahira Naqvi. *Manoa* Vol. 19, (2007):1, 14–19.

Žižek, Slavoj. 2007. 'TRIOS'. *The Neighbor: Three Enquiries in Political Theology*, edited by Slavoj Zizek, Eric L. Santner, Kenneth Reinhard, Chicago, IL: U of Chicago P.

3

Casements of Selfhood

Khakas (pen-portraits) by/of Ismat Chughtai

Fatima Rizvi and Kakul Hai

Introduction

By the first quarter of the twentieth century, fictional genres like the *afsāna* (short story), the *nāvelette* (novella) and the *nāvil* (novel) had become enormously popular. Sociological and realistic in mode, often overtly didactic in tone and aiming at introspection and self-correction, these genres were often conceived as instruments of change. In the second quarter of the century, particularly during the Progressive era (1932 onwards),[1] the writers were radicalised by Marxist political ideology and became overtly socialist in tone, tenor and choice of subjects. The popularity of these genres stemmed from the contemporariness of the issues they addressed as well as the novelty they provided in terms of subject, style and technique, all of which was in keeping with the altering, rapidly modernising social, cultural and political environment. The *khaka* or pen-portrait is a non-fictional genre that developed more or less alongside the novel. Rooted in reality and factual by nature, a *Khaka* is an essay depicting in detail an individual well-known to its writer. It is devoid of ornamentation, flights of fancy and imagination, common to traditional prose and poetry genres such as *dastāns*, the *masnavis* and *marsiyas*, lengthy prose and poetic genres, which include detailed character sketches to depict illusory characters or real people. The twentieth century stand-alone *khaka* may trace its roots to character sketches within these, but differs from them in style and technique. Its origins can be traced to the writings of Mir Taqi Mir's *Niqāt-ush Shu'ara*, (Lives of Poets), Muhammad Husain Azad's *Āb-e-Hayāt* (Fountain of Life; 1880) and Deputy Nazir Ahmad's *Tauba-tun-Nusuh* (The Repentance of Nusuh; 1877). Mirza Farhatullah Beg is generally credited as the first *khaka-navīs* (writer of a *khaka*). His 'Deputy Nazir

Ahmad kī Kahanī, Kuchh Unkī Kuchh Merī Zubanī' (Deputy Nazir Ahmad's Story Partly in His, Partly in My Words) delineating the merits of his mentor objectively (Hasan 51) received much acclaim. *Khakas* by Khwaja Hasan Nizami and Rashid Ahmad Siddiqui are also stand-alone pen-portraits. Sajjad Zaheer's history of the Progressive Writers' Movement, *Raushnaī* (The Light, 1953) contains some of the finest depictions of his contemporaries including one of Premchand. However, these are not stand-alone pieces.

Owing to their biographical and descriptive nature, *khakas* are also described as 'micro-fiction', 'flash-fiction' and *mukhtasar swān-e umrī* or short biography (Suhail 2017, 79). A *khaka* may unfold as anecdote, memoir or reminiscence and hold the readers' attention in various ways—it represents facts and comments upon them; it provides evidence of psychological imprints; it may serve educative purposes. The currency of the *khaka* as an independent genre rose during the progressive and modernist eras of Urdu literature during which experimentation with style and genre was popular. Like other literary genres of this era, *khakas* are specific to the political and sociological culture and depict its zeitgeist. Those penned by the Progressives clearly exhibit the letter and the spirit of their political culture and ideology; those written by politically unaligned writers demonstrate the influence of modernism and a literary order in transformation. The *khaka* therefore, is also a social commentary on the existing times, as manifest in the object's selfhood and his/her writing. The object, which is the unit of analysis in the *khaka* is placed within his/her socio-cultural and political environment. The writer's perception of the object, also betrays his/her own cultural and political leanings. The writer, as the observer, infuses his/her understanding of the context into the interpretation of the object, reflecting the writer's own conceptualisation of selfhood as shaped by the very environment he/she is commenting upon. *Khakas* thus serve as windows into the writers' individualities or selfhoods while they describe another, or comment upon another's art. They exhibit ideas, opinions, perceptions and ideologies espoused by the writer as well as those of the person whose portrait is being sketched. *Khakas* employ a linguistic style that is direct, laconic, informal, conversational, anecdotal and dialogic. Writers often report incidents and anecdotes regarding their objects dialogically as in a play. This technique serves to breathe life into the portrait, making it come alive. Humour, satire and irony may also suffuse a pen-portrait. Imagery and metaphor make it picturesque.

Ismat Chughtai has penned several *khakas* and has also served as the object[2] of those by her contemporaries. Among those she has penned are those on her elder brother and literary mentor Azim Beg Chughtai ('*Dozakhī*' [Hell-bound] 1942), brutal in honesty, and most acclaimed; on Asrar-ul Haq 'Majaz' ('*Ishq Majāzī*' [Illusory Love]1956) and on Miraji ('*Sūkhe Patte*' [Dry Leaves] 1979).

Included in this study are Chughtai's portraits of Patras Bokhari ('*Kuchh merī Yādeñ*' [Memories]),[3] Qurratulain Hyder ('*Pompom Darling*'),[4] and Sa'adat Hasan Manto ('*Merā Dost, Merā Dushman*' [My Friend, My Enemy]).[5] On the surface, these pen-portraits articulate Chughtai's personal opinions regarding her objects. In these, she also unintentionally articulates herself while narrating her perceptions regarding her objects. Chughtai has also been the object of portraits penned by these writers. Included in this study are Bokhari's '*Kuchh Ismat Chughtai ke bāre meñ*' (Some observations on Ismat Chughtai);[6] Manto's '*Ismat Chughtai*'[7] and Hyder's '*Lady Chengez Khan*'.[8] Though they are not responses to Chughtai's portraits, these *khakas* open windows to views of fellow writers on Chughtai the writer and Chughtai the woman. Bokhari's and Manto's *khakas* preceded Chughtai's, and Hyder's is an obituary written for Chughtai. Nevertheless, each text provides evidence of its writer's perceptiveness and relationship with his/her object. This paper reads the *khaka* as a literary genre lending itself to psychological interpretation by virtue of its very nature. It first provides a psychological overview of selfhood and relates the *khaka-navīs* (writer of khaka) and his/her object in an inter-subjective relationship. It then conducts a psychological study of Ismat Chughtai as an individual along ideas contingent to selfhood and intersubjectivity through her *khakas* on Patras Bokhari, Qurratulain Hyder and Sa'adat Hasan Manto. In these, Chughtai consciously discloses about her objects but makes more than a few, unconscious disclosures about herself. Pen-portraits of Chughtai by these three writers are conscious disclosures about Chughtai the writer and Chughtai the woman. All three selections focus on aspects of Chughtai's (and her fellow writers') personae, art and interpersonal relationships. In the process, ideas about objective representation in a *khaka* are under contestation.

Psychological Overview: The *khaka* as a Genre Lending Itself to Psychological Analysis

As mentioned earlier, *khakas* are casements that allow a glimpse into the selfhood of both the writer and the object. It is, thus, imperative to understand the concept of 'self' from a psychological perspective in order to better comprehend the intersubjective reality of both the writer and the object that is formed in the process of writing and analysing a *khaka*. Although the word 'self' is common parlance, its exact meaning is difficult to specify. It is considered an abstract concept, which refers to other abstract concepts related to and constituting the individuality of a person. Hence, a precise definition of the 'self' would be hard to find in psychological literature. However, the psychoanalytic tradition presents two contrasting positions of the self—one by self-psychology and the other by ego psychology (Kirshner 1991). Self-psychology discusses the self as a psychic organisation whose purpose is to serve as a source of intentionality, initiative, and unity that encompasses the structure of the personality and organises it as a whole. The self of this position is created and maintained through an interaction with the other; hence it is a conceptualisation of the self that projects outward. It is a self that develops through interpersonal interaction with another self, in the form of another person or an object. Since this self is dependent on interpersonal and interpsychic processes, known as 'mirroring' or 'self-object transference', its development depends upon receiving understanding and affirmation from the other person. Relationships with another person are considered the building blocks of the self (Hastings 2011). In a *khaka*, even if a personal relationship between the writer and the object does not exist, an intersubjective space of reciprocal relationship and interaction gets constructed through the act of writing by the object, and through the process of reading and internalising that piece of writing by the writer of the *khaka*. As in interpsychic or interpersonal relationships, the focus is mainly on transactions with others, and the unquestionable participation in the social world, the social level of explanation is a major component of the interpersonal conceptualisation of the self. The self of self-psychology, therefore, borrows tremendously from the intersubjective experience with the object, and the social world that they collectively constitute, a process which shapes its structure and constitution. Any *khaka* by virtue of its raison d'être combines interpsychic subject-object sociological relations and the intrapsychic nature of the writer who conceives it, in a dialectic interaction that exposes the self of the writer in his or her interpretation of the other. Since the *khaka* is a perception of the writer about the object, it is strongly shaped by the writer's intersubjective experience with the object, either through personal interaction with the object, or through engagement with the writings of the object, when the object is a writer himself or herself.

The self of ego psychology, in contrast, is a more bounded entity, not guided so much by an intersubjective experience, but is dominated by the demands placed upon the individual by an inner entity equivalent to Freud's concept of the id.

For the purpose of interpreting the selfhood of the authors of the *khaka*s, the position of the self as developed and maintained by an intersubjective experience with the object will be taken.

Another proponent of the interpersonal perspective of selfhood formation was Harry Sullivan (Kirshner 1991). He considered the interpersonal field, and not the individual mind, as the starting point for understanding human behaviour deriving from selfhood. He was greatly influenced by Kurt Lewin's field theory of interpersonal relationships and interaction, which posits the existence of a social field full of actors, with whom the self interacts. According to Lewin, the whole, through its interactive force engaging with the interpersonal field, shapes individual participation, leading to the formation of selfhood. Borrowing from this conceptualisation, the interpersonal field is central to Sullivan's construction of selfhood. In a *khaka*, the interpersonal field is the interaction between the writer and the object, constructed either through an interpersonal relationship of shared experiences between the two. Or, in case no interpersonal interaction between the two has taken place, then the intersubjective and interpsychic relational space that develops between the writer and object through the writings of the object and his/her inter- as well as the intra-psychic impact on the writer of the *khaka*. 'That intimate connection between them is what makes it possible to draw inferences about the subjective even though it cannot be directly observed …' (Grey 1988, 556).

Furthermore in psychoanalysis, D.W. Winnicott introduced the notion of intersubjective formation of selfhood. He brought about a paradigm shift in the formation of selfhood by shifting the focus from the self as an intrapsychic entity to the idea of the self as an interpsychic reality formed through the mirroring process involved in intersubjective experience. According to Winnicott, the recognition of the self by the other is more important than Freud's insistence on the importance of drive and need reduction (Kirshner 1991). The realisation of selfhood is, therefore, an active process taking place in conscious awareness, in which the self is not merely a passive recipient of the fulfilment of innate and instinctual needs and drives, like Freud insisted. In espousing the latter, where Freud presented a 'one-person psychology', Winnicott advocates for a 'two-person psychology' based on the notion of intersubjective experience and its role in the formation of selfhood. Winnicott's two-person psychology, espouses that the self is consistently structured through an internalisation of relational configurations in the shared space occupied by two selves locked in an intersubjective interaction, in this case the writer and object of the *khaka*.

Even thinkers not endorsing the psychoanalytic position have acknowledged the intersubjectivity of the self. For example, Hegel said, 'Self-consciousness exists in and for itself when, and by the fact that, it so exists for another; it exists only by being acknowledged' (1807). This line of thinking rejects the viewing of the world from the inside, leading to an introjected self. The phenomenological notion of the self, from which the psychoanalytic notion of the self heavily draws, pictures the self as being a product of active consciousness that is derived from an intersubjective experience. The notion of a transcendental self that exists a priori is, therefore, rejected. In intersubjective experience, the self comes to recognise qualities in the other person that the self itself possesses, and it is through this realisation that the self discovers itself. Sometimes, the qualities that the self-recognises in the other as a mirror of itself may be qualities that the self is not consciously aware of until it recognises those qualities in the other person. The dialectic involved in this mirroring process that occurs during the intersubjective experience, therefore, lays down the foundation for the formation of selfhood. *Khakas* are a reflection of this process underplay. A close reading and subsequent interpretation of the *khakas* reveals that the writer, while commenting on the object, either through anecdotes and stories of shared experiences or through an interpretation of the object's artistic, social, cultural and political leanings evident in the writings, exposes his/her selfhood also, purely based on the manner in which the writer perceives and interprets the object. Especially so, since no interpretation is possible without an intersubjective experience between the subject and the object, whether through direct contact or through objective observation.

A *khaka* is an essay conceived as an honest representation of a friend, acquaintance or contemporary, along with his/her literary and/or professional attributes. The object should be well-known to the *khaka-navīs* like an 'intimate friend' (Bokhari 'Breaching' 172). *Khaka*s written outside of the writer's personal experiences with his object, or those based on hearsay run the risk of lapsing into falsehoods, exaggeration or understatement. Mushfiq Khwaja's essay '*Khaka-ba Gosh*' in *Roznāmā Jasārat* (Karachi 1986) stresses that:

1. A *khaka-navīs* should have a discerning eye that perceives both overt and covert aspects of his/her object's persona.
2. He/she should have a keen discernment in recognising and projecting facets that constitute the essence of his/her object's nature.
3. He/she should have the ability to make a faithful and factual representation of an event or individual, rather than colour it with his/her perception. In other words, he/she should be objective.
4. He/she should make use of brevity to make as detailed a sketch of the object in as few words as possible. In other words, he/she should be familiar with the art of writing (Suhail 79). In '*Deed wa Daryāft*' (18) Nisar Ahmad Farooqui observes that a good *khaka* depicts an individual such that his appearance, disposition, demeanour, his intelligence, his ideological leanings, his strengths and weaknesses, all come to light. It steers clear of leniency, partiality, exaggeration, and praise (Hasan 52). Objectivity and honesty then, are among the essentials of a good *khaka*.

The art of *khaka-nigāri* (pen-portraiture) is contingent upon the writer's keenness of perception and observation, his/her intimacy with the object, and his/her power of expression. In *khaka*s, the analysis of the object also derives from the writer's engagement with the object, which could be with the public image of the object that has been consciously created by the object, but still represents a manifestation of the object's intrapsychic reality and interpersonal dialectic with the outside world. The writer's keenness of perception permits him or her to perceive the object in a manner that allows him or her to open a window into the object's selfhood, and thereby interact with it. The self and the object of the *khaka* emerge as composite representations of the apparent and the concealed, the positive and the negative aspects of persona, as revealed by means of anecdotes in which they may or may not play integral parts and ideas stemming from intrasubjective and intersubjective experiences. The writer's vision is shaped by his/her own selfhood, where through the process of mirroring, the writer sees an aspect of himself or herself reflected in the object. The intersubjectivity is evident in the writer's interpretation of the object's intentions and motivations. Those qualities of the object's personality that resonate with the writer, through identification, make an impact. The writer, therefore, infuses a great part of his or her own self in the study of the object. What is present before the reader is the interpersonal field shared by two people, in line with Lewin's field theory combined with the two-people psychological perspective. The situation and the context in which the writer and the object engage, constitute the interpersonal field. The dialectical interplay between these two social actors impacts the selfhood of both, in which the latent and the manifest, the concealed and the apparent, interact with one another. In this mirroring process, the intersubjectivity leads to self-recognition for both actors, some of which may be conscious while the remaining may be unconscious realisation. Conscious disclosures are made by the writer as regards the object delineated in a *khaka* on account of sensibilities particular to him or her. However, the writer's subconscious self plays a dynamic role in the sketch without his/her being perceptive about it. As a projection of the author's own individuality, *khaka*s lend themselves quite suitably to psychological inquiry into the formation and sustenance of his/her selfhood.

Ismat Chughtai and Patras Bokhari

Born in Lahore in undivided India, Syed Ahmed Shah or Patras Bokhari (1898–1958) was an essayist, educationist, broadcaster and critic who went on to become Pakistan's first representative at the United Nations. Bokhari wrote in the humourist mode. His portrait of Chughtai, '*Kuchh Ismat Chughtai ke bāre meṅ*', was written as an appraisal of Chughtai in relation to two of her earliest collections of short stories, plays and essays, '*Kaliyāñ*' (Buds, 1941, Maktaba Urdu Adab, Lahore) and '*Choteiñ*' (Wounds, 1942, Educational Book House, Aligarh). The portrait is critical and satiric in tone. Albeit with caveats, Bokhari credits Chughtai with writing in the realistic mode, and for her truthful and keen perception, observation and depiction of the banal and the mundane. He believes that she is best at writing short stories though only when she is dealing with the weaker or marginalised sections of society. He also points out that Chughtai's reader can never break away from the body—male or female, de-romanticised, and at times, even repugnant. He finds her most uncomfortable in the drawing room or in genteel, urbane company. He is particularly severe in his criticism of Chughtai as a playwright, ridiculing what he sees as her limited understanding of dramatic art. He advises her against writing plays, complaining that she is unfamiliar with the performative tradition and tactless with regard to its dialogic style. Bokhari tears down Chughtai's critics (including Krishan Chander) and detractors who are prudish in their estimation of her psychoanalytic depictions of protagonists and her matter-of-fact treatment of human sexuality and sexual desire. He concludes by conceding that she has revitalised Urdu literature. His language is metaphoric, colourful and even picturesque. With regard to her *khakas*, he estimates that the sum of her success rests on '*Dozakhi*'; that nothing in Urdu literature compares with its style and mode ('Breaching' 188). However, it is quite evident that like those of most other critics, Bokhari's observations on Chughtai's short story, '*Lihāaf*' are dated. Though he attempts to look beyond his age, he emerges as a product of a conservative social setup:

> But the value of Ismat's story is reduced because its central focus (or according to Askari Saheb[9], its "*tākīdī nuqta*" [central emphasis]) is not a matter concerning the heart but rather, a bodily requirement. In the beginning one gets the impression that she will unveil Begum Jan's proclivities. Then one begins to expect that perhaps she is interested in the emotions of the child who is narrating the story. However, the story veers away from both these issues and acquires an altogether different direction and fixes its gaze on the mounting quilt. As a result, the poor reader finds himself in the midst of people who, to draw an analogy, are sitting on their haunches by the roadside to watch an exhibition of the amour of animals. (ibid. 187–88)

Chughtai's portrait of Bokhari '*Kuchh merī Yādeñ*'[10] is a memorialising obituary published soon after his death. She begins by quoting his final commendation of her which had evoked uncontrollable laughter, when she first read it:

> "Ismat's person is a source of pride for Urdu. She has made cracks in numerous old battlements which while they were standing, obscured many paths. To deny the status Ismat has in Urdu literature is to exhibit shortsightedness and a meanness of spirit."
>
> I slipped off the divan while in the throes of laughter.
>
> "Please stop, for God's sake," I pleaded, wiping my eyes with a corner of my shirtfront. My stomach contorted, I was breathless, our laughter turned to screams. It seemed as if my stomach would be rent in two if I continued to laugh with such force ('Memories' 177).

Bokhari concludes his *khaka 'Kuchh Ismat Chughtai ke bāre mein'* thus: '*Itnī had-bandī kar lene ke b'ad humeñ is bāt ko taslīm kar lene meñ zarā bhī ta'ammul nā honā chahiye kī 'Ismat kī shakhṣiyat Urdū adab ke liye bā'iś-e fakhr hai* (31) (Having made a note of all her limitations, we must not hesitate to concede that Ismat is indeed a source of pride for Urdu literature) (ibid. 190). Perhaps, Chughtai's uncontrollable laughter stems from the Bokhari's reserved praise, his essay being smattered quite amply with comments on her artistic weaknesses. However, right after, she continues, 'In those days we laughed at every little thing' ('*Memories*' 2015, 177).

Apart from this opening, quite characteristic response to criticism and/or appraisal, most of Chughtai's essay is in confessional mode. It reads like a fond reminiscence of a time gone by. Humour and nostalgia combine to give personal views and opinions which open casements that reveal some intimate disclosures and sensibilities.

Chughtai recalls that Bokhari was a familiar name in her household. She narrates anecdotes about her childhood and adolescent infatuation with him and her adult estimation of him as an individual—of how the whole family read and enjoyed his familiar and tongue-in-cheek linguistic style; how the young imagined that he was young like them, and handsome and perceptive of their sensibilities in relation to him. Chughtai's fascination with Bokhari dates back to her childhood when she was a fledgling writer. She expresses this by narrating an incident when, over-stepping the threshold of moral rectitude expected of a young lady belonging to a respectable Muslim household, she wrote him a letter in a most familiar manner. As a consequence, she was beaten thoroughly and shamed for days together after the letter was redirected to her father. This was possibly a time when she was attempting to discover herself as a writer, which was to become a major aspect of her sense of selfhood. Attraction to Bokhari at this time, despite the fact that it met with ridicule from her family, is a reflection of her rebellious and iconoclastic nature, which later manifests in her stories. Even though she never met Bokhari when she was younger, she shared an intersubjective experience with him through his writings, which is evident from her fascination with Bokhari the writer. Through his stories, she extracted an imagined part of Bokhari's selfhood, which mirrored her own, yet undeveloped, sense of self. This was the part of her selfhood that she held on to keenly and under guard, which is why she was not inclined to meeting Bokhari personally, when the opportunity afforded itself many years later. Chughtai recalls her confusion and bewilderment when he invited her over to visit him while he was visiting India—that she did not want her husband Shahid Latif to accompany her; that in her utter panic over the invite, she mistook a front-office employee, Lakshman, at the radio station for Bokhari; that all her rehearsals of dialogue with him were reduced to a cipher when they began to talk. The conversations she imagined having with him indicate towards an intersubjective experience with Bokhari that she had already experienced, and that part of her was afraid of it being negated when she finally met him, as it was a valued part of her own selfhood. When she mistakes Lakshman for Bokhari, and expresses disappointment in his personality, she reveals how ready she was to reject anything real she discovered about him when meeting him in person. It was a desperate attempt to hold onto the imagined Bokhari, as this version of him had contributed to the development of her own selfhood. And to discover something contrary would require a refiguring of her own selfhood, which she was not yet ready to undertake. In fact, when she actually meets him, she finds him to be 'so well read and knowledgeable that no ordinary approach would bring him down effectively' (ibid., 183). Chughtai finds herself forced to resort to a 'tenacious and regular debate' a 'longstanding asset' of all her family (ibid., 183). In spite of this, she finds that he was 'wiser' and 'more experienced' and finally makes up her mind to be his disciple and accept him as a patronizing elder (ibid., 183). Chughtai also recalls her chagrin at being advised against writing plays and her discomfort when he dismissed her desire to have her stories translated into English (ibid., 188). She also mentions his willingness to help in a personal capacity and his conviction in her literary merit—that one day people would pay well to be able to read her (ibid., 188–89).

Chughtai is most congenial and affable in her recollection of and reflections on Bokhari; she concludes expressing that though he has passed on, he continues to live 'deep in (her) imagination' (ibid., 189). Her vivid recollection of memories of her meeting with Bokhari afford the reader a clear perception of Bokhari the writer, critic and individual. Also brought into the perspective are the socio-political and economic flux of the times, contemporary writers and their writing styles, personal experiences and above all, a sense of nostalgia for the irrevocable loss of an era gone by. The reader stands face-to-face, not with Chughtai the fiery feminist, but a Chughtai who is bashful, fearful, committing mistakes, conceding faults, requesting favours, one who looks up to an elder, acclaimed writer for encouragement and advice, and also one who stoutly rebuffs criticism.

Ismat Chughtai and Qurratulain Hyder

Born in Aligarh, Qurratulain Hyder (1927–2007) is a younger writer and junior at college who remained politically unaligned. Hyder's *khaka* of Chughtai, '*Lady Chengez Khan*' is an obituary opening with the information that Padma Sachdev called to inform her of Chughtai's passing on. This is followed by Hyder's philosophising on the solemnity of dying. Hyder makes several observations about Chughtai's personality, by recalling incidents to which she was witness or by means of which people formed opinions about Chughtai. She also records Chughtai's tenuous association with the Progressive Writers' Association and delineates her against the backdrop of the political and social-cultural instability of her times. Chughtai's candour, her sharp-wittedness, sense of humour, matter-of-factness, her religious sensibilities and even the dementia during her last years are recorded sincerely and sensitively. Throughout the essay, Hyder seems to be elucidating how or why certain ideas about her became fixed or offering apologies for certain misunderstandings regarding her as an individual.

Chughtai's portrait of Hyder, 'Pompom Darling' was written as a response to the latter's short stories and articles published in various journals soon after the publication of '*Sitāroṅ se Āge*' (Beyond the Stars, Khatun Kitab Ghar, 1947). It takes the form of a comprehensive critique, in fact, a diatribe against Hyder's writing and holds her representation of upper middle class protagonists and her political non-alignment as the root cause of the fatalism characteristic of her oeuvre. She disparages Hyder's fiction as 'suffocating' ('Pompom' 2000, 122), with respect to content, characterisation and point-of-view. According to Chughtai, Hyder could never rid herself of her sense of gloom and doom because she failed to come face-to-face with the problems of the teeming masses. She clubs Hyder with her mother, Nazar Sajjad Hyder, claiming that together they constitute a literary lineage. Making a reference to Bokhari's observation with regard to herself that she was no good at representing the 'well-heeled' ('Breaching' 2017, 177) whether in plays or in *afsānas*, she makes a prayer of thanksgiving that her parents did not provide her with the artifice of a well-furnished drawing room, for it would mar her vitality as a writer and make her as cocooned and superficial as Hyder ('Pompom' 2000, 121). In her candid, no-holds-barred style, she clubs all Hyder's characters together as caricatures trapped in an artificial world. Shosho and Fofo (116), Zoofie, Polly and Pompom (118) and Molly and Dolly (124) are all of a category, with minimal differences: 'The same old antiquated mind in new heads forces her to create surrealistic Blanchas instead of drawing beautiful and living pictures. The day is not far when Miss Hyder starts writing stories about mummies and corpses like Miss Hijab Ismail. Already her characters are quite fossilized.' (ibid., 123)

Conceding that 'there is a good deal of individuality and uniqueness' in Hyder's narrative style, Chughtai goes on to add only a little later, that Hyder's multiple points of view leave the reader confused as to whether she believes in the proposition or the opposition (122). Perhaps Chughtai misses that Hyder's multiple points of view and point-counterpoint techniques are meant to state facts as they stand, or point at the existence of multiple truths and leave interpretation to the reader. Possibly, Chughtai's Progressive intent prevents her from perceiving the modernist aesthetic at play in Hyder's narrative or such narrative ingenuity has no scope in her Progressive intent. It is also possible that this points at a personal bias against Hyder.

As readers we may wonder whether Chughtai's cynicism and acerbity points at her biased opinion of Hyder, or perhaps she did not understand her younger contemporary at all. It also denotes a pinch of envy and consequential resistance on Chughtai's part to come to terms with any impact that Hyder's writings might have had on the building of her selfhood. Perhaps Hyder being her junior was the reason for this resistance, because Chughtai felt that Hyder deserved only condescension. The resistance to Hyder could also denote a rejection of the prevalent societal values, marred by capitalist tendencies and class and gender differences, which were part and parcel of Hyder's writing, which Chughtai was opposed to and fighting against. Like she says, 'For there she would meet a Comrade, who has entered the arena after clashing with the world for the sake of his ideals' (ibid., 126), and the fact that it was a woman, Hyder, who was espousing them disturbed Chughtai. Hence, Chughtai makes a concerted effort to avoid identification with Hyder and her writing, despite experiencing a 'strange kind of love' for it which gave her a 'customary stab of pain while trying to disown it' (ibid., 126).

Chughtai's barbed and acerbic account may also be interpreted as unwillingness on her part to associate with Hyder as fellow writer. A comparison between them would be inevitable, as they were contemporary women writers of a shared literary tradition. Chughtai would rather not have such comparisons made at all, and if any were made, they would rather be compared for their contrasting styles and different sensibilities as far as the content and intent behind their writings was concerned. Such unwillingness seems to be present on Chughtai's part, not so much on Hyder's part who depicts her in a subtly reverent manner. This fact is most evident in the titles selected by Chughtai and Hyder for their *khaka*s of each other. Chughtai parodies Hyder as a silly and frivolous 'Pompom Darling', nick-naming her after one of her characters. Hyder is reverential and favourable towards her senior contemporary, burying a hatchet as it were, for surely, she must have read Chughtai's unfavourable estimation. Drawing on her 'remote' (2000, 208) warrior ancestry, Hyder labels Chughtai 'Lady Chengez Khan', '(b)reaching (o)ld (f)ortifications' and '(f)inding (n)ew (p)athways' (170) with her potent pen, like her warrior ancestor Chengez Khan, fighting fierce and bloody battles with his sword.

Drawing inspiration perhaps from Bokhari's essay about her, Chughtai feels that as an elder writer, she is licensed to critique the younger Hyder's oeuvre, and correct what she believes are her errant ways. She is acerbic in her criticism. In terms of selfhood, it can be postulated that Chughtai's sense of self was influenced by Hyder's through non-identification with the qualities of the other, in a process that would be the reverse of the mirroring effect. This is an interesting space in the study of selfhood, one that is not addressed by many psychologists and other thinkers interested in selfhood as a construct of intersubjective experience. Or perhaps the projective identification is of that part of Chughtai's self that she wants to overlook. So if Hyder wrote about the upper middle class, Chughtai insisted that she was the common man's crusader; if Hyder was non-political, Chughtai adamantly projected her political leanings; if Hyder was presenting multiple view-points, Chughtai emphasised a single point of view and underscored the expression of her particular perspective in her writings. The relational configuration of the shared intersubjective space between Chughtai and Hyder, as discussed by Winnicott, functioned in a contradictory manner, where the conscious attempt at non-identification with the object predominated the overt and intentional construction of the writer's selfhood. It might have resulted in intrapsychic dissonance for Chughtai. Her ridicule of Hyder and her writing may have been a reaction to consciously cover up and mitigate her unease of experiencing this dissonance. This process is akin to a defence mechanism to reduce the anxiety, hinted at by Winnicott, which is caused by an insistent detachment of the self from engaging in a dialectic writer-object intersubjective space with a contemporary whom she could not avoid.

Ismat Chughtai and Sa'adat Hasan Manto

Essayist, story writer, playwright, editor and screen-play writer, Sa'adat Hasan Manto (1912–1955) was born in Punjab in undivided India. Manto writes in a matter-of-fact tone tinged with satirical humour or cynicism and deep psychological insight. '*Ganje Farishte*' (Bald Angels, 1952) and *Loudspeaker* (1955) are two of his collections of *khakas*, including those on contemporary writers such as Agha Hasan Kashmiri, Miraji and Ismat Chughtai, and film actors Shyam, Nargis and Ashok Kumar, among others. Manto and Chughtai were contemporaries, fellow progressives and friends, similarly rebellious, with an equally strong sense of individualism which led to fall-outs with the hard line propagated by the extremist wing of the All-India Progressive Writers' Association. In 'Ismat Chughtai' (2003),

Manto's evaluates Chughtai as a friend and fellow writer. The portrait speaks of their kinship, and the fact that they got along famously despite their razor sharp wit; it asserts that they had agreed to disagree, and shared mutual respect for one another; that though they referred to each other as 'Manto Bhai' and 'Ismat Behn', neither had a healthy respect for such a fraternal relationship ('Chughtai' 2003, 233).

Manto recalls several incidents from their years in Bombay, right from their first meeting in August, 1942 at his Claire Road office, while he was editor of *Musawwir*, to the fun they had at the expense of contemporaries, Naseem Bano and Krishan Chander included (235). Manto's earliest estimation of Chughtai, after their first meeting was that '(t)he wretch turned out to be a mere woman after all' (226–27). He could not continue his discussion on '*Lihāaf*' with her because he sensed the embarrassment of 'common, homely girls' on her face when he broached the idea of a weak conclusion to her (226). Time and again, Manto estimates her womanliness and ratiocinates about her as a writer; he appreciates her for her economy of words and is critical of her clumsiness with spellings. Her cleverness with the needle; her unwavering solicitations for her daughter; her obstinacy and her keen perception to the minutiae of human existence, all stand in a balance that make up Ismat the woman and Ismat the writer. According to Manto, if she were not every bit the woman she was, she could not have written with such immense sensitivity (228).

In order to maintain coherence and continuity between the inner workings of the mind and their relationships with others, a dialectic is created by the individual in their intrapsychic and interpersonal lives. Through this dialectic, operating in the shared space of the intersubjective experience of the self-other dyad, individuals 'sometimes enhance each other and are sometimes at odds with each other, forming the basis for powerful conflicts' (Mitchell 1981). This relational matrix, that includes both interpersonal and intrapsychic elements, is most clearly evident in the relationship shared between Chughtai and Manto. In all the pen-portraits discussed in this paper, it is the relational dynamics between Manto and Chughtai that best capture the source of Chughtai's selfhood. Chughtai's womanliness, which Manto refers to in his pen-portrait of her, is clearly evident in 'Mera Dost, Mera Dushman', insofar as her womanliness describes Chughtai's sensitive, deep and nuanced understanding of her relationship dynamics with Manto. More so, Chughtai describes in greater detail the kind of relationship she shared with him, defined by their often conflicting, yet compatible, association. They are like two sides of the same coin, with differing perspectives that, when combined, form a whole.

Chughtai's portrait of Manto, 'Mera Dost, Mera Dushman' is an obituary and Chughtai is evidently distraught. Her memory, vivid and illustrative, makes Manto breathe again. The reader stands face-to-face, not with Manto the writer, but with a very sensitive man, whose inmost sensibilities are brought out with equally perceptive sensitivity. Manto, a friend and severe critic, a very opinionated colleague who scorns most others, a father who grudgingly conceded helpless love for a son who is no more, a husband who spares no occasion to shock a homely wife, but above all, a man who is mostly alienated from and disappointed with practically everything around him, whose relationships with (everyone and everything) are fragile and determined not by robust parameters but by standards dictated by impulsiveness and over-sensitivity. Chughtai's portrait provides more than sufficient indicators about the sensitivity that was mirrored in Manto's fiction. In the process, Chughtai is almost brutally frank with regard to her own estimations and attitudes, or for that matter, her erroneousness and the comparative nonchalance on her part, despite which the relationship flourished for a long time. In fact, Manto's sensitivity stands out the more when visualised against Chughtai's self-confessed tactlessness and self-deprecation. Perhaps, this is a calculated and conscious move of yet another sensitive writer to bring out his sensitivity by highlighting her own lack of it.

The mirroring effect is best depicted in Chughtai's relationship and interaction with Manto, which must have been clearly evident to people around them, and which is why Manto was often questioned about why he and Chughtai were not married. Manto is clearly not an easy personality but Chughtai accepts him as he is, handles him impeccably and also enjoys him. She finds her selfhood enhanced by Manto's selfhood, where her intrapsychic tendencies come to the fore in the shared space of their intersubjective interaction, and find themselves mirrored in the other person's self, and thereby accepted and reinforced. And this mirroring effect is all the more interesting because Chughtai and Manto seem to express rather contrasting and conflicting styles of expression. They are contrasting, yet compatible—that is what makes their intersubjective encounters so much more interesting to unravel and understand.

Language and Objectivity in a *Khaka*

Intersubjectivity can be discerned through the use of language (Thompson 2005) and *khakas* stand testimony to this. The six *khakas* analysed stand testimony to the writers' selves as well as their particular relationships with their objects in terms of linguistic style also. Each writer makes subconscious interventions in his/her portrait that lead to questioning the notion of objectivity in a *khaka*. The dialectic exchange involved in the linguistic discourse between the self and the other, in this case the writer and the object of the *khaka*, unveils aspects of the self that are brought to the forefront of both conscious and unconscious awareness. The writer's individualised writing style, therefore, is influenced by who the writer is describing since the words the writer employs are the ones that come to his or her mind when he or she thinks of the object. Utilising the mirroring concept, the writer's own sense of self can thereby be interpreted from his or her choice of linguistic style applied in the writing of the pen-portrait.

Patras Bokhari's witticisms regarding co-relations between disparate concepts or *fiqre-bāzi*, which Manto disparages in 'Ismat Chughtai' are a case in point where the intersubjective and intrasubjective are at play. 'Patras Saheb's sentence, "As though literature is like a tennis tournament" is typical of his penchant for fiqre-bazi, or witticism. Literature is not a tennis tournament. It is not indecent for men and women to play matches separately." ('Ismat' 2003, 237)

Manto's question directed at Bokhari's witticism elucidates Lacan's perspective (1977) that the language used in a discourse can reveal the underlying unconscious aspects of the relationship between the writer and the subject. Here is a case of one robust writer throwing down the gauntlet at another. 'Will Patras Saheb offer the same insight in the case of literature produced by transvestites? Is there any distinction—natural, internal, fundamental—that differentiates the literature produced by ordinary men and women from that produced by transvestites?' (ibid.) In a similar strain are Chughtai's initial remarks regarding Qurratulain Hyder. Referring to her as a 'new star', an arrow that does not miss it mark, she almost sounds envious of her spectacular success, sulking that the new clutch of writers treads a path already cleared by earlier pioneers ('Pompom' 2000, 115). Chughtai goes on to observe that her star's brightness soon began to fade as nothing in her writing seemed to change. Qurratulain Hyder was trapped in a dying world whose vestiges were crumbling around her. 'Cinderella needed to come down to earth' but she 'continued to twinkle in the sky' and '(w)hen the clock of the world struck twelve, the enchantment of the magic wand began to wane' (ibid. 116). Chughtai's judgement isn't objective.

Manto and Chughtai's *khaka*s of each other resonate with the informal, friendly banter that must have existed between them. Intensely sensitive, they induce as much laughter as they are serious in appraisals of each other's personalities and art of writing, which both describe metaphorically. Interestingly, both Manto and Chughtai have something to say about each other's eyes. Manto recalls: 'Her small but sharp and inquisitive eyes gleamed behind thick glasses' ('Ismat' 2003, 232); and again, quite unrecognisable with colour smeared all over her one Holi, 'Ismat's small eyes rolled behind her eyeglasses stained with colours' (ibid. 235).

Chughtai recalls:

> ... I looked at him from the corner of my eyes. Hidden behind thick glasses were flashing black eyes that suddenly reminded me of a peacock's wings. What's the connection between those eyes and a peacock? ... Perhaps it was the spontaneous glow that went along with the arrogance and impudence in them. My heart skipped a beat when I saw his eyes. ('My Friend' 2015, 191)

Conclusion

*Khaka*s provide comprehensive, first-hand insights about writers and their objects. The format combines a biographical-critical mechanism of analysis that serves as valuable auxiliary reading in studies involving writers' and their objects' literary output. They combine both subjective and objective observations, despite the conscious requirement of objectivity, because the subconscious and conscious minds are continually at play. Subjective observations may fall prey to partiality and objective ones may provide dry appraisals. Opinions or assertions in *khaka*s are open to debate. An informed reader familiar with writers and their objects is free to judge the portrait in accordance with his readings and experiences while an uninformed reader gets an opportunity to familiarise himself/herself. In the *khaka*s analysed in this study, Chughtai's tone is elegiac and commendatory in her portraits or reminiscences of Manto and Bokhari. While she responds to Bokhari's passing on as that of an elder, accomplished writer, her response to Manto's demise is that of an equal—nostalgic and deeply perturbed. Her response to Hyder is jaundiced; her sketch is patronising to the point of being dismissive. All three portraits reveal subjective responses corresponding to relationship and camaraderie. Despite claims to objectivity, Bokhari's appraisal of Chughtai is at times tongue-in-cheek and at times ruthless. This may have to do with his particular ironic-satiric linguistic style. Very likely, his comments on her writings give Chughtai the lead that reverberates in her critique of the young Hyder's oeuvre. Hyder's portrait of Chughtai on the other hand, is balanced, but tilting towards considerate discernment with regard to her as writer and as individual, and giving no indication of ill-will or literary animosity. Manto's portrait of Chughtai elucidates the affection that characterised their relationship, despite the fact that he illustrates how they often held their own, owing to their equally strong personalities.

As a non-fictional genre the *khaka* may lend itself to serious appraisal and evaluation of the writer, object, as well as reader. In fact, the reader may also discover an aspect of his or her own selfhood in the manner in which a *khaka* is read by him/her. Just like Chughtai's selfhood was informed by the writings of Bokhari, Hyder and Manto, in the same manner the *khaka*s written by them will reveal aspects of the selfhood of the reader, depending upon which parts of the *khaka*s resonate with the reader, through their novelty or their familiarity. In this case, a third person, that is, the reader has entered the dialogic space of the writer-object dyad, and though he or she may seem like an objective observer, he or she is in actuality impacted by the writing by partaking in the intersubjective space shared between the writer and the object. And through the process of mirroring, the reader's selfhood is affected. On the part of the writer, he or she imagines a readership for whom the *khaka* is being written. That imagined self of the other, which is the reader, then informs the content and, particularly the linguistic style, of the *khaka*. Although the writer cannot control or predict the readership of the *khaka*, he or she definitely writes it for an imagined other, someone with whom the writer presupposes a sense of familiarity, connectedness, and intellectual and emotional compatibility. Consequently, here we see the writer's selfhood as also being determined by the imagined self of the readership for whom the *khaka* is being written.

Notes

1. The year *Angarey* was published.
2. Melanie Klein, who introduced the concept of the other person as an object, used the object as an underlying referent of an individual's entire psychic life. The construction of the object is therefore not just a matter of mental content; in fact, it is a structuring force in the subjective experience that shapes the formation of the self. Selfhood, therefore, is dependent on the perception and interpretation of the object, who is the other person (Kirshner 1991). Hence, this study refers to the writer as subject and the person portrayed as object.
3. First published in *Nuqūsh*, special issue on Bokhari September, 1959.
4. First published in *Chūi Mūi*, Kutub Publishers Limited Mumbai, 1947.
5. First published in *Nuqūsh*, special issue on Manto, March, 1956.
6. First published in *Sāqi*, Delhi, February, 1945.
7. Written before 1947 and published in '*Ganje Farishte*' (Bald Angles,1952).
8. First published in *Kaliyān*, Bombay edition 1952; the essay used in this study has been edited by the author.
9. Muhammad Hasan Askari (1919–78) was an Urdu scholar, literary critic writer and linguist. He migrated to Lahore after the Partition.
10. Translated as 'Memories' by Tahira Naqvi

References

Bokhari, Patras. 1992. "*Ismat Chughtai ke Bāre Mein Kuch Bāteiñ.*" *Saughat*, Issue II (March): 17–31.

———. 2017. "Breaching Old Fortifications, Finding New Pathways." In *An Uncivil Woman: Writings on Ismat Chughtai*. Edited by Rakhshanda Jalil. Translated by Fatima Rizvi. 170–91. New Delhi: Oxford UP.

Chughtai, Ismat. 2015. "Memories." In *My Friend, My Enemy: Essays Reminiscences, Portraits*. Translated by Tahira Naqvi. 177–89. New Delhi: Women Unlimited.

———. 2015. "My Friend, My Enemy." In *My Friend, My Enemy: Essays Reminiscences, Portraits.* Translated by Tahira Naqvi. 190–212. New Delhi: Women Unlimited.

———. 2000. "Pompom Darling." Translated by Rashmi Govind. In *Ismat: Her Life, Her Times.* Edited by Sukrita Paul Kumar and Sadique. Alt. Series. *Approaches to Literatures in Translation.* 115–26. Delhi: Katha.

Grey, A. 1988. "Sullivan's Contribution to Psychoanalysis—An Overview." *Contemporary Psychoanalysis,* 24: 548–76.

Hastings, C. R. 2011. "Something Happens: Mirroring in Intersubjective Connection. Unpublished manuscript: 1–77.

Hyder, Qurratulain. 2000. "Lady Chenghez Khan." Translated by Deeba Zafir. In *Ismat: Her Life, Her Times.* Edited by Sukrita Paul Kumar and Sadique. Alt. Series. *Approaches to Literatures in Translation.* 204–08. Delhi: Katha.

Kirshner, L.A. "The Concept of Self in Psychoanalytic Theory and its Philosophical Foundations." *Journal of the American Psychoanalytic Association,* 39 (1991): 157–82.

Lacan, J. 1977. "The Mirror-Stage as Formative of the I as Revealed in Psychoanalytic Experience." Translated by Alan Sheridan. In *Écrits: A Selection.* W.W. Norton & Co., New York.

Manto, Sa'adat Hasan. 2003. "Ismat Chughtai." In *Black Margins.* Edited by Muhammad Umar Memon. Introduced and Translated by M. Asaduddin. 221–43. New Delhi: Katha.

Mitchell, S. 1981. "Relational Concepts in Psychoanalysis: An Integration." Cambridge, MA: Harvard UP.

Musanna, Hasan. "*Sajjad Zaheer ki Khaka-Nigāri.*" *Naya Daur,* May–June (2012): 51–56. Edited by Wazahat Hussain Rizvi. Lucknow.

Suhail, Ahmed. "*Urdu mein Khaka-nigari ki rawait aur Javed Siddiqui ka Langarkhanah.*" *Naya Waraq,* January–June (2017) 18/50: 78–83. Edited by Shadab Rasheed. Mumbai.

Watson, Alex. "Who am I? The Self/Subject according to Psychoanalytic Theory." In SAGE Open 4(3) http://nrs.harvard.edu/urn- 3:HUL. InstRepos:12328212.

4

Between the Erotic and the Social in Ismat Chughtai's Short Stories

KIRAN KESHAVAMURTHY

Ismat Chughtai's (1915–91) writings, particularly her short stories, foreground the porous boundary between the public and the private. Her male and female characters are equally engaged, albeit in their own gendered ways, in constantly upholding and undermining the spatial and ideological binary of private and public, a binary produced by the modernising forces of late colonialism. This is most clearly suggested by two themes—the regulation and loosening of the cultural equation between femininity and private domestic spaces, and the romantic and often violent sexual encounters between men and women, that constitute satires of sexual and class hierarchy. The very distinction between the private and the public has to be understood not as a fixed and universal binary, but as I argue, a spatial and discursive metaphor for the inherently shifting, fractured and interpenetrative nature of these categories. A reading of Chughtai's stories reveals the multiple ways in which the private/public dichotomy is repeatedly blurred and reformulated through axes of class, gender and religious identity.

In the course of this paper, I explore two often overlapping themes that temporarily upset the boundary between the private and public; first, the potential of love between outcaste and marginalised individuals to traverse social distinctions and second, the space of the household where sexual and class hierarchies are at once upheld and undermined, sometimes, tragically at the cost of the life of the female character. Chughtai's early stories are satires of men who retain their power over the family and household at the cost of female deprivation and impoverishment. The home in these stories is a fraught space where gender and sexual norms are both established and transgressed. Her early story 'Gainda' (Marigold, 2009) describes the intimate friendship between the unmarried girl-narrator and Gainda, an equally young child-widow. Through the games they play, they enact their fantasies of dressing up as brides, much to the annoyance of the narrator's mother who suspects her young daughter's pretense is a sign of sexual precocity. For both the girls, the imagined possibility of becoming a bride signifies the possibility of self-acknowledgment and social validation. Marriage, for the girls, perhaps unwittingly, is perceived as a brief moment of visibility and recognition in a woman's life that is otherwise eclipsed by and devoted to the men in her life. The ironic contrast between the narrator and Gainda is evident right from the beginning of the story—while the narrator's longing to become a bride is dismissed by the women in the family, Gainda is subjected to the austere life of a widow, a life she unquestioningly accepts. The narrator jealously perceives Gainda as an ideal embodiment of feminine comportment unlike her own awkward and unrestrained self that may be the function of a more secure and privileged life within the interiors of the home: 'How did Gainda walk? With a supple gait as though she had not a bone in her body. When I walked, it was like a galloping mare' ('Gainda' 2009, 6). Both girls are punished when, pretending to be brides, they smear *sindoor* on their foreheads. The narrator's older brother Bhaiya disrupts their play but also pretends to marry Gainda by applying *sindoor* to the parting in her hair. For Bhaiya, Gainda is a seductive and yet forbidden object of desire that has to be regulated and made to conform to social norms of widowhood. She is violently punished for her attempts to appear as a bride even as she is rendered vulnerable by her own beauty. Years later in the story, the narrator discovers that Gainda is the mother of her brother's illegitimate child, for which she is abandoned by the family and left to starve on the streets.

Chughtai's more well-known story, '*Chauthi ka Jora*' (The Wedding Suit, 1946), is an elaboration of a theme that runs across her earlier stories—marriage as an institutionalised affirmation of male privilege at the cost of female disempowerment and impoverishment. The story revolves around Kubra, the daughter of a poor, widowed seamstress whose potential marriage brings ruin to the family. Kubra's mother is known for her ability to stitch and mend wedding suits that have to be perfectly made to ensure a successful marriage. But at the opening of the story, even Kubra's mother struggles to fix the badly cut wedding suits that the women of the neighborhood bring to her. The obstacles that Kubra's mother faces in stitching wedding suits anticipates Kubra's tragic future as she wastes away her youth trapped in the confines of a 'mosquito-infested room' (1946, 36). While she is in purdah, her younger sister Hamida, is the only character in the story who occupies an interstitial space that gives her access to the concealed confines of Kubra's room and the domestic spaces that her cousin Rahat occupies in the house. When Rahat, who is Kubra's mother's rich nephew, visits them, Kubra's mother assumes he will marry Kubra and become her assured source of wealth and comfort. She borrows money to prepare elaborate dishes for him while she and her daughters survive on meagre meals. Kubra's mother orders Kubra to cook special dishes for him and makes her send them through Hamida. Rahat's insatiable greed consumes, as it were, Kubra's fast aging and emaciated body, which embodies the impoverished female household. Kubra's mother and her neighbour, who is like a sister to Kubra's mother, encourage Hamida to tease Rahat and share jokes with him. The social structures of marriage and kinship position Hamida in an ambiguous position of intimacy that is meant to facilitate a marriage that promises material wealth; as Kubra's sister, she is entitled to create a humorously intimate but decidedly non-sexual relationship with Rahat while being exposed to the possibility of sexual intimacy. Hamida almost stands in for her sister, who being in purdah does not have access to her potential husband. Rahat insinuates his sexual interest in Hamida much to her disgust.

> Bi Amma's adopted sister's scheme worked, and Rahat began to spend a greater part of the day at home. Bi Aapa was always busy at the hearth, Bi Amma occupied herself with stitching the jora for chauthi, and Rahat's filthy eyes stung my heart like arrows. He would tease me for nothing while eating, saying that he wanted some water or a pinch of salt. And he would make suggestive remarks. (Chughtai 1936, 32)

Rahat's utter indifference, let alone his contempt for the food he is fed, infuriates Hamida whose sympathies lie with her trapped and unacknowledged sister.

> I was in tears. "These hands", I thought, "that remain busy, like bonded slaves, from morning till night grinding spices, drawing water, chopping onions, laying the bed, cleaning shoes. When will their slavery end? Will there be no buyers for them? Will no one ever kiss them lovingly? Will

> henna never adorn them? Will they never be perfumed with the bridal attar?" (ibid., 32–33)

Kubra is perceived as a burden to the family that has to be exchanged in marriage for the prospect for future wealth. Hamida's observation of her mother's painstaking efforts to impress Rahat and enable her daughter's marriage to him makes this clear.

> Taking just a glass of water herself, she would fry paranthas for Rahat and keep the milk on the boil until a thick layer of cream formed over it. If she could, she would have cut some fat out of her own body and stuffed it in the parantha. And why not? After all, one day he was going to be her very own. Whatever he earned, he would pass on to her. Who does not water a plant that gives fruit? (ibid., 29)

Rahat's marriage to another woman coincides with Kubra's death of tuberculosis. The story ends on an ironic note with Kubra's mother cutting a piece of red cloth to shroud her daughter's dead body with a tragic contentment and peace that comes with a sense of closure of having nothing left to lose. And Hamida is relieved for Kubra who has nothing more to suffer.

> The white expanse of the shroud spread before Bi Amma like death's mantle… Unlike the other suits of chauthi, this one would not have to be stitched… The mark of the white cotton on the red twill. How many young girls would have merged their longings in its red, and how many unfortunate virgins would have mingled its white in the whiteness of their shrouds… Bi Amma put in the last stitch and snapped the thread… The wrinkles on her face glowed, and she smiled. It was as though today she felt sure that Kubra's wedding suit was finally complete and the trumpets would ring out any moment. (ibid., 38)

The eroticism in some of Chughtai's later stories renders their portrayal of female victimhood ambiguous. If Gainda and her child end up struggling to survive, a reading of Rani, the female character in 'The Mole' (1994), suggests her resilience and indifference to her own chastity and reputation even if she similarly ends up becoming the mother of an illegitimate child. Rani, who has been asked to pose for a painting, sexualises the gaze of the painter by provoking his desire for her body. In the process of evoking and parodying the man's desire, Rani appropriates and reflects the male gaze for its desire for the obscene female body, thus blurring the very distinction between male subjectivity and female objectivity. Rani is a poor, illiterate woman who is picked up by the painter, Ganeshchand Choudhry, and made to pose for a painting that Choudhry expects will fetch him a handsome prize in an exhibition. But as she is being painted, she enticingly draws his attention to a hidden mole on her breasts. She provokes his violent jealousy by claiming to have shown her mole to another man named Ratna as she was bathing in the river. She claims she was fed *gurdhani* by another man named Chunnan in his hut. For Choudhry, who is described as a member of the respectable, cultural elite, his desire is constantly evoked and exorcised by Rani's obscene invectives and her apparently free association with other men. That Choudhry is not Rani's exclusive lover makes him a substitutable object of her (imaginary) desire for men. Her ostensible affairs with other men constantly haunt Choudhry's imagination, unsettling his masculine sense of self-ownership. He imagines her frolicking with Ratna in the river and her mole seems to transform itself into a symbol of the impotence of the male sexual gaze that is repeatedly reflected and upset by the woman. Rani clearly mediates Choudhry's desire through her apparent affairs with other men, which suggests that perhaps the true object of Choudhry's desire is not Rani's body per se but her recognition that he requires to redeem his own insecure masculinity. Choudhry drives Ratna out of his house although he knows Ratna was wearing a loincloth when Rani was bathing. He accidentally discovers a piece of gurdhani that drops from Rani's dhoti that again rouses his insecurity. But before he can ascertain the truth of Rani's affairs, she disappears leaving his painting incomplete. Her disappearance compels people to conjecture that Choudhury may have either sold her or had an illicit relationship with her. When Rani is captured by the police days later carrying a baby in a blood-soaked bundle in her arms, Choudhry is wrongly accused of being the father. Although his reputation is lost, he secretly wishes the child had been his as if to validate his masculinity by fathering a child. But the paternity of the child remains a puzzle, for in the court, Rani asserts Choudhry is impotent and claims either Ratna or Chunnan could be the father of the child. Her indifference to the question of paternity puts her in stark contrast to Gainda. If Gainda is resigned to her life as an outcaste widow with an illegitimate child, Rani is more concerned with her own survival and indifferent to social ideals of chastity, reputation, or marriage.

Like the previous story, a later story called 'The Homemaker' (2009) blurs the distinction between the private and public, which operates as a porous distinction between the wife and the whore. The female character Lajo, is a poor and illegitimate orphan who survives by resorting to prostitution. Unlike her name that means 'the coy one,' Lajo seems utterly indifferent to shame or her own reputation. 'She didn't haggle. It was wonderful if it was a cash-down proposition; if not, it was sex on credit. And if someone could not pay even on credit, it was sex on charity' (*'Lifting'* 1994, 79). She is accustomed to being employed and dismissed by those who need her domestic services. When she is employed as a maid by Mirza, an unmarried shopkeeper, she is drawn to the possibility of becoming the mistress of a sizeable house. Unlike her previous employer who exploited her, here she is given the power and freedom to take over the house, particularly the kitchen. She bitterly learns of Mirza's visits to courtesans and although she never expresses a desire to marry Mirza, she believes in love. Her presence draws the attention of the milkman and the boys in the neighbourhood, which rouses Mirza's suspicion. Their first sexual encounter when Lajo seduces him, is described as Lajo's sexual triumph over Mirza's seemingly feminine acquiescence. The encounter compels Mirza to claim a masculine sense of entitlement over her body, her behaviour, and her sartorial appearance. His possessiveness and insecurity are evident when her flamboyant beauty draws the attention of other men. He forbids her from stepping out of the house and he asks her to marry him to seal their relationship. Lajo realizes that marriage would curtail her freedom but Mirza marries her despite her remonstrations. He forbids her from wearing lehngas that expose her legs and orders her to wear tight churidhar pyjamas, which she finds inconvenient and restricting her mobility. Mirza tries to suppress her coquetry that he feels is inappropriate in a wife but the image of Lajo as an ostensibly reformed wife no longer interests Mirza who again turns to courtesans to fulfill his fantasies. His growing indifference compels Lajo to divert her attention to Mithwa, a mason's son who is smitten by her beauty. When Mirza discovers their secret affair, he nearly beats Lajo to death for ruining his honour. The incident promises Lajo freedom from marriage as Mirza divorces her only to learn from a paan-seller who desires Lajo that his marriage to a 'bastard' was never legitimate in the first place (ibid., 93). Mirza and Lajo are relieved that they were never married or divorced.

But by the end of the story Lajo is again in Mirza's employment and the two resume their illicit intimacy.

Chughtai's story 'The Invalid' (2009) is another exploration of an embattled male subject who is torn between his suspicious and possessive love for his wife and the immobility of his body that undermines his masculinity and sexual prowess. There is an ironic contrast between the restlessness of his mind or imagination that believes his wife is having an affair with their neighbour and his immobile body that bears memories of its able, sexual past. He bitterly remembers the times when he was able to intimidate the unmarried women of the neighbourhood with his flirtations but now he feels he is condemned to overhear his wife's lighthearted conversations with their neighbour. His wife is no longer interested in his weak attempts to seduce her and spends much of her time sewing their neighbour's clothes. The presence of the neighbour who is mostly absent in the story is evoked through his clothes that are strewn all over the house. Even his children appear to resemble the neighbour. He is unable to decipher his wife's thoughts and although there is no clear suggestion of an affair, he imbues his wife with his own insecurities. But his wife and the other women of the neighbourhood, the women who once fled from his sexual advances, now trivialise him by discussing their personal affairs in his presence. It is his fierce desire to avenge his desexualised masculinity that seems to fuel his desire to live: 'Let people die of expectations. He wouldn't die. He would live! Let all his children resemble the neighbour—his father, mother, brother and sister… Still he would live! He would live for revenge!' ('The Invalid' 2009, 190).

In another story 'Quit India' the illicit relationship between Sakku Bai, a nanny, and Jackson, a married English officer belies the anti-colonial revolutionary fervour of the pre-Independence years. Like some of Chughtai's earlier stories, love occurs between two socially illegitimate characters who are both marginalised in their own ways. The narrator is an indignant witness to their relationship and the biracial children who are born to them. The sight of Jackson getting drunk and beating Sakku Bai and their children provokes the narrator's indignant patriotism. She perceives their relationship as an allegory of colonial exploitation and a betrayal of the nationalist cause. She is unable to comprehend Sakku Bai's tearful love for Jackson when Jackson's health is ruined by his excessive drinking and doctors admit him to an asylum. He is left behind when his wife and most of his compatriots have left the country to return to England. He refuses to return perhaps because of his love for Sakku Bai. Sakku Bai is delighted when she discovers Jackson has escaped from the asylum. Years later when he is discovered, the narrator learns he was the illegitimate son of an aristocratic woman whose father entrusted him to the care of a peasant to secure the reputation of the family. But he is beaten up by the peasant's sons as he is growing up and finally manages to escape to London where he meets his wife Dorothy, the daughter of an influential man. He hopes his marriage will promise him social mobility and like many other poor and worthless Englishmen, he is sent to India, where he lives an indulgent life. He spends his time at opium houses and has affairs with Indian women while his wife languishes in his absence. He is finally compelled to swear his loyalty to his wife and Dorothy, with her father's help, enables his transfer to Bombay. Sakku Bai is employed as a nanny for the children but Dorothy soon returns to England with the children because of the weather, while Jackson begins to have an affair with Sakku Bai who is then the mistress of a married man, a head bearer named Ganpat Rai. Ganpat pimps Sakku Bai and appropriates her earnings but she eventually gets rid of him with Jackson's help. Sakku Bai does not seem to be troubled by Jackson's marriage and willingly relinquishes her place as Jackson's mistress whenever Dorothy visits India. There is no love between the couple; Dorothy believes she is responsible for her failed marriage while Jackson realizes his position and reputation are a function of his father-in-law's power and largesse. Jackson's love for Sakku Bai is the only thing he can call his own, notwithstanding the fact that they do not share an exclusive relationship. Jackson shares her with his friends but Sakku Bai is grateful for his helpless love which she compares to Ganpat's greed and selfishness. The love between the equally marginalied and disenfranchised Jackson and Sakku Bai traverses racial and national boundaries to become an acknowledgment of all those lives that have been rendered insignificant by their illegitimate birth.

> You've no country… you've no race… no colour. Sakku Bai is your country, and your race, for she has given you unending love… Because she is among the wretched in her country… Exactly like you and like millions of other human beings who are born in different parts of the world… whose births are not celebrated and whose deaths are not mourned. (116)

Some of Chughtai's later stories suggest the porosity between the private and public or between the erotic and the social through the figure of the migrant lower-caste female labourer. Female migrancy, in Chughtai's story, 'Rubs and Fists' (1967), for instance, is a symptom of a larger economic and social phenomenon that captures the illegitimate appropriation of land from lower-caste farmers and the migration of lower-caste women to cities where they earn their livelihood from insecure forms of informal labour. 'Rubs and Fists', describes the lives of two elderly hospital workers, Ratti Bai and Ganga Bai who have migrated to Bombay, through the perspective of an upper-caste woman who has just given birth to a daughter. Ratti Bai wishes to vote for a man who belongs to her caste, convinced that he will ensure she is given back her farmland. Ratti Bai's husband, along with her children, stays back in their village where he cultivates his own land. She appoints a poor woman to take care of her children but the latter ends up having an affair with the husband. The poor woman's husband is a landless labourer who has lost his land and begs and steals his way through neighbouring towns and cities. Ratti Bai seems to have no qualms about her husband's affair, in fact, she facilitates and consents to her husband's affair only because she knows it is a temporary arrangement that will end once she returns to the village. Ratti Bai sends her earnings back home to her husband and supports herself with the help of a man she calls her 'brother' with whom she has a sexual affair. The man's elder brother takes care of their family's lands back in their village. Ratti Bai has no choice but to 'whore around' to pay her pimp and her living expenses. The factory laws of the city are implemented to ensure that workers are retained only for few months of the year to minimise the state's expenses towards their medical benefits. Ratti Bai, like many other women, is unable to retain her job as a mill worker and makes a living by bribing policemen and selling vegetables.

Like Ratti Bai, Ganga Bai also has sexual affairs with men to make ends meet and to support her husband who lost his paddy fields to floods. The contribution that both these women make towards the economy of the city touches the lives of middle-class dominant caste women like the narrator, who discovers to her horror and disgust that Ratti Bai dries and sells cotton, which was once used to clean wounds and for pregnant women in the hospital, to cotton merchants who make cushions and mattresses for rich customers. The story blurs the moral distinction between the 'respectable' dominant caste narrator and oppressed caste women like Ratti Bai and Ganga Bai. While the narrator ridicules Ratti Bai and Ganga Bai's open affairs with other men that violates their marriages, Ratti Bai believes the narrator's husband may punish her for producing another daughter. The narrator is determined to forsake her husband if he punishes her by marrying another man, which for Ratti Bai goes against her perception of dominant caste norms. If the narrator claims to potentially transgress marital norms, Ganga Bai and Ratti Bai are aware of transgressing social norms of caste and gender even if they pretend to uphold them. But the most ironic images of informal female labour towards the end of the story have to do with the eponymous methods that women like Ratti Bai and Ganga Bai use to help women get rid of unwanted fetuses including those of their own. Ratti Bai's gory descriptions of abortions and aborted fetuses, shock and disgust the narrator's sensibilities. The narrator's dreams of sick maternal bodies and mangled fetuses alludes to the dissolution of institutions like the family and motherhood. But there is also the suggestion of a greater entrenchment of caste ties towards the end of the story, where caste becomes a politicised category that promises greater landed power for oppressed caste groups in villages. Caste, in terms of the ownership of land, is privileged as a category that encapsulates and regulates gender and sexuality and forms the economic basis of the socially sanctioned family.

From this discussion of Chughtai's stories, there emerges a sense of how women and their sexualities reconfigure notions of public and private. These reconfigurations occur either within the household or across rural and urban divides as a symptom of larger social and economic transformations that occurred soon after Partition and Independence. Women in these stories occupy uncertain and interstitial positions between the seemingly secure and familiar spaces of the domestic and the uncertainties of a world that is being transformed by economic forces. Men, even those who held landed positions of power are rendered insecure by their desire for women who no longer conform to their definitions of ideal womanhood. If the tragic deaths of earlier female characters mark the contours of patriarchal institutions of marriage, family, and motherhood, Chughtai's later characters parody and subvert the masculine gaze to constitute new articulations of female agency that exceed conventional notions of femininity and resistance. These articulations are affected through intimacies that traverse racial boundaries or even take the form of temporary sexual arrangements that are indifferent to questions of female chastity and marriage, which are imbricated in larger economic and social transformations in caste and land relations.

References

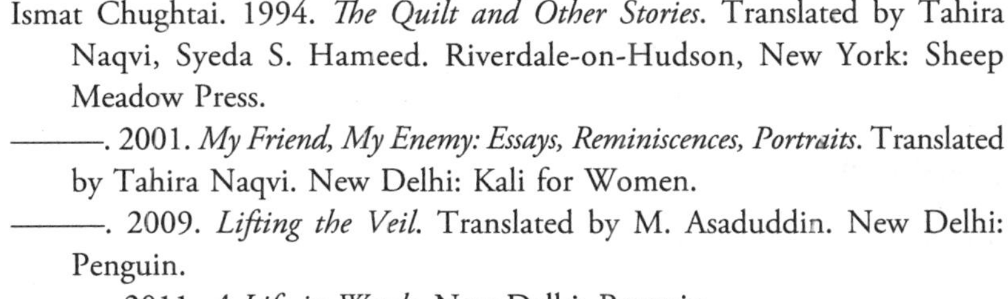

Ismat Chughtai. 1994. *The Quilt and Other Stories*. Translated by Tahira Naqvi, Syeda S. Hameed. Riverdale-on-Hudson, New York: Sheep Meadow Press.

———. 2001. *My Friend, My Enemy: Essays, Reminiscences, Portraits*. Translated by Tahira Naqvi. New Delhi: Kali for Women.

———. 2009. *Lifting the Veil*. Translated by M. Asaduddin. New Delhi: Penguin.

———. 2011. *A Life in Words*. New Delhi: Penguin.

5

Socialist Realism and the Progressive Movement in Urdu Literature

Kunal Chattopadhyay

Socialist Realism

The term Socialist Realism arose in the Soviet Union between 1929 and 1934, and was codified at the (in)famous Writers' Congress. While more intellectual glosses would be put from time to time by a range of Marxist/Moscow–oriented intellectuals, in origin it was worked out as a party line, with Maxim Gorky and Andrei Zhdanov in charge. Indian writers were not often exposed to Lukacs, Brecht, to say nothing of Bloch, Benjamin etc., in the 1930s and 1940s. In the main, they were influenced by what came out of the Soviet Union. With the Communist International having decided, after the downfall of M. N. Roy, to ask the Communist Party of Great Britain (CPGB) to look after India, they were in addition under the influence of CPGB ideologues, which had mixed results. The influence of Ben Bradley (who even presented the India eport at the 7th Congress of the Communist International) and R. Palme Dutt was to produce a deadening, Stalinist rigidity, especially in matters of class collaboration at the political level.[1] However, culturally, this would also mean the influence of Ralph Fox and Christopher Caudwell, who were less rigid Stalinist figures. Caudwell's *Illusion and Reality* had come to India, though the Caudwell debate and its significance were not much understood by many of the participants in the doctrinal debates that broke out in India.

The Socialist Realism model involved presenting either a struggle through which a young hero developed, or else to present happy workers and peasants living in Utopia. A classic model for the latter type can be seen in the Stalin Prize winning novel *Harvest*, written by Galina Nikolaeva. The original models for the former type were Gorky's *Mother*, and Nikolai Ostrovsky's *How the Steel Was Tempered.* But in the 1930s and 1940s, prescriptions tightened, and a flat, monochromatic narrative of growth into proletarian hero-hood through the Bolshevik Party and the great Stalin dominated. Novels had to be rewritten before they could be published, as with Alexei Tolstoy's *The Road to Calvary* (also a winner of the Stalin prize).

To understand how this came about, we need to sketch out the evolution of cultural politics and state-party policy. The October Revolution was intended as a democratic working-class revolution and there was no Bolshevik blueprint. However, a series of blows transformed the revolution. The period 1918–23 saw the failure of the international revolution—in Germany, Austria, Hungary and Italy, among others. 1918 to 1920 also saw a fierce civil war, waged by the capitalists, landlords, and their backers, the Western imperialist powers. The Soviet state emerged victorious, but with the social fabric totally torn up. The working-class vanguard that had led through the Soviets had been smashed, a considerable part dying in the Civil War, as fighters of the Red Army; another large part collapsing with the destruction of industries, and finally another part being pushed into administration. As a result, especially with the end of the Civil War, a bureaucratic layer emerged and came to dominate. Most Bolsheviks, however, failed to see the bureaucracy as a major threat to the revolution. Some feared that Lev Trotskii, a relative newcomer in the party leadership (he had joined only in 1917 and while immensely popular with the workers and soldiers, was looked upon with distrust by a section of the 'Old Bolshevik' leaders) would emerge as a Red Bonaparte, with his grip over the Red Army. Others thought that Nikolai Bukharin, urging peasants to 'enrich yourselves', would open the door to capitalist restoration. In fact, these currents were closer to each other than they realised, speaking a language derived from the left wing of International Social Democracy. And both had objections to party dictatorship over culture (Chattopadhyay 2006). Anatoli Lunacharskii, the Peoples' Commissar for Enlightenment, believed that the proletariat had to be equipped to create its own culture, but did not see this as involving a complete break with pre-revolutionary culture. He was, however, enthusiastic about new cultural forms and styles, leading to the much more traditionalist Lenin occasionally getting upset with him (Fitzpatrick 1970).

The period 1921 to 1928 saw the gradual ascendancy of this bureaucracy and the rise of Stalin. He first allied with Zinoviev and Kamenev to push Trotskii out of positions of influence, then aligned with Bukharin, Rykov, Tomsky and their supporters (the so-called Right) to defeat and oust from the party the most proletarian wing. Thereafter he used 'left' rhetoric to turn on Bukharin. The Left had the support of younger radicals, while the Bukharinists had the support of large parts of the prominent party intellectuals. As a result, the Stalinist consolidation of power also meant a decision to push out the various critical intelligentsia. In the period 1928 to 1934, as a result, what can be seen is a sustained, pseudo-workerist attack on intellectuals and intellectual work of all kind. Stalinism meant, in part, an absorption of the top layer of the workers into the bureaucracy, instead of an expansion of working-class democracy. Thus, while real democratic space was ended (in 1932, sixteen thousand workers carried out a strike wave in four major mills of the Ivanovo Industrial Region, where they targeted the party bosses and the OGPU but left intact the soviet, showing a class orientation, and eventually massive force was used to smash them), an upward mobility of sections of workers into the bureaucracy was visible (Rossman 2002, 44–83). In 1933, out of 8,61,000 recorded management positions 1,40,000 were held by individuals classed as workers in 1928.

This new elite needed new imaginaries suited to its role and function. It no longer wished to be reminded of the heroics of the Civil War or the storming of the Winter Palace. It now stressed 'socialist construction'—a 'mastery' over nature, of economic and social life. In the late 1920s multiple writers' associations had been closed and one organisation, the Rossiyskaia Assotsiatsiya Proletarskikh Pisately (Russian Association of Proletarian Writers, usually known as RAPP) given authority. This was a dogmatic Marxist organisation insisting on stressing 'Proletarian culture', but still autonomous. In the 1930s, this was suppressed and a new Writers' Union formed.

The period 1932–36 saw a series of congresses which laid down full party-state control over everything the bureaucracy could think of. These included control over environmentalists, geneticists, physicists, historians, and philosophers, much of which the present writer has documented in earlier papers.[2] The Writers' Congress of 17 August–1 September 1934 has to be set within this wider context.

The Congress had 591 delegates, including 40 foreign authors. The most serious Marxist analysis came from Nicolai Bukharin on poetics and recent poetry. Bukharin would be murdered a few years later after a fake trial in which he was made to confess to imagined crimes. The dominant figures in the Congress were Maxim Gorky and a secretary of the CPSU(B), Andrei A. Zhdanov. The central issue was Socialist Realism. One recent study says the term was used 228 times during the Congress (exceeded only by praise of Stalin and his contribution to culture—295 times). According to the statutes of the Union, Socialist Realism 'demands of the sincere writer a historically concrete presentation of reality in its revolutionary development. Thus, the veracity and the historically concrete aspect of the artistic representation of reality have to be allied to the task of ideological change and the education of workers in the spirit of socialism'.

In 1932–34, some 400 articles had come out on the subject. These explained Socialist Realism in two ways. One set outlined a space in which the domain of objects to which the notion of Socialist Realism is ascribed. Socialist Realism is given a history—'the path of Socialist Realism', the basis of Socialist Realism etc. The second set lays down prescriptions/injunctions—Socialist Realism is, Socialist Realism is not, Socialist Realism cannot be, etc.

Roman Jakobson, in discussing folklore and literary creation, had suggested that they are analogous to the relationship of langue and parole. He was to argue that folklore is sanctioned and censored by the community, while literature can go beyond repetition and variation. Gorky's speech seemed to suggest that proletarian literature should be closer to folklore, closer to langue than to parole—that is, be based on community (here class) approval, as articulated by the party.

But it was Zhdanov who had the clearest prescription. He stressed that writers had to be engineers of the human soul; they had to depict reality in its revolutionary development, and truthfulness and historical concreteness of artistic portrayal had to be combined with ideological remoulding and education of the toiling people in the spirit of socialism.

The Congress resolutions and discussions resulted in guidelines being laid down for what constituted Socialist Realism. These have been summed up under four heads or points:

- It would be proletarian—that is, art relevant to the workers and understandable by them;
- It would be typical—depicting scenes of everyday life of the people;
- It would be partisan—which meant it would be supportive of the aims of state and party;
- It would be realist in the representational sense.

If we look at the anthology edited by Dhananjoy Das on Marxist Literary Debates in Bengal, it will be evident that by the mid-40s, quite a bit of the foregoing had been taken up by party leaders and party minded writers. One can think of essays by Bhabani Sen, Nirendranath Roy or certain others.

However, the fact that there was a sharp debate in the late 1940s is evidence that before B. T. Ranadive started imposing tight Cominform control, the Progressive Cultural Movement had been rather different. To examine this we need to go back to the 1930s and other languages as well. In particular we need to look at the Urdu current, beginning with *Angarey*. In the 1980s, Ahmed Ali, the only member of the collective still alive, told Shabana Mahmud in an interview that there had been no plan for a literary movement. It was the volume that created the collective. The evidence is inconclusive, but Ahmed may not be fully correct.

The Creators of *Angarey*

The publication of *Angarey* in December 1932 marked a turning point in Urdu literature, especially Urdu literature of the Muslim communities. It also marked a turning point in the literary politics in India.

Several essays talk about the youthful fervour and the immaturity of the authors. Some of this, I will argue, is overdrawn. The effect of this disclaimer, placed at the beginning of discussions, is to downgrade the significance of the work. Four authors came together. They were Sajjad Zahjeer, Ahmed Ali, Rashid Jahan and Mahmud-uz-Zafar.

Mahmud-uz-Zafar is perhaps the least known of the four. A member of the Rampur nawab family, he was educated in Britain and chose not to take the usual route of sitting for the ICS examinations. Instead, he became an educator, and later, a committed communist in India and then in Pakistan. In 1934 he married Rashid Jahan. From 1937 he was an editor of *Chingari*, the Urdu magazine of the PWA. He also attempted to collaborate with Victor Gollancz and publish western leftist books in India, avoiding the Sea Customs Act.

Rashid Jahan was born in a family of social reformers. Her father was a Kashmiri Pandit who converted to Islam and advocated women's education. In 1922 Jahan attended Isabella Thoburn College, where she studied Science. This was followed by an MBBS from the Lady Hardinge Medical College. In 1931 she started working at the Lady Dufferin Hospital in Lucknow where she met Zaheer and the others. Later she set up private practice in Amritsar, where she met young radicals like Mohammad Taseer and Faiz Ahmad Faiz, as well as Mian Iftikharuddin, later a key figure in the Communist Party of Pakistan. In 1937 she published a collection—*Aurat aur Digar Afsane*, consisting of six stories and one play. Repeatedly jailed in the 1940s, she had several operations for cancer, and eventually died in Moscow in July 1952.

Sajjad Zaheer was the most important contributor to the volume; though later he would be active mostly as an organiser. In London as a student in 1929 he helped set up a group of Indian communist students. After the controversy over *Angarey* he was again sent off to London, where he played a major role in planning the Progressive Writers Association. On his return to India in 1935 he was Secretary of the Allahabad Branch of the Congress, and in 1942 he was one of the Communist members of the AICC who voted against the Quit India Resolution. In 1940 he was the UP State Secretary of the CPI. Jailed from 1940–42, he came out and started editing the CPI Urdu paper *Qaumi Jang*. After Partition he served as the General Secretary of the CP of Pakistan till his arrest at the time of the Rawalpindi Conspiracy Case. Repatriated to India in 1954 he revived the PWA and the IPTA.

Ahmed Ali had the shortest period of collaboration with the Left. In the 1930s his position came closest to the Moscow brand of Socialist Realism. At the first Conference of the PWA, which will be discussed more later on, Ahmed Ali delivered a speech on the 'Progressive View of Art', in which he defined art as a product of its environment, asserting that an artist 'cannot escape tendencies which work in that society in that particular period'. (Ali 1986, 39–44). He also attacked the art of the past as mythological, decadent and obscurantist. He ended his speech with an attack on both Iqbal and Tagore. But he did not join the CPI. In fact, he was the only member of the group never to join the CPI, arguing that this stunted the creative spirit of writers and meant accepting one set of dogmas (Ali 1974).

Situating *Angarey* in the Urdu Literary Context

Priyamvada Gopal makes the important point that the study of writers like the members of the *Angarey* collective (or certain others, like Ismat Chughtai, Sa'adat Hasan Manto and Khwaja Ahmad Abbas) enable us to interrogate the influential templates for the 'postcolonial intellectual' (Gopal 2005, 6). As she points out, unlike Bhabha's depiction of gatherings of exiles and émigrés and refugees, we are dealing here with people who were North Indian Muslims from Urdu-speaking middle and upper-class families. They were fluently bilingual, writing and speaking in both English and Urdu, committed to anti-colonialism; members of socially relatively prosperous ('elite') groups who, however, committed themselves to Marxist politics and cultural orientations as well as Muslims presenting important critiques of Muslim orthodoxy while Hindu majoritarianism attempted to construct an image of the nation that would exclude Muslims altogether (2005, 7–8).

One dimension that we need to sketch, however briefly, is the evolution of Urdu literature within which *Angarey* has to be located. Urdu literature and Urdu language are, of course, closely connected, and the origins of Urdu tend to be disputed. The word Urdu is of Turkic origin and refers to a military camp. The language emerged out of the mixture of West Asian and Indic linguistic and literary traditions, and disputes range from whether one should locate it at (and around) the Mughal court, in eighteenth-century Delhi, or across camps with necessary linguistic divergences. Its connections with other languages like Hindustani, Hindavi, etc. have also been noted (Pritchett 1996, 1–36). But a crucial transformation occurred after the failure of the war of 1857. From about this point, one finds a gradual emergence of a group identity among the Muslim elite of North India, with Urdu as the language through which they communicated. The literary legacy of Urdu was viewed as a problematic but authentic repository of an Indian Muslim identity. The Urdu language was itself viewed as the effective medium for reforms among Muslims. One consequence was, when Urdu became a print language for this large group, seemingly literary debates were often closely connected to ideological contestations. For example, calls for reforms of Urdu poetics, according to Qureshi, mirrored reform initiatives in the religious, social and political spheres (1996, 1)

One major strand of modernisation among the Muslims came from Sir Sayyid Ahmad Khan. Through his writings and political activities, and then through the Muhammadan Anglo-Oriental College at Aligarh, Sayyid Ahmad tried to convince his fellow Muslims to modernise through an assimilation of European thought, emphasising rationalism. He argued that Muslim religious beliefs, if rationally understood, did not necessarily conflict with Western insights, but Muslims must still reform their political, social, cultural, and moral values through a selective adoption of Western science and rationality, as that would let the Muslim elite to begin to improve its lot. To achieve his goals, he adopted a precise and functional language for his essays, moving away from the ornate language of the late Mughal court. Qureshi however, locates predecessors of his style 'in the large number of translations from European languages into Urdu that took place at Delhi College (founded in 1825), and in the Urdu works compiled under the supervision of John Gilchrist (d. 1841) at Fort William College in Calcutta (founded in 1800)' (1996, 4). Khan was a prolific writer, and an influential one. At the same time, in opposition to him, there arose the Deoband school, also teaching in Urdu, and defending a different perspective (Metcalf 1982).

Muhammad Husain Azad was to be one of the pioneers through his influential history and anthology of Urdu poetry, *Ab-i Hayat* (1880). Azad had come under the influence of reformist ideas through his association with the Anjuman-i Panjab in Lahore, where he had moved from Delhi in 1864. As part of his activities for the Anjuman, Azad wrote and lectured extensively on the need to reform Urdu literature so that it would be better able to bear the demands of the new society. Altaf Husain Hali was even more important. Hali was also influenced by the British educators associated with the Anjuman-i Panjab during his brief stay in Lahore. This reformist zeal combined with a deep admiration for Sayyid Ahmad Khan and his reform movement to ensure that Hali would go even beyond Azad, whose work he admired, in his call for a new poetics that would serve the interests of the emerging Muslim community in his *Muqaddamah-i Sher o Sha'iri* (1893). Hali calls repeatedly for a poetry that is able to reflect changes taking place in Indo-Muslim society, and which can be true and natural. Hali stood for a careful editing of the literary tradition to save only those elements that were morally uplifting and socially useful (Steele 1981, 1–45). Faruqi, in his essay in the volume edited by K. M. George, argues that the reason for the tremendous influence of Hali's thought was not so much the power of his logic as the emotional and mental state of his audience (Faruqi 1992, 424).

A prose writer who had considerable impact was Shibli Nomani. An associate of Sayyid Ahmad who, however, moved away from what he claimed was the excess of the Aligarh movement, he wrote literary work. His literary work placed an emphasis on the centrality of Classical Islamic literature, especially Persian, as the model for a reforming Urdu. He complicates Hali's critique of the tradition by highlighting the earlier parts as more progressive. At the same time, he draws a stronger distinction between the West Asian and the Indic parts of Indo-Muslim identity. Finally, through his writings, Urdu obtained Western methods of research and historical criticism.

Urdu novels were written by Nazeer Ahmad and Rashid-ul Khairi. Meanwhile ghazals continued to be written, for example by Akbar Allahabadi and Hasrat Mohani, who would, however, be strong critics of colonial rule. While Muslims were the major part of Urdu writers, authors like Munshi Premchand also wrote prose fiction in Urdu Thus, *Angarey* cannot be seen as text coming out of the void. Nonetheless, it did mark a significant departure, and we need to turn to the text and its afterlife.

Angarey

Angarey had ten pieces, five by Zaheer, two by Ahmed Ali, two by Rashid Jahan (of which one was a play), and one by Mahmud-uz-Zafar. Two sets of influences and ideas intersected. They were clearly inspired by the 'strange new world of European culture', as Ahmed Ali recollected. But the primary impulse came from the struggles over reform and modernisation in Urdu literature and within the north Indian Muslim communities. The members of the collective wrote from their own sense that the problems among north Indian Muslims would remain vast and durable, and change would be possible only by forcing the issues out into the open. They saw literature and language as weapons in this struggle.

In her autobiography, Ismat Chughtai wrote of the effect of Rashid Jahan on young minds. In an interview, she said, 'She spoiled me because she was very bold and used to speak all sorts of things openly and loudly, and I just wanted to copy her'(Kumar, www.thehindu.com).[3] Like Jahan, Chughtai would face the charge of obscenity. Unlike in Chughtai's case, Jahan and her collaborators would find their book banned, not republished till 1988 (from Sweden), from Delhi only in 1995, translated into English only in 2014. Even the Jahan centenary in Aligarh could be observed only as private programme. The entire book was attacked. Two stories by Zaheer that raised much hue and cry were 'Can't Sleep' and 'A Vision of Heaven'. In 'Can't Sleep', Zaheer raises the problem of how economic vulnerability and sexual predation are linked to one another. The main character is married, but visits prostitutes as well. Low income makes family life miserable. But the squandering of money by the husband on paid sex means the family does not have any opportunity to be anything other than miserable. In 'A Vision of Heaven', Zaheer scandalously described the pornographic fantasies of a pious Muslim scholar. While this brought on tremendous anger and attacks, I want to focus more on Jahan's two pieces. Jahan was targeted sharply because she was a woman challenging religious and patriarchal domination, writing about women's bodies and the oppression they faced. Threats ranged from cutting off her nose to throwing acid on her face, as well as the well-known incident of obscene cartoons of Jahan being shown, which led to an angry, young Ismat Chughtai writing a response in the *Aligarh Gazette*, defending women's education. In effect, Jahan was planting a flag, asserting that she, and by implication other women, had the right to write in print about women's bodies, sex, and also about science, modernity and progress. Her one-act play '*Parde ke Peeche*' (translated by Shingavi as 'In the Women's Quarters') is mainly a conversation between Mahmudi Begum and her guest Aftab Begum. Mahmudi Begum expresses a desire to die by taking poison. When her guest objects that she is not very old and can now go out and see the world, Mahmudi launches into her life story, which was: Married at seventeen, a child every year, a husband demanding sexual intercourse even when she is ill, infidelity on his part, fear of pregnancy, fear of losing her looks. A long history of a victim's experience is laid out. At the beginning there is a description of the room, which details the everyday life in the women's quarters. Lifting the curtains, the reader is taken to the domestic space, which continues to resist modernisation, and where oppression is ever present. One element of modernity based on Jahan's own experiences was the coming of the lady doctor. Western medical care for Indian women had begun with missionaries saying the majority of Indian women were debarred by custom from seeing male doctors or visiting government hospitals. Colonial officials appropriated this discourse when they decided to support the Dufferin Fund's programme, whereby they could show concern for the cultural sensibilities of their colonial subjects and yet help suffering women (Burton 1996, 368–97). Interestingly, however, lower caste and adivasi women were not welcome to these facilities. It was assumed that they were not modest and so the rules applicable for gentle ladies observing purdah were not applicable to them. Lady doctors worked both in 'purdah hospitals', and were given house calls.[4] But the interaction between the lady doctor and Mahmudi Begum shows us two types of exchanges. On one hand, there is a coming together of the inside and the outside. The lady doctor is a woman, yet one who functions in some ways as the equal of males in a profession. And it is her mediation that lets Mahmudi Begum narrate the crucial things about her body and the embodied womanhood. The lady doctor sees an apparently old woman who, however, claims to be thirty-two. It is the patient who has to explain to the scientifically trained person why this has happened (Zaheer 2014, 116–20). The question of the relationship between science, rational thought and women's bodies was one that Jahan confronts here. Jahan's later stories would develop further. In this play, the division between the public and the private spaces tend to remain unproblematised, though the revelations about the private sphere can be made only because the figure of the lady doctor can move between the two spheres.

In later stories, the universalist claim of the term woman is questioned at times by class. In 'Who', included in Tharu and Lalitha vol 2, the editors see Jahan as looking at the working-class woman cut out to the measure of the middle-class woman's requirement (Tharu and Lalitha 1993). I cannot discuss the story at length here. But this erases possible meanings that do exist. The middle-class rejection (nobody wishing to sit in the chair she had used) is there. But the 'other' woman tries to find an existence that would ignore the class bound reality of her existence. Gopal suggests that she enters a school, because it is a space crucial for the emancipation of one class of women (Gopal 2005). Indeed, it can be suggested that for the more exploited classes, education does stand as the gateway to social mobility. Jahan's other story in *Angarey* is a very short one. 'Seeing the Sights of Delhi' is the story narrated by one woman to her friends of a trip from Faridabad to Delhi by train. It is a commentary on the project of emancipating women from above. The Delhi station is seen from the perspective of a woman. Her husband leaves her sitting on the luggage while he pushes off with a friend. Burkha clad, she sees men around her trying draw her attention. But it is not all a tale of woe. She sees European men and women chatting and holding hands, sees the 'black men' who live in the engine. Indeed, all space is viewed in terms of living spaces. The station is bigger than a fort. Men live in the engine. She also watches hawkers sell cigarettes and toys. When, two hours later, the husband returns, having eaten at a hotel, and offers to buy her some pooris, she tells him she wants to return. The demand to return can be seen as a resistance to a compulsion in 'coming out'.

I want to discuss the shifts brought about by *Angarey* in the world it was addressing. As we have noted, Premchand and others had written powerful prose stories in Urdu before this, so it is not that *Angarey* was the first short story collection. But when we are looking at north Indian, Urdu-speaking and reading Muslims, we need to remind ourselves of the immediate background. The reformist versus traditionalist disputes had been mainly among the elite. While the *Angarey* collective also came out of that elite social milieu, the nature of their critique went well beyond what the Urdu-speaking Muslim reformists had been saying so far. They were writing in a prose style oriented to the urban middle class and talking much more about them. So both Urdu literary conventions among their own social groups, as well as religious and social orthodoxies, were challenged. This cannot be understood unless we now also examine the wave of hostility the book generated.

The Central Standing Committee of the All-Indian Muslim Conference passed a resolution, saying that the meeting: 'strongly condemns the heart rending and filthy pamphlet called *Angare*... which has wounded the feelings of the entire Muslim community by ridiculing God and his Prophets and which is extremely objectionable from the standpoints of both religion and morality' (*Hindustan Times* 1933).

Inevitably, in the light of this claim to be speaking for the entire community, the resolution also demanded an immediate ban on the book.[5] Shabana Mahmud cites an article in *Medinah* written in Urdu, fiercely denouncing the book, saying that 'To mock at the creator of the world, to ridicule religious beliefs and to make indecent jokes are the main characteristics of this bundle of filth … one finds a bold and shameless display of every kind of foul language' (1996, 448–9).

In Aligarh, a conservative mullah, Shahid Ahrarwi, led a smear campaign against the Women's College, which he called a brothel. His campaign was what provoked the young Ismat Chughtai into responding in the *Aligarh Gazette*, leading to a student protest and a demonstration against Ahrarwi (Ahmed 2009). Fatwas started being issued against the book. The issue was also raised on the floor of the United Provinces Assembly. Eventually, the Government of the United Provinces banned the book in March 1933, under Section 295A of the Indian Penal Code (Zaheer 2014, 158–9). Ahmed Ali wrote later that while they expected that the book would create a stir, they had indeed not expected the degree of rage directed at them. 'Our lives were threatened, people even lay in wait with daggers to kill us' (Coppola 1981, 61).

But the writers refused to be browbeaten, refused to issue any apology or go into hiding. Instead, Mahmud-uz-Zafar issued a statement on behalf of all four. It asked, 'Shall we submit to such gagging?' and responded to critics by saying, 'They have chosen the particular field of Islam, not because they bear it any "special" malice, but because, being born into that particular Society, they felt themselves better qualified to speak for that alone' (Zaheer 2014, 165–66). The statement ended with a call to set up a League of Progressive authors (2014, 167). This provides us with the Indian roots of the PWA, and shows why it would not be a simple clone of a Zhdanov-inspired Socialist Realism.

The European Connection

Which, however, does not mean that the European influence can be denied. That existed, and was a major reason why a revolt within Urdu literature led to an all-India and multi-lingual movement. Indeed, the Progressive movement was the first occasion where Urdu literature took the lead in forming an all-India tendency, and gave a strong boost in creating a distinct multi-lingual cultural movement. Sajjad Zaheer had been sent to London by his father. There he met fellow Indian students and academics. By late 1934, a group had formed, including Mulk Raj Anand, Promod Ranjan Sengupta, Mohammed Taseer, and of course Zaheer. Anand prepared the first draft of the manifesto for the proposed PWA. After further discussions, drafts were written by Dr Jyoti Ghosh, and then by Zaheer. His draft was published both in Britain and in India. In November 1934, the first meeting of the Progressive Writers Association took place and Anand was elected president, and the manifesto was finally adopted with minor amendments. We may have occasion to return to the text later. What is necessary, at this point, is to look at the international influences at work. When *Angarey* had been planned and published, a thoroughgoing sectarianism had been imposed on international communism. The present writer has argued that this was due to a conscious policy of the Soviet Union, which was under the belief that the rise of a far-right regime in Germany would result in tensions between the Western 'democracies' and Germany, and thereby provide the Soviet Union with greater elbow room (Chattopadhyay 1998, 103–31). Though formally the line would change only with the Seventh Congress of the Communist International in 1935, the triumph of Hitler and the brutality of Nazi rule brought about a revulsion, so that in practice, 'all but the communists are fascist' was not a tenable stance any longer. Many writers and artists were shocked at the violence on cultural workers in Germany, the confiscation of books etc. on the ground of being 'anti-national', 'communistic' or just 'undesirable'. In 1933, Louis Aragon inaugurated La Maison de la Culture. Aragon, Henri Barbusse and Andre Gide edited a journal, entitled *Commune*, which proclaimed itself as 'a review of struggle… In face of the confusion by which existing culture moves towards fascism, the *Commune* proclaims that the only revolution is the proletarian revolution' (Ahmed 2009, 23). On 6 February 1934, there was a crisis in France. Activists of the Action Française (AF) and the Fédération Nationale des Contribuables worked together on 9 January, as did members of the Jeunesses Patriotes (JP) and the Solidarité Française on 11 January. On 23 January, the call to demonstrate saw the names of the AF, the JP and the Contribuables on the same poster. On 6 February, the arranged meeting time for each group would see them converge on the Place de la Concorde, over the river Seine from the French parliament building, between 8 and 9 p.m. Right-wing action on the streets was aimed at changing the government to the right. On 9 February 1934, a socialist and communist counter-demonstration took place while Daladier was being replaced by conservative Gaston Doumergue. Nine people were killed during incidents with the police forces. On 12 February, Socialist and communist–led unions called a general strike. As left and right faced off, the left waged a cultural war as well.

In 1935, an International Congress of Writers for the Defence of Culture met in Paris, with over 200 delegates from 38 countries. Andre Gide presided over the gathering, and participants included Andre Malraux, Barbusse, Romain Rolland, Heinrich Mann, Aldous Huxley, E. M. Forster, Stephen Spender, Virginia Woolf, Pablo Neruda, H. G. Wells, Bertolt Brecht, Boris Pasternak among others. Gide was at that time very sympathetic to the USSR, and his speech on 'The Individual' attacked those who claimed individuality would wither if writers organised collectively. He insisted that great literature always came from below, through the experience of ordinary people.

The Congress debated the defence of culture and of democracy. Intellectuals spoke about their public role, and many people other than writers came in to hear them. Talat Ahmed argues, using Zaheer's 1952 'Reminiscences', that contrary to what used to be thought (that no Indian had been present at the Congress), Zaheer was probably present (2009, 26). Zaheer met both Ralph Fox (in London) and Louis Aragon (in Paris). Both were interested in the initiative to form an Indian Progressive Writers' Association, and Fox was very critical of sectarianism of the type that simply derided Rabindranath Tagore as a supporter of the Indian bourgeoisie, calling this approach, a 'caricature of Marxism' (Zaheer 1952, 50). And Aragon warned Zaheer that organising writers was a difficult task, because each writer wanted an exclusive path for oneself.

The PWA: Role of the Urdu Group in Its Formation and Spread

While the PWA as it was eventually formed was a truly all India effort, it is necessary to highlight the role of Urdu writers and speakers in organising it. Journals like *Payam* in Hyderabad or *Zamana* in Kanpur corresponded with Zaheer or printed articles by authors sympathetic to the Angarey group.

When Zaheer returned to India, he set about the task of forming the association in reality, and in India. In late December, Dr Tara Chand organised a meeting of Hindi and Urdu writers, where apart from Tara Chand, Premchand, the Angarey collective, Josh Malihabadi, and others met. Premchand was enthusiastic about the proposal for the PWA, and he had printed the manifesto in *Hans*.[6] Sikdar avers that the Writers' Association in Bengal was the most active, indeed the real dynamic force of the all India PWA. He also sneers at the creators of the PWA as people who wrote in English (Sikdar 2013, 70).[7] This illiterate rant is interesting as a piece of Bengali chauvinism, which, notwithstanding its ill-informed anti-communism, must insist that Bengali communists were the best of the lot.

The PWA's draft manifesto echoed the sentiments initially expressed by *Angarey*. It stated:

> It is the object of our Association to rescue literature and other arts from the conservative classes in whose hands they have been degenerating so long, to bring the arts into the closest touch with the people.... We believe that the new literature of India must deal with the basic problems of our existence today—problems of hunger and poverty, social backwardness and political subjection. (*Left Review* 1936, 240)

Zaheer was aware that to make it a successful movement it had to cover at least the bigger language groups and their literary traditions. While Punjabi, Bengali, Marathi, and other writers responded quickly, there was a clear division between the Hindi and the Urdu world, no doubt since this was the period from when communal divisions would sharpen further, in the wake of the Government of India Act of 1935, followed by the election campaign and then the election results of 1937. So when Firaq Gorakhpuri, who wrote in both Hindi and Urdu, supported Zaheer, it was a great step forward. Then at the end of 1935 he was able to meet Munshi Premchand, who responded extremely favourably. Premchand signed the draft manifesto of the PWA, and in early 1936, after some hesitations, also agreed to preside over the proposed conference of progressive writers. The biography of Premchand by his son stresses how excited Premchand was at this striving of young writers to organise a new literary movement (Rai 2002, 339–42).

On April 10, 1936, the Rifah-e-Aam hall in Lucknow witnessed the founding Conference of the All India Progressive Writers Association.

In his speech, Premchand declared that if literature 'does not arouse in us a critical spirit… does not make us face the grim realities of life in a spirit of determination, [it] has no use for us today' (Premchand 1986, 186). He went on to explain that for him, progressive literature meant 'that which creates in us the power to act; which makes us examine those subjective and objective causes that have brought us to such a pass of sterility and degeneration; and finally which helps us to overcome and remove these causes, and make us men once again' (1986, 187). And he ended with a ringing declaration:

> We shall consider only that literature as progressive which is thoughtful, which awakens in us the spirit of freedom and of beauty; which is creative, which is luminous with the realities of life, which moves us, which leads us to action and which does not act on us as a narcotic, which does not produce in us a state of intellectual somnolence. For if we continue to remain in that state, it can only mean that we are no longer alive. (1986, 191)

Two years later, Premchand was no longer alive when the second All India Conference of the Association was held in the Asutosh Memorial Hall in Calcutta. Rabindranath Tagore, unable to attend due to ill health, sent a message in which he made a self-criticism, saying, his nature had become to live in seclusion, but that he accepted that writers should not do so. Writers had to understand society, and to show the path of progress they had to listen to the beating of its heart.

The conference heard Mulk Raj Anand, one of the founders of the group in London, who had recently returned, after having been to Spain in solidarity with the Republicans. Anand also called upon Indian writers to adopt the point of view of the man in the street in their writings, and to take their place in the struggle against imperialism, fascism, feudalism, and other exploitative and reactionary forces (Anand 1979, 5–24).

There were only a limited number of people stressing sectarianism of the type that the Zhdanovist brand of Socialist Realism advocated. Ahmed Ali's speech on the 'Progressive View of Art' has already been mentioned. Zaheer recollected in his memoirs that it had not been discussed earlier, and felt that would have been better. Ali's views about Iqbal were not shared by all the Urdu Progressive writers. In a 1939 article, Ali Sardaar Jafri argued that there were contradictory elements in the poet's philosophy. He argued that Iqbal's belief in an Islamic cultural renaissance should have been based on radical principles, but his belief in pan-Islamism enabled conservatives and separatists to gain (Jafri 1939).

Organising the writers for the progressive cause was a major effort. As Coppola notes, prior to 1936 there had been very little effort by Indian writers to organise themselves. And here, the association was committing itself on one hand to the cause of freedom, and on the other hand to practical ways in which countrywide connections could be made, including by promoting the translation of progressive literature from one language to another (Coppola 1974, 10). From Coppola's reconstruction, there were several meetings organised by the Urdu PWA in the 1930s. These meetings and their achievements need to be examined, to trace in greater detail the role of the Urdu group. The first of these was in Allahabad, in 1937. It was attended by not only Urdu writers, but also some Hindi writers, like Narendra Sharma and Ramnaresh Tripathi. Acharya Narendra Dev and Jayprakash Narayan, the Congress Socialist Party leaders, were also present (Coppola 1975, 186). The presence of the CSP was significant. This was the period of the Popular Front. In India too, by this time the Dutt-Bradley thesis had led to the adoption of the Popular Front line. The Congress Socialist Party, founded in 1934, had been critical of Gandhi, but had also been critical of the CPI's sectarianism of that era (internationally, the 'Third Period' Stalinism, when all non-Communists were seen as fascists). The CSP included diverse elements. Jayprakash Narayan at that time was on the left, and was a Marxist. Narendra Dev was by contrast a believer in non-violence. By 1936, the CPI was calling for an anti-fascist, and anti-imperialist united front. So it was keen to forge closer ties with the CSP.

This meeting discussed, among other things, an issue that has repeatedly haunted progressive writers in India, Pakistan and Bangladesh. The writers come from a middle class (in those days, some also from upper class) background, and are making workers and peasants the subjects, or should be doing so. But how far were middle class authors really identifying with workers and peasants? Faiz Ahmad Faiz, the primary organiser of this meeting, argued that class background was relatively unimportant, and what was important was for the writers to familiarise themselves with the lives and conditions of workers and peasants. Following this meeting, Zaheer and Kunwar Muhammad Ashraf [8] went to Lahore, where they enlisted the support of Iqbal for the PWA.

In 1938, another Urdu meeting was held in Allahabad, again including a certain number of Hindi writers, such as Maithilisharan Gupt, Sumitranandan Pant and Amrit Rai (Coppola 1975, 193). Pant was also elected one of the Co-Presidents. Also, at this conference, Jawaharlal Nehru made a speech, stating that while as an artist the writer was an individual, this did not mean that the writer could remain apart from society (Coppola 1975, 195). The third and the fourth conferences were held respectively in Delhi and Haripura (the latter coinciding with the AICC Session). At Haripura, Sarojini Naidu presided over the session. And at the third conference, an Anti-Fascist Committee was set up to generate support for the Spanish Republic (Coppola 1975, 199).

Apart from the conferences, Zaheer for a time edited a periodical, *Chingari* (Spark), which also had on its editorial staff Ashraf, Rashid Jahan, Sohan Singh Josh, Tika Ram Sukhan, Firoz Din Mansur and Har Kishen Singh Surjeet (*Chingari* 1938). The editorial board is evidence that the Urdu Progressive world was not a community-based group. An English quarterly was also planned, and its first issue, as *New Indian Literature*, did come out in 1939. Hindustani, English, Bangla, Gujarati, Marathi, Tamil, Telugu, Malayalam, and Kannada were represented in the editorial board.

With this survey, we now need to move to the consideration of certain specific dimensions of the work of the Urdu PWA and individual writers. Specifically, we will look briefly at its relationship with nationalism and the freedom struggle, and anti-fascism and World War II.

Freedom Movement and the PWA

The formation of the PWA came at a time when major changes were occurring in the political struggles in India. The Government of India Act, 1935, followed by the elections of 1937, saw the Congress emerging victorious in a number of provinces, with the left wing providing the motive force but the right firmly in control of the party organisation and hence also of candidate selection. Out of 1585 seats across all the Provincial Legislative Assemblies, the Congress won 711, winning absolute majority in five provinces (Madras, Bihar, Orissa, Central Provinces, United Provinces) and close to a majority in Bombay (86 seats out of 175). Among the 864 seats assigned 'general' constituencies, it contested 739 and won 617. Of the 125 non-general constituencies contested by Congress, 59 were reserved for Muslims and in those the Congress won 25 seats. Dr Ambedkar's Independent Labour Party won 13 of the 15 seats reserved for the depressed classes/Harijans in Bombay. Most other Scheduled seats were won by the Congress. Nehru, Jayprakash and other leftists were hesitant about entering government, but Gandhi prevailed over them. This had contradictory results. Masses streamed into the Congress. Mass organisations grew in size, with leftists gaining among students, workers and kisans. On the other hand, corruption, factionalism, and a rightward trend was visible in the functioning of Congress-led governments. Perhaps even more critical, for the long run, was the arrogance with which the Congress treated the Muslim League. While Jinnah's claim that the League was the sole spokesperson for Muslims was clearly trounced in the elections, Nehru's remark that in India there were only two parties, those who wanted to perpetuate British rule and others who were fighting to end it, made claims for the Congress as the only legitimate party for freedom, and antagonised Jinnah. After the elections, too, the Congress, in negotiating joint governments with the League, for example in UP, insisted on the merger of the League party with the Congress party inside the Assembly.[9] As a result, from 1937, Jinnah moved from what Bipan Chandra termed a liberal communalist to an aggressive communalist phase. The calling-off of the Civil Disobedience Movement by Gandhi, the Gandhi-Irwin Pact, and the elections, had created considerable dissatisfaction among activists within the intelligentsia. Ashraf, for example, had been involved in nationalist politics since his days as a student in Aligarh. The hanging of Bhagat Singh while Gandhi was present in London for the Round Table Conference indicated to him the failure of Gandhian politics. Within the Congress, he moved left, to the CSP, and eventually to the CPI. Premchand, previously a staunch Gandhian, also developed a perspective that could not be contained within the Gandhian framework. In his earlier works, he had depicted the hardships of peasants, but in these, a social peace was eventually possible between zamindars and kisans. In *Godaan* (*Gift of a Cow*), the social conflict and exploitation is much more stark. Hari's search for salvation compels him to make the gift of a cow to a brahman, and in order to do so he hands over his daughter in marriage to an elderly man, and is at the mercy of money lenders and the landlord. One of those writers who do not settle down to accept the existing order as they grow older, Premchand became more critical, and it was to shape his literature. In *Mangalasutra*, his unfinished novel that Amrit Rai cited (and that was published in 1948), he sharply criticised class power as well as the power of the state and its officials as defenders of class power. As he wrote,

> Some poor man goes and eats a few ears of corn from another's field, and he is punished by the law. Another, a rich man robs others in broad daylight, and he is honoured and titled. Some men come armed with all kinds of weapons and terrorize poor helpless workers and turn them into slaves.... They draw fat salaries, go hunting, go dancing, indulge themselves in all kinds of pleasure. Is this God's own creation? Is this justice? (Rai 2002, 363)

What *Godaan* and this unfinished novel show are, on one hand, a deepening of the understanding of what independence needs to mean, and on the other hand, a deepening of a literary orientation that highlights social realism, without being Socialist Realist. A closer relationship (certainly not deliberately) can be made with the orientation proposed by Trotskii. He rejected the repudiation of past cultural traditions though he was clear that the past had to be viewed critically. And in one of his last pronouncements on art, the manifesto, 'Towards a Free Revolutionary Art', (signed by Andre Breton and Diego Rivera, but written mainly by Trotsky), which was followed by the formation of the FIARI (Fédération Internationale de l'Art Révolutionnaire Indépendant), Trotsky argued that 'the artist cannot serve the struggle for freedom unless he subjectively assimilates its social content, unless he feels in his very nerves its meaning and drama and freely seeks to give his own inner world incarnation in his art'.[10]

At the same time, he was stressing that:

> We recognize, of course, that the revolutionary State has the right to defend itself against the counterattack of the bourgeoisie, even when this drapes itself in the flag of science or art. But there is an abyss between these enforced and temporary measures of revolutionary self- defense and the pretension to lay commands on intellectual creation. If, for the better development of the forces of material production, the revolution must build a socialist regime with centralized control, to develop intellectual creation an anarchist regime of individual liberty should from the first be established. (ibid.)[11]

In a letter to the US periodical *Partisan Review*, he would write close to this same time, that

> But a truly revolutionary party is neither able nor willing to take upon itself the task of "leading" and even less of commanding art, either before or

after the conquest of power. Such a pretension could only enter the head of a bureaucracy—ignorant and impudent, intoxicated with its totalitarian power—which has become the antithesis of the proletarian revolution. Art, like science, not only does not seek orders, but by its very essence, cannot tolerate them. Artistic creation has its laws—even when it consciously serves a social movement. Truly intellectual creation is incompatible with lies, hypocrisy and the spirit of conformity. Art can become a strong ally of revolution only in so far as it remains faithful to itself. Poets, painters, sculptors and musicians will themselves find their own approach and methods, if the struggle for freedom of oppressed classes and peoples scatters the clouds of skepticism and of pessimism which cover the horizon of mankind. (Trotsky 1938)

Talat Ahmed makes out a case that a similar perspective was developed by Antonio Gramsci. Like the present author, Ahmed argues, not that the proponents of the Progressive movement (she considers Jahan and Anand along with Premchand) were aware of this convergence, but that there was an unwitting convergence (Ahmed 2009, 56–60).

Premchand's dissatisfaction with the freedom movement under Gandhi led him to fiction that would highlight the upper class, conservative character of the run of the mill Congress rightist. In *Gaban*, his character Devdeen Khatik asks such leaders, 'Saheb, tell me the truth, when you mention self-rule, what sort of picture comes before your eyes? Like the English, you'll draw a big salary too, live in bungalows too, enjoy the mountain air, and travel around wearing English styles …' (Premchand 2000, 159).

Activists of the PWA were also keen to rope in left-leaning Congress leaders, above all Nehru, on whom a lot of left hopes rested at that time, especially after his 1936 Presidential Address. So Ashraf would be a major figure in proposing the Muslim Mass Contact movement. Young intellectuals were in the forefront of the mass contact movement, but the overall reluctance of the Congress to take up the campaign seriously meant that the League was able to consolidate its grip. Hindu Mahasabha elements were afraid, and there was even deliberation on whether all Hindu Mahasabha members should enter the Congress in UP to counter the Muslim influence. By 1939 the mass contact movement was disbanded. Ashraf would feel that Nehru had let them down very badly (Kruger 1966, 413).

Linked to this was also the question of class. Nehru had said, at the beginning of the Mass Contact Movement, that the League's 14 Points did not address the concerns of the poorer Muslims. But how far did the Congress address the poorer Indians, regardless of religious identity? When there was a pressure from zamindar or capitalist, how far was mainstream Indian nationalism willing to take a stand? As the experience of the Congress-led provincial governments showed, their progressivism did not go very far. And this was where the Progressives did mount a challenge. If they failed to do more, this has to do with issues that can be barely mentioned here. This was the twist and turn in CPI policy, the fractured relationships between the different sectors of the Indian left[12] and the resulting weaknesses.

War and the Progressives

When World War II began, India under colonial rule immediately declared war. While the Congress condemned the Nazis, it stated that if the war was to retain the status-quo then India had no interest in the war. The CPI condemned the war as an imperialist war. Hundreds of CPI members including Zaheer were arrested, as were Mahmud-uz-Zaffar and Sohan Singh Josh. But when Germany invaded the USSR things changed. The CPI shifted its position in a sharp turn. The Communist International, and the CPGB, which handled contacts with India, made sure that the struggle against fascism had to be unconditional, regardless of whatever promises the rulers made or did not make. Zaheer would be released in March 1942. Meanwhile the Congress was moving towards its most intense anti-British battle ever. As the Quit India Movement began, the CPI not only opposed it openly, but denounced the more militant participants, like the CSP, the RSP and the Forward Bloc as fifth Columnists of fascism. Around the same time, the CPI changed its attitude to the Muslim league and the Pakistan demand.

The rise of the Progressive Movement had involved a partnership between activists committed to the CPI and the wider left nationalist-progressive circles. With an open split between these two, the progressive movement faced difficulties. However, the PWA was not simply a CPI 'front', and in the period when P. C. Joshi was General Secretary, the party leadership appears to have operated with sufficient astuteness and flexibility so that political differences did not mean driving all possible allies away. Of course, the CPI opposition to the Quit India Movement, and then its attacks on Subhas Bose, created major strains. But more perplexing were the turns in CPI policy and how they were internalised by CPI authors. Two of the Urdu poets, Ali Sardar Jafri and Kaifi Azmi, attacked imperialism. Azmi's poem was a response to a British official asking Indians to pray for the British war effort:

Your Lordship how is it possible
For us to repay you for your gift to us?'
How can we, the broken hearted, cry?
Our lips are sewn shut; how can we beseech? (Coppola 1975, 212)

How indeed, can a people who have no rights of their own be expected to pray for the well-being of those who have behaved like tyrants and have sewn shut the lips of the oppressed? And Makhdoom Mohiuddin wrote the poem 'Sipahee':

Jaane waale sipaahee se poochho
woh kahaan jaa rahaa he
kon dukheeyaa he jo gaa rahee he
Ask the departing soldier
where exactly is he going?
Who is the sorrowful one singing (Translation by the author)

This was an equally trenchant attack on imperialism, stressing that the youth of India were being taken away to fight an imperialist war while the freedom struggle lay unfought. So it was not surprising that the PWA was under severe repression, including not only arrests, but suppression/censorship of writings, and the failure of the PWA to hold a conference till 1942. A statement issued by Josh Malihabadi and Saghar Nizami called for an independent India and socialism, but also stressed that in view of aggression by Japan, it was the duty of every Indian to defend their country (Coppola 1975, 218). An AIPWA Conference held in Bombay in 1943 heard CPI leader and trade unionist S. A. Dange emphasise that in the war, remaining unconcerned about the 'victory of the nations led by the Soviet Union' was 'aiding a worse slavery' (Dange 1943).

This change in outlook, strange though it seemed to nationalists who were unconcerned about international issues, and though criticised by the anti-Stalinist revolutionary left (who, however, were smaller both overall, and particularly in the cultural world), made the Urdu poets turn around. Makhdoom Mohiuddin now wrote the poem 'Jung e Azaadi'.

Ye jung hai jung-e-azadi, azadi ke parcham ke tale
Hum Hind ke rehne vaalonki, mehkoomonki, majbooronki,
Azadi ke matwaalonki, Dehkaanonki, majdooronki
Saara sansaar hamara hai
This war is the war for freedom, under the banner of freedom
Of the people of Hind, of the condemned, of the helpless
Of those drunk in freedom, of the peasants and of the workers
The whole world is ours...[13]

Similarly, Ali Sardar Jafri also now called upon his fellow Indians to wage war against and imperialism. But Britain now seemed to disappear from the list of imperialist powers, being part of what Dange had called 'nations led by the Soviet Union'. The attitude to the war would, of course, be taken up by Ismat Chughtai in *The Crooked Line* (1944).

Since this is a conference devoted to Chughtai, it is worth finishing the paper by looking briefly at her work, but also because there will be many papers devoted to her, I do not propose anything like a proper discussion of the novel. My aim is to relate it to the earlier discussions on war and the Urdu PWA.

Chughtai, like Shaman, the protagonist of the novel, grew up in a reasonably well-to-do north Indian Muslim family. Aware quite early of double standards that existed within liberal families regarding assertive women vs assertive men, Chughtai convinced her parents to let her finish schooling in a hostel, and then went on to do a B.A. in English and the Arts at Isabella Thoburn College, where she was a voracious reader. She then studied at Aligarh Muslim University to train as a teacher, becoming a Headmistress in a girls' school. Chughtai had read *Angarey*, and had idolised Rashid Jahan. With support from Jahan, she attended the first PWA Conference of 1936. However, Chughtai was independent minded, and as the pressure of Socialist Realism began to mount, she would resist. As she explained later,

> For instance, when the policy of the Party rigidly concluded that Progressive literature is only that which is written about the peasant and the labourer, I disagreed. I cannot know and empathize with the peasant class as closely as I can feel the pain of the middle and lower class. And I have never written on hearsay, never according to any set rules, and never have I followed the orders of any party or the Anjuman [Association]. Independent thinking has always been my nature and still is (Gopal 2005, 69)

The Crooked Line is written from the standpoint of a middle-class woman, and presents an examination of the politics of gender and family, class and nation in the years just before India's Independence. Shaman, as she grows up, meets progressive forces including the CPI activists, and has sympathies with the latter. She is totally convinced of the need to go all out in opposing colonialism, and donates money for the underground CPI through Iftikhar. Iftikhar is portrayed as a radical who is critical of marriage, but is blind to the inequalities between genders that would inhabit the free unions he proposes. But if we focus only on the war, we find how Chughtai presents a critical commentary. Till mid-1941, Nazi Germany and the USSR were allied. While defenders of the USSR have pointed to its need to save itself, or the dubious role of Britain in the period just before the Molotov-Ribentropp Pact, it also needs to be stressed that the Russo-German Pact was not just a defensive action. Using it, the USSR also annexed a part of Poland, and then went on to annex the three Baltic States. Chughtai would write, talking about the war on Poland, 'At this end, Russia too felt some tingling and joined the ranks of martyrs. In the flash of an eye two greedy children cut up Poland in half as if it were a sweet biscuit, and devoured it' (2003, 228). Then came the outbreak of Hitler's war on the USSR, when Shaman feels, 'Until yesterday Russia and Germany were in an embrace, cuddling each other, and today this battering had started' (2003, 277–8). She goes to a meeting of communists to discuss the attitude to be taken to the war now that this transformation has occurred. The meeting is described thus: 'The debate at the meeting was riotous. But everyone was somewhat flustered. No one knew which viewpoint to endorse and which to oppose; there were as many opinions as there were voices' (2003, 279). Shaman, however, does not appear to be convinced about solely supporting the allied cause while putting the freedom struggle on a back-burner. The following brief passage indicates a less than reverential attitude to the new 'People's War' line:

> Literary and progressive meetings also lost their edge and were about to fall apart. Two or three people went to jail and the policies underwent change. Most of the members now shifted their attention to "work" related to the national war. The battle for Russia was transformed into the world's battle, and for this reason was now mankind's battle. (Chughtai 2003, 285)

What I would emphasise, from the above, is not simply Chughtai's independence of thought. Rather, this suggests that the Progressive movement still remained an independent movement, with plurality of ideas, critical concepts. This was a far cry from what the CPI would try to achieve during the Ranadive period, when party leaders would quote Zhdanov and Stalin to lay down the line on literature. It is by ignoring these, by reading all references to looking at the conditions of workers and peasants as compulsory Socialist Realist writing, rather than sensitive, social realism, that recent anti-communist writings have tried to trash the Urdu PWA.

Notes

1. For a full account of the Comintern and the CPI, using archival material obtained since the collapse of the USSR, see Sobhanlal Datta Gupta, *Comintern and the destiny of Communism in India: 1919–1943: dialectics of real and a possible history*.
2. '*Bijnaner Itihas Charcha, Marxbadi Itihas Darshan O Boris Hessen*', Sectional Presidential Address, Countries Other than India, Paschim Banga Itihas Samsad 22nd Annual Conference, Narendrapur, 2006, published in Itihas Anusandhan -21, (Proceedings of the PBIS 22nd Session) PBIS, Kolkata, 2007; 'Class Struggle among the Molecules: The Rise of "Proletarian Science",' *J.U. Journal of History, vol. XV*, pp. 35–46; and 'Early Soviet Commitment to Environment Protection and its Decline', in Amit Bhattacharya and Mahua Sarkar (Eds), *History and the Changing Horizon: Science, Environment and Social Systems*, in association with UGC-SAP Phase II, History Department, Jadavpur University.
3. Cited by Kuldeep Kumar, 'Rebel with a Cause', http://www.thehindu.com/todays-paper/tp-features/tp-metroplus/rebel-with-a-cause/article6202000.ece
4. Because the Dufferin Fund, and then the Victoria Fund, focused on generating jobs for women (European women) in the medical profession, the nature of women's response was different from how it was to develop in the West. Class, caste issues and how they prevented certain categories of women from gaining access to decent allopathic medical care have been more significant in south Asia, while in the West, there have sometimes occurred anti-hegemonic feminist critiques demanding 'female centred' home-birth. This is not to argue that if women are employed then sexist assumptions cannot dominate, but merely to stress that the ways in which class, gender, caste and race played out in India was very different.

See Cecilia van Hollen, *Birth on the Threshold: Childbirth and Modernity in South India.*

5. 'Urdu Pamphlet Denounced: Shias Gravely Upset', The Hindustan Times, February 21, 1933.
6. *Hans*, a Hindi periodical, was originally quite a Gandhian venture, with Gandhi and K. M. Munshi being associated with Premchand. But it was his energy that kept it going, and it shut down after his death.
7. Asru Kumar Sikdar, *Kil Marar Gosain*, Deep Prakashan, Kolkata, 2013, p. 70. Of great interest is this author's uncritical swallowing of a colonial government's police circular, ignoring the names that even he cannot avoid citing as being present at the Conference. In p. 72–3, he further claims that by sitting side-by-side with the CPI Conference in 1943, the relationship between the PWA and the CPI became open. This presupposes that the relationship had been the same previously, only hidden. This further raises the question whether the PWA should have met in one of the jails where Congress leaders were kept arrested. And, as I discuss briefly at the end, even in 1943, the PWA was not simply a CPI 'front'.
8. Ashraf was at that time a young CSP activist who was in charge of the minorities cell of the Congress. For his life, see Horst Kruger, Ed., *Kunwar Mohammad Ashraf: An Indian Scholar and Revolutionary 1903-1962*, and M. Farooqi and N. L. Gupta, *Life and Works of Dr. K. M. Ashraf.*
9. There were problems on both sides, including Jinnah's demand for control over a community which cannot be discussed in detail here.
10. http://www.generation-online.org/c/fcsurrealism1.htm
11. Ibid.
12. One should enumerate at least the following currents: The CPI, the Congress Socialist Party, the Bengal (as well as some outside Bengal) left that supported Subhas Bose as a left nationalist and would go on to form the Forward Bloc, the anti-Stalinist Marxist current inside the CSP that would eventually separate out as RSPI(ML) (subsequently just RSPI), the anti-Stalinist current that would form from the expulsion of Saumyendranath Tagore as the Communist League/Revolutionary Communist Party of India, and the supporters of M. N. Roy who would form the Radical Democratic Party. In addition, it is necessary to stress that major mass organisations, like the All India Kisan Sabha, the All India Trade Union Congress, and the All India Students Federation, all on the left, were not in the1930s or early 40s all under tight CPI

control, as would happen later on. So when discussing Left forces, these organisations require autonomous examination.

13. https://cbkwgl.wordpress.com/2017/02/08/jung-e-azadi-maqdoom-mohiuddin/

References

Ahmed, Talat. 2009. *Literature and Politics in the Age of Nationalism: The Progressive Episode in South Asia, 1932–56*. London: Routledge.

Ali, Ahmed. 1986. "Progressive View of Art." *Years of PWA: Golden Jubilee Celebrations Souvenir*. Lucknow: Golden Jubilee Celebrations Committee: 39–44.

———. 1974. "The Progressive Writers' Movement and Creative Writers in Urdu". In *Marxist Influences and South Asian Literature, Vol. I*. Michigan: Michigan State University, East Lansing.

Anand, Mulk Raj. 1979. "The Progressive Writers' Movement." In *Marxist Cultural Movement in India, Chronicles and Documents (1936–1947), Vol. 1*, Edited by Sudhi Pradhan. Calcutta: Santi Pradhan.

Burton, Antoinett. "Contesting the Zenana: The Mission to Make "Lady Doctors for India" 1874–1885." *Journal of British Studies* 35, (1996): 368–97.

Chattopadhyay, Kunal. "The Communist Party of Germany, The Theory of Social Fascism, and Hitler's Rise to Power." *History: Journal of the Department of History* Vol 1, (1998): 103–31. Burdwan: The University of Burdwan.

———. 2006. *The Marxism of Leon Trotsky*. Kolkata: Progressive Publishers.

Chughtai, Ismat. 2003. *The Crooked Line*. Translated by Tahira Naqvi. New Delhi: Women Unlimited: 228.

Coppola, Carlo, 1974. "The All-India Progressive Writers' Association: The European Phase." In *Marxist Influences and South Asian Literature, Vol. I*, edited by Carlo Coppola. East Lasing: Michigan State University, East Lansing.

———. 1975. *Urdu Poetry, 1935-1970: The Progressive Episode*. Chicago: University of Chicago.

———. "The Angare Group: The Enfants Terribles of Urdu Literature." *Annual of Urdu Studies* 1, (1981): 61.

Dange, S.A. 1943. "Literature and People." Address to the 4th AIPWA (Conference). Bombay: People's Publishing House.

Datta Gupta, Sobhanlal. 2006. *Comintern and the Destiny of Communism in India: 1919–1943: Dialectics of real and a possible history.* Kolkata: Seribaan Publication.

Farooqi, M and N. L. Gupta. 1973. *Life and Works of Dr. K. M. Ashraf.* New Delhi: CPI Publications.

Faruqi, Shamsur Rahman. 1992. "Modern Urdu Literature." In *Modern Indian Literature: An Anthology*, edited by K. M George. Delhi: Sahitya Akademi.

Fitzpatrick, Sheila. 1970. *The Commissariat of Enlightenment: Soviet Organization of Education and the Arts under Lunacharsky, October 1917–1921.* Cambridge: Cambridge University Press.

Gopal, Priyamvada. 2005. *Literary Radicalism in India: Gender, Nation, and the Transition to Independence.* London and New York: Routledge.

Jafri, Ali Sardar. "Review." *New Indian Literature* 1(1939).

Kruger, Horst (ed.). 1966. *Kunwar Mohammad Ashraf: An Indian Scholar and Revolutionary 1903–1962.* Berlin: Academie-Verlag.

Kumar, Kuldeep. 2014. "Rebel with a Cause." The Hindu. http://www.thehindu.com/todays- paper/tp-features/tp-metroplus/rebel-with-a-cause/article6202000.ece.

Mahmud, Shabana. "Angare and the Founding of the Progressive Writers' Association." *Modern Asian Studies* 30:2, (1996): 448–9.

Metcalf, Barbara Daly. 1982. *Islamic Revival in British India: Deoband, 1860–1920.* Princeton, N.J.: Princeton UP.

Premchand, Munshi. "The Nature and Purpose of Literature." *Indian Literature,* Vol. 29, No. 6 (116) (1986): 184–91.

———. 2000. *Gaban.* Translated by Christopher R. King. New Delhi: Oxford UP: 159.

Pritchett, Frances W. 1994. *Nets of Awareness: Urdu Poetry and Its Critics.* New York: Columbia UP.

Qureshi, Omar. 1996. "Twentieth Century Urdu Literature". In *Handbook of Twentieth Century Literatures of India.* Westport, CT: Greenwood Press.

Rai, Amrit. 2002. *Premchand: His Life and Times.* Translated by Harish Trivedi. New Delhi: Oxford UP.

Rossman, Jeffrey J. "A Workers' strike in Stalin's Russia." In *Contending with Stalinism: Soviet Power and Popular Resistance in the 1930s.* Ithaca and London: Cornell UP: 44–83.

Sikdar, Asru Kumar. 2013. *Kil Marar Gosain.* Kolkata: Deep Prakashan: 70.

Steele, Laurel. "Hali and His Muqaddamah: The Creation of a Literary Attitude in Nineteenth Century India." *Annual of Urdu Studies,* No. 1, (1981): 1–45.

Tharu, Susie and K. Lalitha (eds). 1993. *Women Writing in India, Vol. 2.* Oxford: Oxford UP.

Trotsky, Leon. "Art and Politics in our Epoch." *Partisan Review,* (1938). https://www.marxists.org/archive/trotsky/1938/06/artpol.htm.

van Hollen, Cecilia. 2003. *Birth on the Threshold: Childbirth and Modernity in South India.* Berkeley and Los Angeles: U of California P.

Zaheer, Sajjad and others. 2014. *Angaaray.* Translated by Snehal Shingavi. New Delhi: Penguin Books.

Zaheer, Sajjad. "Manifesto of the Progressive Writers' Association." *Left Review 2,* no. 5 (February 1936): 239–42.

———. 1952. "Reminiscences." *Indian Literature 2.* Bombay: Peoples' Publishing House: 50.

6

The Fabric of the Story

Chughtai's Craft

Sucheta Bhattacharya

> Granny was … a first-rate liar. And her biggest lie was her burkha, which she always wore. (Chughtai 2009, 146)

In *Tiny's Granny,* Granny's *burkha* was a lie because she deployed it for functions that the burkha was never intended for. She used it nonchalantly as the situation demanded—as a pillow, a towel, a prayer mat, even as a shield when the street dogs attacked her heels. When they went for her calves, they found the voluminous folds of the burkha hissing back at them. It was an old and frayed burkha, patched many times over, the original white of the material turned multi-coloured, marked as it were by the colours of moments of past happiness and unhappiness, and desire and expectations, of disappointments and denials, and useful in more ways in the present, so she refused to part with it. Who knows if it would not serve as her shroud as well in future?

The burkha was a lie because Granny no longer used it for the purpose for which it was intended, that is, the preservation of modesty. The veil had disappeared long ago and Granny wore it without properly closing it in the front (even when she was wearing a transparent kurta with no vest underneath).

Chughtai's writings ask what constitutes resistance or subversion for women crushed under patriarchy. When one does not have resources like education or family support or money to establish one's agency, does one get crushed unrecognisably under the heavy wheels of the juggernaut of patriarchy?

Chughtai's Granny does not. Her weapon for survival and resistance is the very object with which patriarchy had sought to subjugate her, her burkha. But she has shaped and trimmed it according to her necessity and will.

It is not only in this story, but in many others by Chughtai that the use of attire has more than one significance.

In '*The Homemaker*' ('*Gharwali*') for instance, Lajo's intense dislike for *churidar* pyjamas is funny but also moving. I will take the liberty of getting into this story a little more deeply.

> [After the wedding] Mirza put on a ban on the *lehenga* and instructed her to wear tight-fitting churidar pyjamas. Lajo was used to open space between her legs. Two separate legs joined by a strip of cloth were truly bothersome. She kept pulling at the strip and then, at the first opportunity, took off her pyjamas and was going to slip into the lehnga when Mirza appeared on the scene. She got so nervous that she forgot to hold the lehnga around her waist and let it fall. (Chughtai 2009, 88)

Lajo's refusal to be sexually subjugated to a patriarchal law governing marital loyalty and morality is reflected in her suspicion of the churidar-pyjama. It is not that she is immoral or disloyal. In fact, Lajo does not have a single disloyal bone in her body. It is only that she has her own brand of loyalty as well as morality. Of illegitimate birth, uninitiated into the patriarchal system where men call the shots, she refuses to abide by the rules of a legal marriage which she sees as an absurd and irrational bond. She lusts not after a man, but a home that she can call her own. Mirza provides her the space, but she does not see him as owning it. He is an excuse for a home that Lajo has been looking for all her life. She wants a home of her own, a space where she can be what she is. However, she also believes that she needs the home as much as Mirza needs a homemaker. Lajo does not see any sense in selling herself body and mind and soul to the man for this privilege, for she does not see this as a privilege but an equal transaction. She doles out sexual favours to Mirza happily and freely without ever relinquishing her ownership of her own body. For her it is a fair and equal exchange, the highest price she can pay for buying something she needs so desperately. She pays with sex but refuses to subjugate herself to Mirza. For Lajo, a home is not what it has come to connote to generations of women: a place for exploitation, restrictions, subjugation. For her home is not a place where one is always supposed to keep one's legs covered. She needs a home where she would have freedom to be herself. She needs to be the queen of her home and

Mirza, her poor vassal, whom she would keep happy by granting sexual favours. Mirza's attempts to possess her body as well as her soul make her feel claustrophobic and she does everything in her power to wriggle out of the marriage, to get back the happiness of feeling the free movement of her legs beneath the comforting spaciousness of her lehenga. Poor Lajo does not accept that a woman can never have a home of her own.

I start my essay with the given that Ismat Chughtai is one of the greatest writers that the subcontinent has produced. My specific interest lies in trying to understand what constitutes her greatness as a writer, not in terms of the issues that she explores, not only as a feminist writer but in terms of her crafts(wo)manship, the actual building of the stories she creates.

Any discussion on Chughtai and her art, I imagine would necessarily draw a reference to Sa'adat Hassan Manto, her great contemporary. There is a certain similarity between the approaches of Manto and Chughtai in their approaches to life and art. They apparently have the same dispassionate, clinical outlook on their environment as well as the same irony. It is also not an insignificant fact or a mere coincidence that they were both charged with obscenity for *Bu* (Manto) and *Lihaaf* (Chughtai) at the same time, which should tell us something about the similarity in their sensitivity. The style that both use is ironic, non-judgmental, not overtly or violently critical. The human subjects or the ideas they focus on are seemingly ordinary. Both treat commonly available material in terms of themes and believable situations. Both are conscious about issues related to class. But this mildness is misleading, as this apparent ordinariness leads to scathing criticism of social structures and their oppression of the weaker sections. But we have to look at the elements in Chughtai's writing that distinguish it from Manto's to understand the nature of her greatness.

I would argue that the difference lies in the variation of patterns she creates as a woman. Most authors writing in her time and historic context use the same idealistic threads perhaps but there are certain threads Chughtai uses in her inimitable way, and therein lies her exclusiveness. I would also argue that her uniqueness and greatness lie in the woman's sensitivity that she brings to her stories. The question that interests me here is whether we can look upon Chughtai as a great author because she wrote with a woman's sensitivity, enriching a seasoned writer's expertise and mastery over plots and characters. In *The Laugh of the Medusa* (1981) Hélène Cixous says,

> . . . It is by writing, from and toward women, and by taking up the challenge of speech which has been governed by the phallus, that women will confirm women in a place other than that which is reserved in and by the symbolic, that is, in a place other than silence. Women should break out of the snare of silence. They shouldn't be conned into accepting a domain which is the margin. . . (250)

Chughtai brings the margin into the discourse when she, as a woman, writes about women in their everyday life, of their desires, pains, resistances, and small victories as well. But we often confuse the nature of the art which only a woman can bring in, with feminist politics. These two can be allied, obviously, and they both are political but apart from this one similarity, they are ontologically different. There can be no argument that Chughtai was a feminist, in her writing as well as her activism. But feminist positionality does not necessarily translate into great art. In this respect I would like to quote a few lines from Adrienne Rich regarding the burden that the early feminist writers had to contend with, as she analyses it.

On re-reading Woolf's *A Room of One's Own*, Rich was struck by 'the sense of effort, of pains taken, of dogged tentativeness, in the tone of that essay' (1972, 20). She found in Woolf,

> . . . the tone of a woman almost in touch with her anger, who is determined not to appear angry, who is willing herself to be calm, detached, and even charming in a roomful of men where things have been said which are attacks on her very integrity. Virginia Woolf is addressing an audience of women, but she is acutely conscious—as she always was—of being overheard by men. . . . (18–30)

Rich here talks about the anxiety that the early twentieth century feminist writers experienced about articulations in their own voice. While that anxiety did not detract from their art, their approaches were often hesitant. The anxiety they felt at the possibility of being ridiculed by male intellectuals if they gave vent to their own voices was a palpable one and therefore, they often pretended to sound like their male contemporaries, emotionless and dry, because in the western philosophical discourse, dry reason has always been considered superior to emotion which is associated with femininity. Even feminism during the initial period of its turbulent journey would often have entailed denial of womanliness, of woman's imagination and language. Early history of women's writing is anyway replete with examples of these denials—of style, ideas and even one's identity. Taking up a 'male' pseudonym has been a very common phenomenon in the world of women's writing. Feminist writers were not totally free from this hesitation as well and were acutely sensitive about this judging male 'aural' presence as Rich points out.

In Chughtai's writing, which was also being born in a world dominated by male writers, much before the concept of écriture feminine becomes almost a slogan, we experience an absence of this fear, not simply when she is talking of tabooed ideas, not simply about writing outside the veil, but also in terms of talking in her own voice, that is, as a woman. She is fearless, insouciant about the dictates of 'patriarchy'. She uses women's experiences and the metiér of women for exploring the world. Her images, metaphors are 'feminine' in essence. But there is also a lightness of touch, a subtle but very powerful satirical attitude, criticising and even condescending to the world of 'men'. I personally find her use of certain metaphors very significant, particularly the imagery of clothes, which comes up quite frequently in her short stories, as an integral part of this attitude. This engagement with clothes rather interestingly continues to inform even Chughtai's autobiography which is titled 'The Paper Attire' ('*Kaghazi Hai Pairahan*'). I would also argue that Chughtai's writing uses a very specific kind of weave, and her use of the clothes in her stories, as images or objects or metaphors, takes on a special significance, because they do not merely lend themselves to being tools for narrative purposes but because they emerge metonymically as well from the world of women's experiences. It is an engagement that only a woman can perhaps understand fully, as clothes become an integral part of her existence the way a man's attire never can be.

The clothes in Chughtai's writing do not only become a narrative necessity but establish the close, complex and conflicted relationship between women and their attire, the fact that clothes mark the different phases of life for women, and that it is through them that women connect to society in complicity or resistance, or clearly establish their distinct identities. If clothes symbolically are used to mark a separation between the desiring female body and the patriarchy-imposed social identity, they can also be used subversively to defeat patriarchal restrictions.

Chughtai's female protagonists are ordinary women. The sexually dissatisfied wife (*The Quilt*), the worn-out spinster who dies waiting futilely for a suitable groom (*The Wedding Suit*), or the triply marginalised low caste girl-widow in love with an upper-class boy, victim of a forbidden and doomed love which is imperfectly understood by the narrator, herself a young girl (*Gainda*)—none of these characters nor the situations are alien to the reader.

These women do not make conscious political statements through what they wear, their attires are a combination of survival instinct and innate resistance. It would seem they become subversive without consciously intending to. The constant tussle that goes on between the desiring, aspiring female body and the stereotypes that society would like women to be reduced to, is marked upon the clothes they wear. The romanticism usually attached to women's clothing is significantly absent in Chughtai's writing. Instead she uses her insight as a woman in subtle ways that mark her approach as very different from that of her male contemporaries. Begum Jaan, the sexually deprived wife in 'The Quilt' all through the years of her marriage wears Hyderabadi *jaali karga* kurtas and brightly coloured pyjamas to cover her white, fleshy, well-oiled body. All the lightness, brightness and colours of a happy and satisfying conjugal life that she has been deprived of seem to have found their place in her attire, another lie she wears on her body while her husband spends his day teaching and caring for the male orphans whom he shelters in his mansion. The jaali karga kurtas, made of diaphanous material also have an erotic overtone that her husband is apathetic to, most probably because of his own unrevealed sexual orientation. In 'The Wedding Suit' (*Chauthi ka JoRa*), the wedding veil so lovingly embroidered by Kubra's mother gets lovelier as Kubra herself wilts. The red veil, like a vampire, seems to suck the youth and finally even the lifeblood out of Kubra, as she works herself to the bones nurturing the veil. Finally, the resplendent wedding dupatta is replaced by a white unstitched shroud, the *kafan*, as Kurba succumbs to tuberculosis in her unrelenting desire to someday wear that lovely veil adorned with pretty gold stars made out of Kubra's mother's gold eardrops sewn on it. In this story the narrative is held together primarily by the image of the veil of a ghostly new bride; at the same time the veil in its demand to be made beautiful devours Kubra, her mother and her sister in various ways. The veil moreover is the product of a demand by patriarchy, the imposed cover every woman must assume in different ways even if it kills her.

If we look at the plots carefully, these are stories which would have been narrated in the melodramatic mode in the hands of most writers. These situations are capable of being painted in stark white and black, in the binary of moral right and wrong, in scathing words of criticism about social ills.

M. Asaduddin in his introduction to Chughtai's selected writings in English translation, titled *Lifting the Veil,* says that the literary influences that Chughtai imbibed were of Tolstoy, Gorky, Chekhov, Dostoevsky, Maupassant, Balzac, Zola and Bernard Shaw. Interestingly these are all male realist writers. The other influence was that of Rasheed Jahan, one of the first feminist writers and thinkers in Urdu, slightly older than Chughtai, who remained a literary model and ideal for Chughtai. As she writes, 'The handsome heroes and pretty heroines of my stories, the candle-like fingers, the lime blossoms and crimson outfits all vanished into thin air. The earthly Rasheed Jahan simply shattered all my ivory into little pieces… life, stark naked, stood before me' (Chughtai 2009, xviii).

If the feminist impulse in Chughtai's writing owes its existence to Jahan's influence, perhaps the other influence, the realist one, comes from the great nineteenth century European realists. However, what is also interesting is that as Peter Brooks in his 'The Melodramatic Imagination' argues, realist fiction in the nineteenth century used melodrama unreservedly. He says,

> … there is a convergence in the concerns of melodrama and of psychoanalysis—and indeed psychoanalysis is a kind of modern melodrama, conceiving psychic conflict in melodramatic terms and acting out the recognition of the repressed… the hystericized body offers a key emblem of that convergence, because it is a body preeminently invested with meaning—a body that has become the place for inscription of highly emotional messages that cannot be written elsewhere, and cannot be articulated verbally. (Brooks 1995, xi)

Chughtai obviously did not inherit the melodramatic element from the realist writers, even if she did imbibe the realist impulse of addressing social ills. To me it seems that the absence of the melodramatic temperament in Chughtai's writing is due to the identification and excellent use of images that she, as a woman found in her creative world. Women's experiences do not need external melodrama to heighten the degree of truth. Melodrama is an expression of repressed articulations and acts as symbolic. For Chughtai melodrama is not needed because repression—whether in terms of the psychological state or of writing truth—does not exist in her narratives. She employs images and metaphors that consolidate and manifest the emotions, and even register protests without turning into propaganda. The image of the clothes is one such tool. Chughtai was a writer who wrote not about violent, articulated resistance on the part of women but of silent ones. Chughtai's women characters are not hysterical for the same reason that they are not melodramatic, and more importantly, they are not victims. They suffer but with knowledge, they struggle but they are dignified and in control even in misery, even in the face of injustice and helplessness. They reduce the antagonist, patriarchy, by the immensity of their suffering and the dignity with which they resist it. The felt suffering somehow gets written on the clothes they wear. The characters use clothes in different ways—like Lajo and Granny, they manipulate the system through clothes, or they get manipulated by clothes, the handmaiden of patriarchy, as in the case of Kubra, but clothes become important parts of both their life stories and the narratives told about them.

I will conclude this brief attempt to understand Chughtai's craft by going back to the story I started my essay with.

The indomitable Granny in *Tiny's Granny* is defeated finally not by human beings but the monkeys of the mohalla. They had detected the object that she cherished in secret, which was an old pillowcase stuffed with things. The monkeys steal it, tear it open and expose the treasures that Granny had collected in the long course of her life. The torn pillow rains down not the cotton wadding but '…Shabban's quilted jacket … Bannu the watercarrier's waist cloth … Hasina's bodice … the baggy trousers belonging to little Munni's doll … Rahmat's little dupatta and Khairati's knickers … Munshiji's muffler … the sleeve (with cuff) of Ibrahim's shirt … a piece of Siddiq's loincloth …' (154), and much more. The departed had been preserved in Granny's life and memory in these pieces of clothing. Inside the pillowcase, hidden from public eye, they had a dignity which their exposure in public view robs them of. They look ridiculous, and grotesque. Granny's whole life with all its pains and sufferings, like those pieces of clothing with their hidden and forgotten histories, had been kept concealed, but now lay exposed with all its vulnerability. The brazenness of Granny's old burkha was defeated finally by the exposure of all her weaknesses forcibly torn out of the secret recesses of the pillowcase, which perhaps is a metaphor for her memory. Her burkha, a liar, remains strong, albeit patched over, but those disparate unsewn, unorganised pieces of clothing from different origins that escape from the depth of the pillowcase project the truth about her miserable, unsewn life which she had bravely sought to hide from people's pity and charity.

Life, Chughtai seems to imply, is potentially a patchwork quilt. Some women manage to connect those patches seamlessly, but most fail, because bigger structures intervene and prevent those pieces from being sewn together. Fragmented lives, memories scattered and unstitched are what suffering is all about. Chughtai's own art is a perfect tailor's art. That is how she understands life—both as an artist and as a woman—the importance of patching pieces of clothes for that perfect pattern that most women fail to achieve.

References

Brooks, Peter. 1995. *The Melodramatic Imagination, Balzac, Henry James, Melodrama, And The Mode of Excess*. New Haven and London: Yale UP.

Chughtai, Ismat. 2009. *Lifting the Veil (selected writings)*. Selected and translated by M. Asaduddin. New Delhi: Penguin Books.

———. 2013. *A Life in Words: Memoirs*. Translated from the original Urdu *Kaghazi Hai Pairahan* by M. Asaduddin. New Delhi: Penguin Books.

Cixous, Hélène. 1981. "The Laugh of the Medusa." *New French Feminisms: An Anthology*, edited by Elaine Marks and Isabelle de Courtivron, translated by Keith Cohen and Paula Cohen, 245–64. New York: Schocken Books.

Gilbert, Sandra M. and Susan Gubar (eds.). 2007. *Feminist Literary Theory and Criticism, A Norton Reader*. London: W.W. Norton and Company Inc.

Rich, Adrienne. "When We Dead Awaken: Writing as Re-Vision." *College English* 34, no. 1 (1972): 18–30. https://doi.org/10.2307/375215.

7

A Changing Mind, a Changing Body

Understanding the Journey into Female Adolescence through *Terhi Lakeer* and *Lal Tin Ki Chhat*

Urmi Sengupta

When Muhafiz Haider lauds the Urdu *Pragativadi* writer Ismat Chughtai for her prerogative to 'present woman in her essential form' (Haider 2000, 218) that is, free from social norms and categorisations that strive to construct and control her sexuality and sexual desires, he is not talking about the de-contextualisation of her protagonists but rather about her tendency to look within and beyond the forces of socialisation which operate within the patriarchal and essentially heteronormative society that strives to 'maintain an oppressive hold on the life and behaviour of its (female) members' (Naqvi 1995, vii) . One of the important aspects of this process of socialisation is perhaps the coercive silence that society maintains on the subjects of female sexuality and sexual desire, and certain biological phenomena like menstruation, female orgasm, pregnancy and childbirth—the very issues that plague the minds of young girls caught between childhood and adulthood. Unanswered or evaded questions about the physical and mental changes they are undergoing may turn the journey into adolescence a traumatic one. While the emotional upheavals go largely unnoticed by the adults, the bodily changes are greeted with the imposition of certain dictates about dressing and behaving in a 'feminine' way without an initiative to explain their significance in real biological terms. The 'First Phase' of Chughtai's first novel *Terhi Lakeer* (1945), one of the earliest among her coming-of-age stories about young girls, exemplifies this intention by tracing the transformative experience of Shaman, a female-child at the brink of attaining puberty, who struggles to come to terms with her newly awakened sexuality and the rapidly changing contours of her body and mind. This paper aims to explore the mysterious pathways of a girl child's journey into adolescence in a patriarchal society through *Terhri Lakeer* by Chugtai on the one hand and *Lal Tin Ki Chhat* (1974) by Nirmal Verma (1929–2005) on the other. Best known for pioneering the *Nayi Kahani* movement in the Hindi short story, Verma is believed to have been instrumental in shifting the focus of Hindi prose fiction from the *Pragativadi* (progressive) concerns of social inequality and political subjugation to an exploration of the *'gahan antarik samasyae'*(deep psychological turmoil) (Singh 2013, 52) of individuals struggling to negotiate the crisis of values within the urban middle class Hindi-speaking population of India due to the changing dynamics of gender and the 'postcolonial' consciousness vis-à-vis individual/social identity and regional/national identity in the mid-twentieth century, post-war, post-Independence society. *Lal Tin Ki Chhat*, his second novel after the autobiographical *Ve Din* (1964), sees 'his masterful pen dip into the palette of senses and repressed feelings' of eleven-year-old Kaya, thereby embarking upon an exploration of 'a childhood unfolding into the bewilderment of adolescence' (Kak 2017, 1) This paper, therefore, will strive to interrogate the thematic and formal representation of the social, cultural and psychosexual determinants that shape the awakening and expression of female sexuality in the two works, thereby establishing connections across the two *bhasa-sahityas* and the literary consciousness that informed them in the middle decades of the twentieth century.

As one of the major literary figures associated with *Pragativad* movement in Urdu literature, Ismat Chughtai was among the first Progressives to deal with gender in such a way that 'themes with a more familiar connection to the "woman question"—education, domesticity and familial politics—came to intersect with the questions of citizenship, political responsibility, labour, sexuality, class, caste, religion and ethics' (Gopal 2005, 5). Though she considered herself to be a part of the *Pragativad* Movement ever since she attended the first conference of the Progressive Writers' Association (PWA), held in Lucknow in 1936 and presided over by Munshi Premchand—widely accepted as the pioneer of the movement in both Urdu and Hindi literature—Chughtai admits to ambivalent reactions from her fellow *pragativadi*s on her boldness in articulating what society would prefer to push under the carpet (Chughtai 1972, 172), especially in the context of her representation of repressed female desire and same-sex relationships in '*Lihaaf*' (*Adab-e-Lateef* 1942). While some fellow progressives such as Sa'adat Hasan Manto, Krishan Chander or Manjoo Gorakhpuri came out to support her, many considered her preoccupation with such issues as 'a betrayal of their working-class politics' (Batra 2010, 28). It was her literary predecessor and fellow *pragativadi* Rasheed Jahan whom Chughtai hails as having been the chief source of inspiration for the frankness and in-your-face attitude that informed not only her literary exploration of female desires and sexuality but also her interrogation of the socially constructed notion of 'shame' that threatens to curb the freedom of expression of Shaman of *Terhi Lakeer*:

> She (Jahan) influenced me a lot; her open-mindedness and free thinking. She said whatever you feel, you should not be ashamed of it, nor should you be ashamed of expressing it, for the heart is more sacred than the lips. She said that if you feel a thing in your mind and heart and cannot express it, then thinking it is worse and speaking it better, because you can get it out into open with words. (Chughtai 1972, 172)

Written over the months of her first pregnancy, a period that saw her being strongly criticised and shamed for '*Lihaaf*' by many a critic and reader, the hard-hitting language of the novel aims to shock readers into realising the repercussions of the lack of constructive discussions (or for that matter, any discussion) about the physical and emotional needs of a female child fast moving towards puberty within a patriarchal society. The third person narrative with a tight knit, action-driven plot and a linear chronology of events narrated in a matter-of-fact tone, hardly leaves space for digressions and overt sentimental musings. The character of Shaman, loosely based on that of the author herself, is the ninth child of a middle class Muslim family based at Aligarh. A victim of acute neglect from her immediate family, especially her mother, her childhood need for emotional attachment and physical caress is satisfied by her caregivers, her wet-nurse Unna and her elder sister Manju. It is they who unwittingly provide her with the very first exposure to a fully developed, naked female body. Her undisguised, non-judgemental curiosity and a feeling of wonderment about female nakedness as an infant, transforms into a guilt-ridden, voyeuristic interest about the same, as the forces of socialisation gradually begin to instil in her a feeling of shame about the female sexual organs and their alleged role in sexual intercourse, pregnancy and childbirth. Half-baked and convoluted ideas gathered through stealing glances while accidentally chancing upon the so called 'forbidden' terrains of adult sexual encounters and eavesdropping upon adults' conversations, especially in the context of the wedding of her sister Sanjhu, finds expression in her fantasies and games:

> And then one day summoning up great courage, they (Shaman and her Bari Apa's daughter Noori) secretly staffed two balls of cotton in the doll's *koti.* They felt such shame, they couldn't even look at her. Draped in a filmy crepe *dupatta,* the doll looked like a woman alive and real. Allah forgive them! One day Bari Apa stumbled upon the doll and such beating they received! She tore off the *koti* and stitched up the shirt. From that day they lost all interest in the doll. What was she except a bundle of rags? (Chughtai 1995, 43)

According to the French feminist and philosopher Simone de Beauvoir, as mentioned in her seminal work *The Second Sex* (1949), play-acting, games and fantasy imbued with sexual undercurrents often emerge as alternative avenues to channelise the newly awakened and largely repressed sexuality of a girl child standing at the threshold of adolescence. The first stirrings of sexual desire in Shaman sparked by her strong physical attraction and emotional dependence on her teacher Miss Charan and her classmate Najma, fills her waking hours as well as dreams with wishful fantasies. In fact, the play-acting through which Shaman and her roommates tend to replicate the rituals of marriage (like exchanging garlands) to validate their 'feelings' for their female friends, emerges as an unconscious attempt on the part of the girls to blur the lines between their same-sex erotic desires and their realities governed by the patriarchal machinery that harps upon heteronormativity in order to perpetuate itself. As Beauvoir says,

> What is really the truth? In the area in which she (a girl in her early adolescence) has been shut up, this is a word without sense. Truth is reality unveiled, and unveiling occurs through acts: but she does not act. The romances she tells herself about herself—and that she also often tells others—seem better ways of expressing the possibilities she feels in herself than the plain account of her daily life. (2015, 427)

Juxtaposition of the character of the protagonist with that of her older female relatives like Bari Apa, who are instrumental in internalising and perpetuating the patriarchal norms of female propriety and imposing the socially-assigned gender roles on their younger counterparts, is enough to vouch for the fact that 'one is not born, but rather becomes, a woman' (Beauvoir 2011, 295). Fiery and free-spirited, Shaman is a rebel even as an infant. While her niece Noori is gradually conditioned to follow the footsteps of Shaman's Ammi and Sanjhu*bi* in slipping gracefully into the socially approved role of a 'respectable daughter' and 'obedient wife', whose individuality is stifled within the vicious cycles of pregnancies and childbirth, Shaman strives to emerge as the *terhi lakeer* (crooked line), the defiant deviant. Condemned, rebuked and punished for her inquisitive nature, assertiveness and strong-willed personality, she tries to claim and reclaim her agency through deliberately transgressive acts of violence and insubordination, only to succumb to some extent to the dominant patriarchal discourse of gender. Her very first stirrings of sexual desire for her teacher leave her with a feeling of pleasant wonderment, but even though she is unable to comprehend the actual gravity of the (misplaced) charges (of molesting a student) that cost Miss Charan her job, she holds herself responsible for the unfortunate turn of events to some extent. This incident coupled with her first real sexual encounter with her roommate Rasul Fatima, that finds her the unwilling recipient of the one-sided affections of the latter, slowly but steadily conditions her to associate sexual desire with a feeling of 'shame' that almost bordered on revulsion. While the lack of proper understanding of the manifestations and outcome of pregnancy makes her equate it with her state of being infected with roundworms (or 'snakes' as she calls them), in her early childhood, her missionary education leaves her with a wish to become a 'virgin mother' like the Holy Mother Mary without really comprehending the implications of virginity:

> The sacred mother was a virgin! Thinking of this made her smile. She too was a virgin, was she not? If, God forbid, the Holy Father caused her to have an innocent baby Jesus, what would she do? Certainly Amma would refuse to give him any milk, but yes, she would use her own kurtas to make clothes for him. Then she remembered that when the washerman's daughter had had such a baby boy, everyone ostracised the girl. Shaman tried her best to explain: 'So what if you are a widow? Who can interfere with Allah's will? He can do what he wants.' But the girl kept repeating, 'No, Bibi, I've committed a sin.' And even after hours and hours of thinking, Shaman couldn't understand what this sin was and why people committed it. (1995, 53)

Yet to form a comprehensive understanding of the biological coordinates that connect pregnancy with a sexual intercourse between members of the opposite sex, she chooses to interpret her pre-pubertal hormonal syndromes as pregnancy and takes pleasure in fantasising about her imaginary motherhood till the moment her roommate Saadat points out that marriage is a prerequisite for pregnancy. Through the inability of the girl to associate the socially constructed notion of 'sin' with pregnancy outside marriage, an issue which is later explored in greater detail in the short story 'Gainda', the author strives to interrogate and subvert the politics underlying the concept of 'chastity' that helps the patriarchal machinery to assert its control over the free will and sexuality of a woman. It is interesting to note that though the 'First Phase' of the novel is replete with autobiographical elements, Shaman's journey into adolescence, unlike that of the author's, mostly unfolds within a 'closed situation'—whether it be her joint family or the girls' schools which she gets to attend—where most of her interactions are limited to the members of her own sex (members of the opposite sex, mostly her male relatives, flit in and out of her life without leaving any significant mark on her psyche till well into the 'Second Phase' of the novel). Chughtai's upbringing, however, took place in close association with not only her Amma and her sisters but also her sensible father and six brothers. It was this family full of 'peculiar mad people' (Chughtai 1972, 170), that was instrumental in shaping the 'rebel woman' in her, who aspired to push the traditional boundaries of gender-based social learning and explore the subversive potential of art in empowering a girl child to take charge of her own body and sexuality.

The avant garde works of Nirmal Verma emerged as a force to reckon with at a time when *Pragativad* began to lose its relevance in the light of the new age sensibilities of the urban, middle class Hindi readership in the decade following Independence. With his 'attractive, crystalline fiction' impressive 'in its commitment to form, in its self-awareness, its vivid, poetic imagery, (and) its sensitive psychological texture' (Jaidev 1989, 26), the author laid the foundations of the *Nayi Kahani* movement in Hindi literature, whose characteristic features have been identified by Roadarmel as 'the heightened questioning of (older) values, the disillusion, the alienation, the introduction of previously taboo subjects, reflection of modern consciousness and experimental narrative patterns'(1989, 5). One of the major areas of thrust, in this context, emerged as the interrogation of the patriarchal values that have traditionally controlled female desires and sexuality in the light of the new age sensibilities pertaining to a woman's agency over her body and mind, that had emerged as a direct outcome of the change in the gender dynamics in the society—a change that was facilitated by sociological factors such as the gradual disintegration of joint families and greater physical mobility and economic emancipation of women—that informed the mid-twentieth century 'modern consciousness' of urban India. Verma's second full-fledged novel *Lal Tin ki Chhat* written during the early 1970s when the author had already established himself as a *nayi kahanikar,* though not motivated by any revolutionary zeal, displays a rare sensitivity in exploring the stages of development of this newly emergent female consciousness in all its strength and vulnerability, As Verma himself says, quoting the words of the Italian filmmaker Michelangelo Antonioni:

> When someone asked Antonioni about this (the importance of women characters in his films), he replied, "The loneliness and the contradiction of our society can be best summed up in the character of a woman." On reading this I felt that he had said something close to my heart. What I find in a little compromised men, I see fully manifested in women beyond their limit and in complete nakedness and totality. (Kengari 2007, 175)

Set in the hill station of Simla, the novel delves deep into the *antarik yatharth* (inner experiential reality) (Singh 2013, 30) of the adult Kaya by inviting the reader to embark upon a journey through her memories of that one year that marked her passage from childhood into adolescence.

Many of the storytelling techniques and stylistic devices of Verma's *nayi kahani,* also inform his experimentations with the genre of novel, lending it a form distinctly different and unique from that of its *pragativadi* predecessors. The absence of a linear, action-driven plot marks the narrative that 'centers on the consciousness of an individual: (her) frustrations, lack of communication, loneliness' (Singh 2016, 320), letting the past and the present coalesce into a seamless thread of thoughts and emotions of a girl left to deal all by herself with the physical and psychological changes that mark her onset into puberty. With her mother struggling with a difficult pregnancy, her father away in Delhi for work for most of the year and her brother Chhote too young to be her confidante, Kaya is mostly left to the care of the manservant Mangtu, her Bua and her neighbour, old Mrs Joshua in the last few pre-pubescent months of her life. While Shaman craves for attention and companionship even within the structure of a joint family or a pulsating hostel life, Kaya's loneliness is of a different nature. Mature for her age, introverted and imaginative, it is her solitary wanderings in the mountains or the night time strolls in and around her house that help her to take stock of her life and seek answers to the numerous questions that are mostly evaded by the adults in her life. This situation finds parallels in some other examples of Verma's *nayi kahani* like 'Andhere Me' (*Parinde,* 1959) which also deal with a similar subject matter. 'Kaya did not fear the loneliness; she was just a little mystified, as though it grew within one like a sickness, out of sight of people—of Chhote, of Mother, of Mrs Joshua. She was growing up unnoticed, unlike Mother, whom everyone noticed' (Verma, *The Red Tin Roof* 61). The *vatavaran* or the 'ambience' emerges to be of paramount importance in this context. The mountains almost become a living entity that revel in her moments of pain, ecstasy and bewilderment. Nature seems to take cognizance of her physical and psychosexual changes that go unnoticed by her family and acquaintances, through a corresponding change of seasons. As Verma himself admits in his 'Samvad ki Maryadayein',

> I am deeply fascinated by the action of the story and its ambience... To me what is interesting is that it is not important to name the city or the name of a particular specific locality but a sort of an unformulated, invisible but very sensuous and tangible sort of an environment in which the characters are operating—whether it is the mountains or the cityscape or a season, this depends on the theme that I have chosen. The thing that particularizes the situation, that itself seems to give the story a certain universal dimension. (Quoted in Kumar 1990, 15)

While summer that brings Kaya's Babu back home on a vacation spells happiness for her, the dreary autumn months are witness to her sudden awareness of her own sexuality and are filled with a sense of foreboding at the steady infiltration of the forces of gender-based social conditioning into her hitherto carefree childhood existence. Kaya's journey uphill towards her Chacha's house in Falkland becomes symbolic of her journey into the uncertainties of adolescence, ones that would fill her life with exciting new experiences, and yet leave her with a strange longing for the wooden house with the red tin roof, that she had left behind, one that symbolises her once uncomplicated days of childhood. The use of symbolic imagery, thus, forms an integral part of what Gitanjali Shree calls 'a unique "Nirmalesque" quality of writing' lending a subtlety of tone and a suggestiveness to literary representation of matters pertaining to the female body and sexuality, that is distinctly different from the frankness and the matter-of-fact tone adopted by Chughtai in *Tehri Lakeer*.

The use of *sanket* (symbols), though, does not necessarily entail subtlety; at times ending up being extremely hard hitting in its own way. This tendency is beautifully enunciated in the way in which the life-force of Ginny, Kaya's adorable pet, is projected as being symbolic of the repressed sexuality of Lama, the rebellious older cousin she looks up to, who strives in vain to break free of the shackles of rules and regulations imposed by society that threaten to thwart her aspirations of economic and social autonomy.

> "You know how Ginny suffers? She keeps howling outside my door at night. Don't you ever hear anything?" she (Lama) laughed quietly. "Listen, Ginny wants release—as do I: I want to get out. Do you know how to go about it?" A numbness spread through me. The vestiges of happiness in me were instantly clipped as though by pincers and doused in cold water. Release? That can't be found—it's given. (Verma 2003, 53–54)

The starkness of Ginny finding her 'release' only in death (by jumping onto the railway tracks), and Lama, condemned as a 'witch' by Mrs. Joshua and married off against her will by her mother and aunt, never finding hers, shocks the reader into a critical examination of the patriarchal machinery that perpetuates its domination through its very own victims. It is interesting to note the unmistakably ecofeminist undercurrent that underlies this situation. As the defiant girl continues to fight a losing battle against gender-based social conditioning, she is able to identify the disruptive behaviour of an otherwise docile animal for what it is: a desperate attempt to assert her will to live a life on her own terms. For, as Josephine Donovan argues in her essay 'Feminism and the Treatment of Animals: From Care to Dialogue', 'Indeed most women are acutely aware of what it feels like to have one's opinions ignored trivialized and rendered unimportant. Perhaps this experience has awakened their sensitivity to the fact that other marginalized groups—including animals—have trouble getting their viewpoints heard.' (2006, 306) Later in the novel, as Kaya begins to feel the cumulative weight of the social conditioning, moral policing and body shaming curb her autonomy, a hitherto absent empathy for the tormented dog fills her heart. The complete realisation of this identification provides the novel with a proper closure, the scene of Ginny running along the railway tracks to meet the approaching train being recreated, where the former subject seeking a 'release' through self-annihilation, is replaced by the protagonist herself. Positing menstruation, as a liberating force that does restrict but emancipates a girl inducing her to realize her full potential as a freethinking and sexual being, that finally prevents Kaya from putting an end to her life, is subversive in its own right.

The use of the 'grotesque' in order to explore the deep dark crevices of the human mind, another crucial narrative strategy of the author, takes up new dimensions through the first person narratorial intervention within the predominantly third person narrative that describes how Kaya, who tries to help Lama to break off her marriage by posting a letter that defames the potential groom, feels an eye staring at her from within the letterbox, every time she opens it, long after Lama is gone. This letterbox looks like a dead bird hanging upside down to her. What is this but a reflection of her feeling of guilt at her very first act of transgression, and eventual deviation from the well-trodden path of being 'a well-bred girl' by social standards? Her accidental encounter with the act of childbirth, which incidentally is also her first exposure to a fully developed naked female body, however, has none of the characteristic elusiveness of Verma's fiction:

> She watched spellbound, awestruck, as that quivering body writhed like a worm under the rock. Each wave bore Mother into a deeper dungeon of pain. Only Dai Ma's hands crawled forward between Mother's thighs, clutching in her wizened hands Mother's arched body. *No! No!* Kaya cried, her nails clawing the sheet of glass, her dry, chapped trembling lips chafing against the window frame... Mangtu shook her by her shoulders even as she swayed like a drunk—"Don't you have any sense of shame Kaya?" Kaya stared at him. She had heard that word before many times but it never had anything to do with her. Even the world between mother's open legs—her naked body racked by spasms—was above shame: chaste, pure. (2003, 81–83)

Though the shame that Kaya has been conditioned to feel every time someone mentioned her mother's 'growing body' in the months leading up to the stillbirth is purged to a large extent, she realizes that her elders would never approve of her sharing this experience with anyone, even if invited to. Her first exposure to male nakedness, however, takes place in the form of the crucified naked body of Christ glimpsed during her chance visit to a dilapidated church. Though never openly rebellious like Shaman, Kaya, too, is free spirited in her own quiet way, exploring her newly awakened sexuality from within her very private world of playacting. A familiar childhood role play involving the offering of adulation to goddess Chandika transforms unconsciously into her very first attempt at self-pleasuring:

> Kaya had a strange feeling that the hands that stroked her were Kali Ma's, not her own. *What a courageous devotee! This little girl, braving the cold naked.* Kaya's hair flowed down, her hand slid down from her throat to her small breasts. Massaged, pinched, a wave of intoxication bearing her along without her realizing that she had gone beyond play-acting to enter a messy world where she was her own witness.... "Orre Kaya, don't you even have an iota of shame?" It was Chandika Ma. Kaya scrambled into her clothes, casting about in utter despair. (2003, 107)

The goddess emerges as the reflection of her inner turmoil, representing her sexuality that seeks expression on the one hand, and the patriarchal social norms that strive to repress it on the other. As her body and mind take cognition of her first stirrings of sexual desire for her adolescent cousin (Chacha's son) Beeru and later for the mistress of her Chacha, the 'forbidden' finds expression in dreams and fantasies, in which the naked body of Christ becomes one with that of Beeru and the goddess takes on the shape of the living *pahari* woman.

> I have grown up, she told herself. Her eyelids drooped with sleep. Her dry scaly lips mumbled *Beeru Beeru*, while she led herself into believing that he might just hear her. Her thoughts were in turmoil buffeted by nebulous longings. There was a sudden gnawing memory of a body nailed to a swinging piece of wood. It stood near her pillow, utterly silent but pleading. (2003, 166)

It is interesting to note the way in which sexuality, sexual desire and the causality between sexual intercourse and pregnancy is understood through religious metaphors in both the novels. What prompts these two writers make their young protagonists take the likes of Virgin Mary, Jesus Christ or Goddess Chandika, who are emblematic of institutionalised religions that have traditionally frowned upon same-sex (non-procreative) relationships, sexual encounters outside the 'sanctity' of marriage, incest and any assertive expression of female sexual desire, as the points of reference to come to terms with their newly awakened sexuality? This deliberate and conscious act of subversion strives to overhaul one of the most important power structures of the patriarchal machinery that threatens to smother any constructive discussions on sexuality and sexual desire, under an overtly judgmental shroud of 'shame' and 'sin.'

Unlike the closed world inhabited by Shaman, Kaya finds her growing up years informed by a strange craving for the approval of the father figures, who hold authority in the family. Babu's indifference to her wishes and opinions is in strong contradiction to the importance her Chacha accords to her views, a phenomenon that marks her journey into the new phase of her life with a new found self-confidence. Her first full-fledged sexual encounter with her Chacha's mistress, though strongly reminiscent of what comes to pass between Begum Jaan and her young guest in Chughtai's '*Lihaaf*', finds the young girl a slightly bewildered but willing reciprocator of the older woman's affections. Contrary to the claustrophobic atmosphere in which the sexual intimacy unfolds in the former, Verma designs the latter to unfold amidst nature, beside a waterfall surrounded by pine trees. The fact that Kaya identifies the waves of sexual pleasure gushing over her with the spontaneity of the waterfall, an unrestrained 'happiness', and yet not completely free of the prickle of pine needles, reflects her keen attempt at enjoying her sexual escapade without succumbing to the social taboos associated with it. The moments that mark her first taste of sexual pleasure and her first flow of menstrual blood reaches an epiphanic stature transforming into what Verma calls *anayas samay* or involuntary moments 'which glow at small intervals across the entire landscape of the past' (*Shabd aur Smriti* 119). These are the moments that the middle-aged Kaya keeps returning to in order to seek answers to certain existential questions that plague her adult life.

The two novels, separated in time by three decades, harp upon an issue that never loses its relevance in a patriarchal society. Though not motivated by a 'progressive' ideology or a revolutionary zeal like Chughtai, Verma's exploration of the female consciousness pertaining to the changing contours of the body and the mind at the brink of adolescence, is subversive in his own subtle, often symbolic way. An exploration of the formal as well as thematic representation of the expression of the newly awakened female sexuality in both the works that harp upon the authors' deep-rooted commitment to the respective literary sensibilities that inform their creative endeavours, thus helps trace a trajectory of interconnectedness across *bhasa sahityas* in mid-twentieth century India.

References

Batra, Kanika. "The home, the veil and the world: reading Ismat Chughtai towards a 'progressive' history of the Indian women's movement." *Feminist Review* 95, (2010): 27–44. JSTOR. (Accessed March 15, 2017).

Beauvoir, Simone de. 2015. *The Second Sex (Vintage Feminism Short Edition).* S.L.: Random House.

Chughtai, Ismat. "Mahfil Interviews Ismat Chughtai". *Mahfil* 8.2/3, (1972): 169–88. JSTOR. (accessed March 3, 2017).

———. 1995. *The Crooked Line (Terhi Lakeer).* Translated by Tahira Naqvi. New Delhi: Kali for Women.

———. 2001. "In the Name of Those Married Women." In *Lifting the Veil: Selected Writings of Ismat Chughtai,* translated by M. Asaduddin. New Delhi: Penguin Books.

Donovan, Josephine. "Feminism and the Treatment of Animals: From Care to Dialogue". *Signs* 31.2, (2006): 305–29. JSTOR (accessed 3 January 2015).

Gopal, P. 2005. Print. *Literary Radicalism in India: Gender, Nation and Transition to Independence.* London and New York: Routledge.

Haider, Muhafiz. 2000. "The Essential Women of Ismat." Translated by Promila Puri. In *Ismat: Her Life, Her Times,* edited by Sukrita Paul Kumar and Sadique. New Delhi: Katha Books.

Jaidev. "Brilliance Sans Significance: The Fiction of Nirmal Verma." *Jadavpur Journal of Comparative Literature* 26–27, (1989): 26–33.

Kak, Manju. Review, *The Red Tin Roof,* by Nirmal Verma. http://www.academia.edu/9258771/The_Red_Tin_Roof_Nirmal_Verma (accessed 9 August 2017).

Kengari, Vandana. 2007. *Nirmal Verma ka Stree Vimarsh (Discourse on Women in Nirmal Verma).* New Delhi: Vani Prakashan.

Kumar, Sukrita Paul. 1990. *The New Story: A Scrutiny of Modernity in Hindi and Urdu Short Fiction.* New Delhi: Allied Publishers.

Naqvi, Tahira. 1995. "Introduction." In *The Crooked Line* by Ismat Chughtai. New Delhi: Kali for Women.

Roadarmel, Gordon C. 1972. *Modern Hindi Short Stories.* Berkeley: U of California P.

Singh, Madhu. "Translator's Introduction: *Maya ka Marm* and the Experiential reality of Nirmal Verma." *Sagar* 21, (2013): 28–33. (Accessed June 26, 2014).

———. "Altered Realities, New Experiences: Bhisham Sahani, Nirmal Verma, and the 'Nayi Kahani' Movement." *Comparative Literature Studies* 53.2, (2016): 312–33. Project Muse. (Accessed 22 July, 2017).

Singh, Namvar. 2009. *Kahani: Nayi Kahani.* Allahabad: Lok Bharati Prakashan.

Shree, Gitanjali. "Nirmal Verma." *Economic and Political Weekly* Dec. 3, (2005). https://www.epw.in/journal/2005/49/commentary/nirmal-verma.html.

Verma, Nirmal. 1976. *Sabd Aur Smriti.* New Delhi: Bharatiya Jnanpith.

———. 2003. *The Red Tin Roof (Lal Tin ki Chat).* Translated by Kuldip Singh. New Delhi: Penguin Books.

8

Codes of Censorship in Pre-Independence India

An Analysis of Chughtai and the Progressives

DEBJANI CHAKRABARTY

> Better a thousandfold abuse of free speech than denial of free speech. (Charles Bradlaugh 1908, 134)

Discourses on censorship often invite spirited calls for freedom of speech not unlike Charles Bradlaugh's speech at the Hall of Science in 1880 mentioned above. While the censored group cites nefarious intentions, the group doing the censoring calls for censorship as a tool in the practice of 'pragmatic vigilance', necessary to maintain some modicum of peace in a functioning social set-up (Kaur and Mazzarella 2009, 10). Although censorship is often associated with State-mandated proscriptions, broadly defined, censorship represents, 'a variety of processes … formal and informal, overt and covert, conscious and unconscious, by which restrictions are imposed on the collection, display, dissemination and exchange of information, opinions, ideas and imaginative expression' (Jones 2001, xii). In this paper, I have tried to extend the definitions of censorship to underscore that while legal actions are the most common tools of censorship, they are but the manifestation of a hidden yet dynamic network of multiple forms of repression. Additionally, this paper also asks whether there can be a productive consequence of what is essentially a restrictive process. Censorship, some scholars argue, is particularly effective when it comes to the prohibition of certain ideas and discourses because its effect does not stop at the single, isolated act of proscription or ban. When an element is chosen to be censored it is very publicly vilified for being unworthy of existence, consumption or consideration in civil society. Psychologically, this creates a negativism whereby individuals reject any further notions that might even be tangentially related to it: 'They furnish the individual with guide posts in his associative thinking which keep him within the boundaries set by the moral codes' (Young 1930, 636–37). Therefore, the act of censorship becomes more effective and continues to exacerbate by dint of becoming naturalised with the passage of time. This, in turn, becomes an intrinsic part of a society's self-fashioning, through a rejection of what it chooses *not* to be.

Social regulations are, therefore, often developed according to what is considered despicable and maintenance of these social regulations is dependent, in a large part, on individual and collective acts of self-censorship. Hobbes, for instance, has argued that self-censorship is a conscious public performance of censorship and not an unconscious act that is perpetrated by powerful social forces. He postulated that opinions cannot be coerced; they form organically, through internal processes that are immune to the commands and demands of external society. Therefore, peaceful existence entails that everybody is tolerant of everybody's beliefs that are performed or expressed privately. Publicly, however, one needs to adhere to the commands of the sovereign irrespective of their private beliefs but without any compulsion to change these beliefs either (Parkin 2015, 293–317). To cite an even older example, performances of comedy in ancient Athens, for instance, also entailed a tightrope walk of pushing one's beliefs but also practising deliberate self-censorship to avoid prosecution (Baltussen and Davis 2015, 1–17). Needless to say, Hobbes' theories do not work in the post-truth age that we inhabit, where not only are private beliefs very much susceptible to social malleability, but there are institutions that operate almost exclusively on that premise. Beliefs are constantly challenged, moulded and altered on social media platforms. Censorship has taken on the form of cancellation and self-censorship—whether performative or organic—is very palpably present. This paper, however, explores the questions surrounding censorship not through present day scenarios but within the historical context of pre-Independence India and the rise of the Progressive Writers' Association. The first section of the paper elaborates on the history of State-mandated censorship in colonial India and tries to establish that both the colonial State and the anti-colonial intelligentsia utilised various modes of censorship in order to create an ideal Indian womanhood that would serve some, if not all of their purposes. One of these modes involved self-censorship such that women were expected to abide by specific restrictions to aid the group that they belonged to, which in this case was their national identity. Self-censorship is expected from individuals within a group in order for the group to sustain itself. For instance, members of a family are expected to keep secrets for the welfare of the family (Bar-Tal 2017, 41). As a result, when Ismat wrote 'Bachpan' and sent it for publication, it was sent back along with a letter that disapproved of her writing about how the Maulvi would punish her (Chughtai 2012, 38). Similarly, M. Aslam was indignant that she had referred to her brother as 'hell-bound', as rules of loyalty to one's kin dictated that she be kinder to her brother (Chughtai 2012, 33).

Bar-Tal theorizes self-censorship as a restrictive practice of 'intentionally and voluntarily withholding information from others in the absence of formal obstacles' (Bar-Tal 2017, 40) and juxtaposes it against conformity and obedience. I would put forth, however, that while self-censorship is often purposeful, acts of self-censorship take place almost unconsciously and ubiquitously in order to try and adhere to what Foucault would call 'epistemes', particularly when it comes to exploited groups. Additionally, Bar-Tal defines 'formal obstacles' as official mandates, orders and laws. But censorship, as highlighted earlier, is far more nefarious than that. Mazzarella and Kaur, for instance, ask whether unofficial acts such as *gheraos, bandhs, hartals, dharnas*, and *morchas* would constitute censorship? (Kaur and Mazzarella 2009, 5). If it promotes, generates and contributes in any form to restrictive practices, I posit, then it is an act of censorship, the source notwithstanding. This line of scholarship is pursued by the New Censorship Theorists who argue, for instance, that censorship 'encompasses all socially structured proscriptions or prescriptions which inhibit or prohibit dissemination of ideas, information, images, and other messages through a society's channels of communication whether these obstructions are secured by political, economic, religious, or other systems of authority'. This definition urges us to look into the 'implicit structures of censorship' that work towards 'control, conditioning and silence' (Freshwater 2003, 225–27).

New Censorship Theorists would argue that the expansive networks of censorship also give rise to productive practices that are uniquely built to respond to the censorship. Restriction, therefore, naturally births resistance. Drawing from Foucault's work on the history of sexuality, scholars postulate that censorship can also be 'a relentless proliferation of discourses on normative modes … of being in the world … a productive part of the apparatus of modern governmentality' (Kaur and Mazzarella 2009, 5). How this brand of productivity is manifest in literature has been explored in the second section of the paper. Chughtai, for instance, responds to the manufactured sanctity of the domestic sphere by completely de-mystifying it. She fills her *afsanas* with detailed accounts of the politics, intrigue, manipulations and repressions that take place within familial structures. She never uses expletives but explicitly describes those elements that will inspire disgust: disease, phlegm, blood, odour. She also rails against the idealisation of women's lives and the products of the same surrounding like herself by highlighting that it was reading Rashid Jahan's realistic stories that contributed to her self-hood, not the frivolous romances that were largely peddled to the female readers.

Economic Censorship of Women and Their Emancipation

Working with the theories postulated by Marxist feminists, this section of the paper analyses how the socialist writers of the PWA represented the complex structures of gendered economics by looking at the treatment of domestic work and sex work. This paper, therefore, utilises the lives and works of the Progressive writers to ask three questions. 1. After the publication of *Angarey* in 1932 and its consequent proscription a year later, Progressive ideas, discourses and works inspired a multitude of responses from the colonial authorities, from the Muslim intelligentsia, from the Hindu reformers, from women and various other groups. How far have these responses, a lot of them censorial, influenced the creation of newer literary articulations? 2. Whether, if at all, economic repression of women was an important element of anti-colonial exertions? 3. And, perhaps most importantly, how does 'ideal womanhood', an artificial and repressive category created by Indian patriarchy in collusion with the British, stand apart from and simultaneously create women's subjectivities across religious and class lines. Although different kinds of suppression of free speech and curbs on opinion have existed for centuries, India's tryst with censorship can be definitively mapped in the contours of its colonial legacy. In 1780, James Augustus Hicky's *Bengal Gazette* was gagged soon after its birth on account of publishing gossip directed at Marian Hastings, the wife of Warren Hastings, the Governor-General of India. However, it was the backdrop of the annexation of Mysore in 1799 that set the stage for what has come to be considered the first formal act of press censorship in India when Governor General Wellesley introduced a stringent policy of pre-censorship, and decreed that anybody who failed to comply would be promptly packed off back to Europe (Jones 2001, 1159–60). So far, however, censorship remained limited to English language print productions and was established and sustained through regulation as opposed to law. Following the battle of 1857, the government was wary about what would be deemed 'seditious' writing and contested that those who produced and/or read English newspapers, were, whether European or Native, far too responsible as citizens to be seditious (Chatterjee1993b, 24–25). Instead measures, therefore, had to be introduced to strangle 'sedition' written in native languages which led to the passing of the Vernacular Press Act of 1878: 'a coup d'etat to pass a very stringent gagging Bill' (Gopal 1964, 118).[1] Two aspects of this description are of importance to us. First, the underlining of the stringency of this bill which is evinced in its provisions that stated that local officials could demand security bonds from printers or publishers whom they suspected to be potentially dangerous. This security as well as the machinery of the press could be confiscated if they published anything considered objectionable. In addition, any appeal to the courts against such confiscation was disallowed. Second, the feature of the 'coup d'etat' is symptomatic of a consistent feature of the British colonial government's stance on censorship: confusion. The governance of India was split between the Secretary of State for the colonies based in London, who was the overseer, and the government of India, led by the governor general, in conjunction with the local governments (Ross 2001, 323), effectively swinging 'back and forth from strict controls to virtual freedom of expression' (Barrier 1974, 4). Such a split therefore entailed that the government of India would not only be answerable to the overseers in London but would also have to take into account the political climate that was prevalent at each given time. Consequently, 'The Vernacular Press Act of 1878 was enacted in great haste so as to forestall long debates over principles, especially in Britain' (Chatterjee 1993b, 25). Nonetheless, despite the urgency and the arguments in support of it, the Vernacular Press Act was repealed in 1881 by Lord Ripon. The oscillation between the government in India and the often-liberal overlords in London, resulted in disruptive actions when it came to the policies of state censorship. State censorship in British India, therefore, 'waxed and waned to an awkward rhythm' (Kaur and Mazzarella 2009, 14), being not innate and unswerving but disjointed and reactive. Although all of the regulations mentioned thus far belong to the arena of political fracas and intrigue, the disjointed nature of British censorial intervention can be observed within the realms of the social and cultural networks as well. With its quagmire of religiosities, castes, communities, languages, rituals and ethno-cultural practices, the geo-political entity that is now India represented a puzzle when it came to governance. Cohn had explicated how the British in India at once failed to recognise the complexities of Indian society and over-simplified them (Cohn 1996). This resulted in the British creating a number of over-arching 'truths' about India that the Indians were supposed to conform to following its creation (Cohn 1996, ix–xviii). Partha Chatterjee terms this the 'rule of colonial difference' (2001, 20)[2], that the legitimising principle of colonialism relied on establishing and essentializing differences between India (the colonised) and Britain (the coloniser). Furthermore, the civilising mission of the colonisers was undergirded by what was considered the abominable treatment of its women, leading to a layered and complicated anti-colonial response to the 'women's question'.

The 'women's question' in India's history, particularly the history of the struggle for Indian independence has been a contentious one, and not just in terms of the lens of academic retrospection but through the cacophony of voices that asked and answered, very rarely to the benefit of—and often to the woe of—the woman. Reformers, scholars, politicians, religious heads of both sexes asserted their opinions concerning it and their efforts brought forth welcome but also at times disastrous consequences. This was an intriguing intermeshing of the exercise of nation-building and emancipation of women, with most of the audible voices claiming that that the former could not be feasible without the latter. The exact nature of this 'emancipation' will be tackled in some detail later. There were alternative opinions as well, ones that placed ontological primacy on the paradigm of national freedom as opposed to gendered freedom. One notable advocate of such a view, for instance, was Bal Gangadhar Tilak who had jokingly shrugged off the women's question, saying that he would ensure the re-marriage of a thousand widows but only once the country was free (Chakravarti 1999, 73). These opinions are doubly significant, not simply because they played a role in galvanising a certain brand of political practice that spurred other reactions but also because their (recorded) presence in the past offers up insights into the gender politics of the present. Further, these opinions were responses to the creation of the 'orient' by the colonial forces. Said's treatise on orientalism revealed how a large part of the colonial enterprise comprised of the creation of academic and literary materials that delineated features of the Orient that were believed to be true. In other words, 'truths' that would fit comfortably within the confirmation bias of the peoples of the Occident and legitimise colonial rule. Said also mentions that the project of orientalism is not merely a structure of falsehoods that would cease to exist in due time. He writes that orientalism is a network of knowledges, a discourse such that it is a system of signs corresponding to and inextricably linked to other systems. He further elaborates that since this network empowers both political and socio-economic stability, it can lay claim to a significant amount of durability. 'After all, any system of ideas that can remain unchanged as teachable wisdom (in academies, books, congresses, universities and foreign service institutes) from the period of Ernest Renan in the late 1840s until the present in the United States must be something more formidable than a mere collection of lies' (Said 1979, 6). The Occident, therefore, is continually 'producing' the Orient, spawning a dialectical relationship whereby, the Orient is continually responding to its own production. Criticism and collusion are working hand-in-hand. The anti-colonial intelligentsia is criticising the colonial enterprise but also accepting parts of its narrative and colluding to change them into favourable outcomes. Conversely, the representatives of the colonial nation are acknowledging the moral backwardness of the Indian populace but also participating in exercises that would underscore that this backwardness is not innate to their civilisational history. A significant example of this collusion can be found in Lata Mani's work on sati whereby she explains how 'Indian traditions' were often created by the colonial machinery (Mani 1999, 88–126). Utilising this example, Partha Chatterjee writes, 'It was colonialist discourse that, by assuming the hegemony of Brahmanical religious texts, defined the tradition that was to be criticized and reformed. Indian nationalism, in demarcating a political position opposed to colonial rule, took up the women's question as a problem already constituted for it: namely, as a problem of Indian tradition' (1993b, 119).

Chatterjee further posits that the Indian responses to the colonialist discourse comprised of a manufactured binary, splitting the national identity into two domains: the material and the spiritual. In the material or exterior domain, Indians had to learn and emulate the precepts of science, technology and rationality from their Western masters. However, this emulation was discouraged in the internal sphere which was the *ghar* (home) and represented the spiritual realm. The West was considered not only spiritually bankrupt but also the ghar would be central to the weaving of a distinctive national identity and the fulcrum of this spiritual realm would be the woman. Therefore, women's lives call for reform not by dint by of being important human lives but because they are crucial to the creation of the nation. Nonetheless it would be measured reform such that Western influence would not be able to corrupt that which was considered essentially indigenous.

> It followed, as a simple criterion for judging the desirability of reform, that the essential distinction between the social roles of men and women in terms of material and spiritual virtues must at all times be maintained. There would have to be a marked difference in the degree and manner of Westernization of women, as distinct from men, in the modern world of the nation. (Chatterjee 1993b, 126)

Consequently, the Orientalists were far more successful than the Reformists, who advocated a complete overhaul of women's rights based on Victorian Christian values, in forging a path to improve women's lives. The technique employed by the Orientalists was one of evoking the glories of the past, particularly the Vedic ages and use the examples of Vedic heroines Gargi and Maitreyi to explicate that in earlier days, the woman was the man's spiritual companion, participating in *yajna*s and spiritual studies and exercises. It was claimed that without the aid and companionship of the women, the men would not be able to gather the strength to free the motherland of her shackles. The note of rescue of the woman by the man notwithstanding, what is significant here is the division of labour when it comes to attaining independence. The man will play the central role in this quest, with the, albeit indispensable, aid of the woman. Gandhi, for instance, asserted that the wife was a comrade, the better half, and a colleague (Norvel 1997). However, even in his calls for women's equality, is implicit his tacit but firm recognition of difference. In a speech on women's education in 1918, Gandhi emphasised,

> Man and woman are of equal rank, but they are not identical… Man is supreme in the outward activities of the married pair and, therefore, it is the fitness of things that he should have a greater knowledge thereof. On the other hand, home life is entirely the sphere of women and, therefore, in domestic affairs, in the upbringing and education of children women ought to have more knowledge. (Gandhi 1970, 273–75)

The contentious nature of state censorship in Britain earlier discussed is also in display within the complex network of nation-building and the woman's place in it as can be evinced in the events surrounding the practice of sati. Lata Mani speaks about the anxieties of the British government when it came to interventions within what they considered to be the domain of faith and religious practices (Mani 1999, 92). Thus, despite wide-ranging assent about sati being a symbol of primitivism and barbarity, Lord Bentick muses, 'Whether the question be to continue or discontinue the practice of suttee, the decision is equally surrounded by an awful responsibility' (Bentick 2004, 350–51). According to him, ending 'suttee' risks the stability of British rule and long-term social reform, yet allowing it to continue condemns hundreds of innocent victims to needless death posing acute moral dilemma.

Even after a span of ninety years, similar concerns are echoed by Vincent Smith in the wake of the Montagu-Chelmsford proposals such that he cautions the government against any censorial reform measures lest they witness a repeat of 1857 (Chatterjee 1993b, 17).

Censorial state intervention in British India worked hand-in-hand with other brands of censorship and repression that were utilised to engage in the creation and protection of the spiritual realm discussed earlier. Through the story of Rukma Bai's life, Uma Chakravarti has explicated how these networks worked. Rukma Bai refused to honour a marriage she hadn't consented to and her husband moved the court which judged in Rukma Bai's favour. Consequently, the Indian male milieu protested vehemently against such a decision.

'They threatened the British government with public displeasure … Large sums of money were collected in the husband's support to appeal against her stand. When she adamantly refused, the court ordered her arrest' (Chakravarti 1999, 73). Similar circumstances led to the ban of the literary collection *Angarey* as well: the British government was being asked to ban this volume and even prosecute the writers very vehemently by the Indian Muslim population. The government too had little sympathy for the Progressives because not only were they anti-imperialist but also communist.

Progress, Gender, and the Unexpected Virtues of Censorship

While writing about the nationalist discourse, Partha Chatterjee theorises that '"passive revolution" is the general form of transition from colonial to post-colonial national states in the 20th century' (1993a, 50). Developed by Gramsci, the concept of 'passive revolution' broadly signifies a revolution that takes place without mass support or participation and is essentially engineered by the social elite and represents social and political reforms (Gramsci 1971, 44–120). The birth and development of the Progressive Writers' Association can be analysed as tools that participated in the sculpting of this 'passive revolution' that was integral to the processes of nationalism in India. Faiz, for instance, while writing about the Progressives, says, 'If the message of the progressive writers does not reach the uneducated workers at least it reaches the middle classes. The war between the capitalist and the proletariat is not the exclusive war of the proletariat; it is a battle challenging all of us. Are we not part of our society?' (Faiz 1967, 649–64).

While the message may not reach the 'uneducated workers', the masses, of which these workers were a part of, were certainly a point of interest for the Progressives, as will be explicated later in this section. Priyamvada Gopal explains the rise of the Progressive Writers' Association utilising the conceptions put forth by Terry Eagleton whereby he writes that in order to work towards liberation, an oppressed group needs 'to generate a positive particular culture without which political emancipation is probably impossible. Nobody can live in perpetual deferment of their sense of selfhood, or free themselves from bondage without a strongly affirmative sense of *who they are*' (Eagleton, 1990, 37, quoted in Gopal 2005 27, emphasis mine). The Progressives, like many others in the arena of Indian anti-colonial movements, embarked on the project of defining 'who they are' but underscored their aims by stating what they did not want to be. The Progressive Writers' Movement began in the wake of several and severe acts of censorship that greeted the publication of *Angarey*. Aijaz Ahmad, in his blistering critique of Jameson's argument that all third world literatures are responses to the imperialist past and are hence national allegories, utilises the oeuvre of Urdu literature to point out the reductive nature of Jameson's theories. Ahmad writes:

> I do not know of any fictional narrative in Urdu, in roughly the last two hundred years which is of any significance and any length (I am making an exception for a few short stories here) in which the issue of colonialism or the difficulty of a civilizational encounter between the English and the Indian has the same primacy as, for example, in Forster's *A Passage to India* or Paul Scott's *The Raj Quartet*... The "nation" indeed became the primary ideological problematic in Urdu literature only at the moment of Independence ... it came together with the Partition of our country ... the worst bloodbath in the memory of the subcontinent ... Our "nationalism" at this juncture was a nationalism of mourning.... A critique of others (anti-colonial nationalism) receded even further into the background, entirely overtaken now by an even harsher critique of ourselves. (Ahmad 1987, 22)

While agreeing with Ahmad's in-depth analysis of the richness of the Urdu literary sphere I would, however, argue that the spectre of the 'nation' was very much present, subtly and otherwise, in the literatures being produced at this time, as a result of the preoccupations of the PWA collective. First, it is important to note that the PWA, as Ahmad himself writes, became 'the strongest and proximate shaping force' in Urdu literature and 'defined the parameters of the broad social agenda and cultural consensus among the generality of Urdu writers, including those who were not members of the associations; those who did not subscribe to the broad consensus were relegated to the fringes of the writing community' (Ahmad 1993, 18).

Second, as exhibited in the earlier section, the nationalist project did not merely involve a critique of the other but also a critique of one's own civilisational lack such that one recognises what parts of the Western milieu to adapt and emulate and what elements of Indian indigenous traditions needed to be preserved and this was very much an agenda of the Progressives as well: '[w]e can discuss, criticize and remould our varying ideals and develop our national culture' (ibid.). Third, the overarching communist principles that guided the actions of the PWA also involved a strident criticism of imperialism. Premchand, for instance, in his inaugural address of the first meeting of the PWA in 1936, said: 'Then our self-respecting humanity will raise the standard of revolt against capitalism, militarism and imperialism' (Premchand 1985, 188). Fourth, the exercise of 'nation building', which was an anti-colonial response, was so deeply intertwined in everyday life that its presences can be observed in a variety of literary responses. Note, for instance, Priyamvada Gopal's observation of Ismat Chughtai's novel: 'Ismat Chughtai, wielding irony as her weapon of choice in her semi-autobiographical novel, *Terhi Lakir* (translated as *The Crooked Line*), would . . . satirise the whims and vagaries of the male family members with regard to women's emancipation' (Gopal 2005, 35). Fifth, while there were different schools of thought when it came to the exercise of 'nation building', what they all had in common was that although they were subject to State censorship, they would, in turn often utilise diverse techniques of proscription to render invisible and eventually prune that which they considered undesirable to the creation of a new nation. Large number of works produced by the Progressives were also responses to and protests against such actions. Gail Minault writes that the Muslim intelligentsia, not unlike their Hindu counterparts, were engaged in reform work. For them reform was necessitated not only as a nationalist programme but also to nurture and exhibit the pride of belonging to noble (*sharif*) lineage. However, the Muslim woman presented a barrier in the creation and maintenance of this image of the sharif, for she represented all that was wrong with Muslim society: educational, moral and spiritual backwardness. However, just like their Hindu brothers, the Muslim reformers also believed that women, their backwardness notwithstanding, were also the axis on which their pride revolved. 'If women personified the plight of their community: its backwardness, its ignorance of the faith, its perilous cultural and historical viability, they were also at the core of family life, the potential purveyors of ethical values and religious ideals' (Minault 1998, 6).

However, Muslim reform was not a homogenised movement. Rakshanda Jalil explicates how it was primarily divided into two schools of thought—the Deobandi and the Aligarh schools. The former advocated for reform that aligned with the scriptures and was spearheaded by *ulemas*, leaning more towards pan-Islamic unity as opposed to national unity. The latter was the more liberal branch, boasting of names like Sir Syed Ahmad, and working towards nationalist pride and vigour. Nonetheless, Jalil observes, both these strands 'failed the Indian Muslim, failed that is, in giving them realistic ways to seeing themselves' (Jalil 2014, 157–58). It is in the midst of this lack that *Angarey* burst forth, delineating all evils that needed to be gotten rid of in order to energise anti-colonial movements. 'A few of us, filled with dreams of freedom and independence, made bold to publish in 1932 a collection of our short stories in Urdu, *Angarey* (Burning Coals) to show a mirror to society' (Ali 2017, xiv).

It is this very act of showing the mirror that invited the ire of the society around them and prompted the State to intervene and censor their work. As has been earlier explicated in this essay, censorship takes on a variety of forms. Drawing from the work of Kimball Young (1930), I would posit that the enraged reaction and the consequent censorship is a manifestation of a social taboo. A taboo that forbids everyone from engaging in anything that might adversely affect the group morale and encourages them to inhibit anything that might catalyse questions against the validity of existing social mores. Young justifiably terms it a 'contagion' (1930, 634), rapidly spreading with the potential to upend prevailing structures. The 'group' in this situation is the Indian Muslim community, which, already dealing with the possibility of Hindu majoritarianism side-lining it 'from the life of the Indian nation' (Gopal 2005, 7) was rudely shocked that people from eminent Muslim families engaged in such blasphemy (Jalil 2014, 164–5). One contemporary newspaper report stated, '…We could not find in them [the stories] anything intellectually modern except immorality, evil character and wickedness.… There is no regard for the greatness and majesty of God nor any respect for the sanctity and honour of prophets, nor any respect for human dignity' (Jalil 2014, 166).[3]

The question of human dignity has often dictated censorship norms. Alan Segal writes that censorship can be read as not a protectionist action that seeks to shield society from depravity but that which proscribes subversions of human dignity. He defines dignity as that 'which bestows some kind of worth, elevation or excellence upon humans in the sense of ideal qualities of morality, thought, appearance or behaviour' (Segal 1970, 64). The being and practice of this 'dignity' is what contributes to the perpetuation of any social structure within a given paradigm such that not only is it fragile, inorganic and often arbitrary, but also any threats to this notion of human 'dignity' also threaten social relations. The primary subversions of human dignity are sex and violence. The general outrage that Sa'adat Hasan Manto was consistently exposed to can be traced to this notion. His infamous story '*Bu*' was charged with obscenity not because it depicted sex, but because it elaborated on the subversive power of lust while simultaneously exposing the hypocrisies of class structures. His Partition-inspired vignette 'Mishtake', on the other hand pointed to the absurdity, variety and the alarming regularity of violence human beings are capable of. Finally, '*Thanda Gosht*' (Cold Meat) represented the disturbingly bestial amalgamation of sex and violence, highlighting that human beings are constantly on the edge of depravity and degradation, held back not by good sense but the tenuous and agenda-driven structures of social nicety. Manto and the Progressives' works also invoked discomfort and indignation because they exemplified a specific brand of 'transgression' such that they irradiate that which is integral to the functioning of social structures but is supposed to stay hidden, that is 'forms of knowledge or representation that are generally, even obsessively known insofar as they must not be overtly acknowledged' (Taussig1999, 8). Hunger, for instance, is a common enough occurrence in society but depiction of hunger reveals that it is artificially created and that it is in the best interests of some sections of society.

Consequently, such a depiction critiques the very economic foundation on which society thrives and represents a threat. Works like Sukanta Bhattacharya's '*Hey Mahajiban*' and Rafik Azad's '*Bhaat Dey, Haramjada*' and even the Bengal Famine paintings by Chittaprosad have revealed the potential for rebellion embedded in the evocation of hunger. In the *Angarey* volume, Sajjad Zaheer portrays hunger in the stories '*Neend Nahi Aati'* (Unable to Sleep) and '*Garmiyon Ki Ek Raat*' (A Summer Night), underscoring its relentlessness and the piercing indifference it meets with from people who are not subjected to it. It is important to note that these stories drew the ire of the State not simply because they dealt with hunger but also because they emerged from the ideological grounds of communism, and communists were severely censored by the State.[4] After the formation of the PWA, in 1936, the Home Secretary of the Indian Government had sent a private circular to several authorities warning them about the Left-leaning proclivities of the group.

> The proclaimed aims of the association are comparatively innocent… The inspiration however comes from … organisations and individuals who are… advocating policies akin to those of the communists…. I am desired to suggest therefore, that suitable opportunities may be taken to convey, preferably in conversations, friendly warnings about this association to

> journalists, educationists and others who may be attracted by its ostensible programmes. (Jafri 1959, 7–8)

Furthermore, the stories carry within themselves a rebellious potential because they seek to eliminate all other differences except the ones between the haves and the have-nots[5] and everything else is either utilised to maintain this dichotomy or ensure that it is not visible, as is evinced by the way the Munshi uses religion to distract Jumman in '*Garmiyon Ki Ek Raat*'. In the end, there is no dent in the system, everything keeps moving, only Jumman stays fixed, rendered inert by hunger and helplessness.

More pertinent to the point of transgression, perhaps, is Ahmed Ali's story '*Badal Nahi Aate*' (Clouds Do Not Come) which records the lament of a married Muslim woman. Not only does the narratorial voice exclaim that Hindu and Christian women have better lives than their Muslim counterparts but also brings to the fore that which is privately known but never publicly acknowledged—physical and sexual abuse suffered by women in the confines of the home, the prized spiritual realm, the very fulcrum of indigenous Indian society and thought. The description of the abuse is not written in the form of a protest but to register the cyclical pattern of her imprisoned life.

> Beats me like a dog; gives me a bone just to beat me; calls me close and then beats me; beats me all around; beats me and yells; makes love to me and beats me; caresses me and beats me; forget everything else, he beats me after he beats me. And he treats me as though I'm descended from dogs, and still I keep licking his boots. (Ali 2014, 87)

The relentlessness of the violence is interspersed with anti-British rants, the abruptness and the juxtaposition signifying how women's issues are either trivialised or, worse still, weaponised in favour of the anti-colonial struggle. Even the hallowed halls of the PWA were not immune from the suppression of women's issues. Priyamvada Gopal mentions how Rashid Jahan and Hajrah Begum were relegated to jobs that were disliked by everyone else in the organisation and how they had to slowly infiltrate and find their foothold in an essentially male-dominated space. (Gopal 2005, 28–9). Susie Tharu and K. Lalitha note how the rhetoric of women's reform formulated by anti-colonial intelligentsia was endorsed and emulated by the socialist Progressives. Like the reformists, the progressives too placed ontological primacy on a specific mission, arguing that gender issues would resolve themselves after successful completion of said mission. '(women's) issues remained marginal in an analysis that considered the "woman question" a social problem that would be resolved with the overthrow of capitalism' (Tharu and Lalitha 1993, 81).

Indeed, anything that resolved to go beyond the sanitised confines of the women's issues considered apposite by the reformers, progressives or the general intelligentsia, would be considered transgressive, inviting censure and censorship. I would postulate, for instance, that the point of contention in the '*Lihaaf*' controversy, was neither the act of sexual intercourse nor sexuality but the gender of the person who dared to depict it. Hans Baltussen and Peter J. Davis write that the 'most extreme form of free speech is no doubt frank speech, parrhesia, which etymologically originates in pan ("everything") and rhesia ("speaking"): in other words, the freedom to "say all"' (Baltussen and Davis 2015, 2). Parrhesia, therefore, engages in Taussig's brand of 'transgression' but it is only the property of one who is not a slave and not an exile, entailing that parrhesia is a privilege limited to only a few. In the context of twentieth century India, needless to say, parrhesia was made available to and utilised by upper-class/caste male intelligentsia. Consequently, although depiction of sex was 'transgression', it was acceptable (only) when men wrote it; progressiveness, after all, has to pay premium to social comfiture. When Bangalore Nagratnamma decided to republish Muddupalani's *Radhika Santwanam*, social reformer and novelist Veerashalingam severely criticised the poet for describing sex in her work. Nagratnamma retorted that many celebrated male poets describe sex even more 'crudely' than Muddupalani. Nonetheless, all the copies were seized by the State in 1911 and the publishers were charged with obscenity (Tharu and Lalitha 1993, 2-4). Similarly, detailed descriptions of sexual intercourse in M. Aslam's '*Gunah Ki Raatein*' (Nights of Misdeeds) were acceptable but allusions to sex by Chughtai were not. '"...You've even described the details of the sexual acts merely for the sake of titillation," I said. "My case is different. I'm a man... You're an educated girl from a decent Muslim family.... Do you want to compete with men?"' (Chughtai 2012, 29–30).

Evidently, not only was she supposed to adhere to gender norms but also norms that are specific to her class and religious identity for she was also a representative of the 'Muslim woman' in the newly emerging nation. The fact that the contents of '*Lihaaf*', isolated from its creator, had very little to no impact on the furore it caused is further revealed by the reaction of Chughtai's sister-in-law who did not think it was obscene and recognised the person it was based on, highlighting the fact that same-sex relationships of the nature portrayed in the story were not uncommon. Furthermore, the idea of women writing about sex was so outlandish that readers often believed that 'Ismat Chughtai' was a pseudonym for a male writer (Naqvi 2004, vii). It is also important to note here that Chughtai's depiction of a queer relationship was by no means a celebration of the same. She calls lesbianism a 'disease' and an 'aberration', and is overjoyed to find out that the inspiration for her story had divorced her earlier husband, remarried and was now a grandmother. The radical nature, the 'transgression' of the story lay in the fact that it portrayed that women need emotional and sexual satisfaction just as much as men but it was neither radical nor kind in its depiction of a queer relationship: Rabbu is repulsive and Begum Jaan is frightening. Their interactions invoke discomfiture and reprobation from the other characters in the story as it is supposed to achieve the same effect on the readers. Chughtai states her reason for writing the story. '"My objective was just that. How I wanted that some brave fellow release her from Rabbu's clutches, encircle her within his strong arms and slake her life's thirst. It is a virtuous act to provide water to a thirsty creature"' (Chughtai 2012, 41). What she is attempting, in effect, is what I have chosen to call 'productive provocation' (Kaur and Mazzarella 2009, 3), an act of deliberate and socially uncivil provocation performed with the hope that it would lead to immediate and affective change, which can be found also in works such as Sajjad Zaheer's '*Dulari*' and Chughtai's own 'Tiny's Granny'. These stories are not provocative by dint of their theme which is the sexual exploitation of the domestic labourer, which, once again, was a relatively common and adroitly hidden part of the upper echelons of society. What sets them apart, is the treatment of the theme. While Chughtai delves into child sexual abuse and the impact of poverty on mental health, Zaheer explores the possibility of assertive subjectivity even within the most marginalised. Zaheer's eponymous protagonist chooses the avenue of sex work, becoming a social pariah and economically even more unstable than before, rather than tolerate an insult, an affront to her emotional well-being. That women who are subjected to the worse kinds of social censorship and repression can still find newer, more novel ways to assert their beings, find their freedom and claim their place is explored in stories like '*Neech*' and 'The Homemaker' as well. In Sajjad Zaheer's '*Neech*', Shyamali, having survived abuse at the hands of her husband, refuses to be repressed by anybody anymore, leaving her lover when he starts complaining that he might lose his living because of her. 'I have the courage to feed to ten like him!' becoming her mantra and her pride. Lajo, in 'The Homemaker' rejects the hypocrisy of reform. Her husband Mirza desires her as long as she is not reformed; as soon as she is turned into the ideal Muslim wife, he begins to neglect her. She reverts to her old, socially unacceptable behaviour, is promptly divorced by Mirza, and peace and happiness is once again restored in their relationship. Lajo does not much care whether Mirza is her legal husband, as long as she is his homemaker. 'She could share Mirza with another woman, but as far as her home was concerned, she was the undisputed mistress' (Chughtai 2009, 90). For Lajo, empowerment comes not from social sanction of being an ideal Muslim woman and wife but from having a domain of her own. This is a particularly powerful assertion; in the absence of avenues that provide women with complete economic, sexual and emotional freedom, the domain of the interior becomes significant in the lives of women, reformed or otherwise. Rashid Jahan's works in the *Angarey* volume deal with enunciations of female subjectivities within domestic spaces. In '*Parde ke Pichhe*', for instance, Mahmudi Begum reacts to her incessant emotional, sexual and physical exploitation by expressing herself with alarming honesty and over-the-top actions. She cries uninhibitedly, screams and curses her children and even threatens suicide. In a familial setting where her opinions are disregarded, expressing her anger provides her with an outlet. In a relationship where even her body is regulated such that she's not allowed to breastfeed her children, the histrionics of spitting and beating her forehead is a claim to her own selfhood. This is the stark difference in the way men and women viewed the *ghar* (home). While for men it was an abstract tool of nation-building, for women it is the one space where they can exhibit and assert, if not fully, then at least honestly, their subjective being and becoming. The significance of the space becomes even more acute as a result of male intervention in it. Minault writes, 'Ironically enough, reform movements involved the assertion of male authority and value judgement over those areas of women's lives that in pre-colonial society was largely autonomous'

(1998, 6). This, in addition to the repression and censorship faced in the exterior, material realms, leads to the creation and articulation of an alternative rhetoric of resistance. In her memoirs, Ismat tells the story of Mangu who was physically and psychologically tortured by her mother-in-law for not producing a male heir. Soon, Mangu would come to be possessed by spirits, would attack both her husband and mother-in-law. The exorcists then advised the husband to live separately from his mother who was cursed and at the root of this evil. Consequently, Mangu and her husband moved to a different city. Chughtai writes, 'That was when I realized that… a woman may be weak but does not have to be stupid' (2012, 12). Rani, in 'The Mole', responds to her situation in life by gladly capitalising on that which is solely hers, her sexuality, and is unashamed about it even in the court of law. What is important to note here is that in most of the works written by the Progressives, the marginalised and exploited woman figure has been able to better her circumstances as a result of economic independence and when she hasn't, has lamented the lack of it thereof. In the final section of this essay, I explore the connections between economic repression and women's emancipation.

'I have the courage to feed to ten like him!': What about the means?

All exploitative systems function with the intention of creating profit and sustain themselves as a result of the same. However, they gain legitimacy through moral and religious arguments. Noel Rae has shown how pro-slavery polemicists would interpret the Bible in a way that justified slavery although it is abundantly clear that the primary motivating force for the enterprise of slavery was economics and not the civilising mission of Christ (Rae 2018). Nicholas Dirks mentions how animal slaughter, hook-swinging and human sacrifices were just a few of the several aspects of rituals undertaken by the tribal communities that drew the ire of the missionaries and consequently that of the colonial administration. Dirks is also quick to mention how economic and political interests would earn a hasty scaffolding of moral repulsion. 'In fact, the practice of human sacrifice had only come to the attention of the government after they developed an interest in controlling the highland tracts of central and eastern India' (Dirks 2001, 191). Similarly, the presence of women being limited to the domestic sphere contributes to the creation of profit for the exploiter.

There is a wealth of Marxist feminist scholarship on the argument that domestic labour is productive labour and contributes to capitalism by creating exchange values in one way or the other. However, there are also those that assert otherwise. One strand of argument states, for instance, that the very definition of 'labour' is that that it produces surplus value on being exchanged for wages and since domestic labour of the women in the family is not 'sold', housework cannot be considered unpaid labour (Menon 1982, 37). Similarly, Coulson argues that domestic labour's 'immediate products are use-values and not commodities; they are not directed towards the market, but are for immediate consumption within the family' (Coulson, Magas and Wainwright 1975, 62). Such a stance, however, de-legitimises women's role in the capitalist system. Additionally, Bennholdt-Thomsen writes that domestic work does indeed engage in commodity production: 'the homemaker produces use-values which are turned to exchange values after a certain delay in time' (Menon 1982, 34).[6] I would, however, draw attention to Jean Gardiner's subsistence postulate which states that in order for labourers to maintain subsistence level they require wages as well as domestic labour (Gardiner 1975, 47–58).

Therefore, there are certain aspects of a labourer's existence—hygiene, nutrition and all-round physical and mental well-being—that is being ensured by a category of people that would work without wages: the women. Consequently, within the Indian context, this role is not only codified but also idealised. The 'decent' woman is not supposed to indulge in the vagaries of the external material world; that is the realm for men, the lower class and lower caste, 'indecent' woman, the indecent 'other'. This is also why the portraiture of sexual exploitation of the domestic labourer in decent families would constitute a transgression. Apart from unveiling the fact of it, the Progressives' works also upended the social discourse that women who join in the work-force are sexually promiscuous, which, in turn undergirded the dichotomies of the 'decent' woman and the 'indecent' woman. These works show that these women are victims and not debauched and/or willing participants.

As such, for the socialists, economic strength is a necessary catalyst for resistance. The defiance of women like Shyamali in '*Neech*' or Lajo in 'The Homemaker' emerge from their ability to economically fend for themselves. Ahmed Ali's stories in the *Angarey* volume depict the helplessness of women without financial freedom. In '*Badal Nahin Aate*', the protagonist laments this very fact by exclaiming: 'Why are we powerless? If we had our own money, we wouldn't have to endure this humiliation. We could do whatever we wanted whenever we wanted. But then again, we don't have permission to earn a living. We are rotting slowly, trapped behind the veil ... Death doesn't come either' (Ali 2014, 82–3). In '*Mahavaton Ki Ek Raat*', the readers are acquainted with the anxiety and grief of a poor, widowed mother of three, as rain pours down through the damaged roof onto their cold, hungry bodies. This story almost foreshadows her inevitable turn to sex-work, for society has not provided her with the means to sustain herself and her children in any other way. Nonetheless, there were also stories like '*Dulari*' where the protagonist, despite being a domestic servant, an employee, is not paid and has no financial freedom whatsoever and has to resort to sex-work when staying in the house becomes unbearable. In the story, the other servants of the family would claim their respectability by emphasising that despite their station in life, they are in fact, paid workers, not a slave like Dulari. Gopal writes, '"Dulari" ... posits as a problem the naturalising of domestic work as familial obligation rather than visible and waged labour' (Gopal 2005, 34). Geraldine Forbes cites the plight of widows in the family to suggest that it was intrinsic within the Indian milieu to trivialise and render invisible the domestic labour performed by women in the family and, by extension, the maid servants as well. Forbes says, 'Maid servants were often employed in every middleclass home, yet their employers seldom thought of them as workers. Perhaps this was because the distinction between dependent relative and domestic servant was often slight. One of the legitimate criticisms of Indian families, for instance, was that they made drudges out of widowed female relatives' (Forbes 2004, 180). '*Dulari*' is also an important work because, along with Mahmud-uz-Zafar's '*Jawanmardi*', it develops a self-reflexive critique of the reformist stand. Both Kazim in '*Dulari*' and the protagonist of '*Jawanmardi*' are educated, sensitive men, not unsympathetic to the woes of the women around them and seek to reform their lives. However, these men fail to enact any worthwhile change in the lives of the women because of the limitations of their politics as well as moral cowardice. Indeed, their sympathy and reformist zeal make matters worse. This further strengthens the Progressive argument of women's improvement being birthed by economic freedom as opposed to rescue by the reformer. Chughtai, in her memoirs mentions how finding an employment transformed her life for the better. She looks back on her childhood with deep despair, noting that each day comprised of beatings and reprimands. There was little to no tenderness in the familial relations and absolute dependence on others caused her to feel stifled. When she is slightly older, the fate of her cousin, Khanam Sahib terrifies her. Caught in a legal trap, Khanam Sahib is unable to get a divorce and escape the confines of a loveless marriage. Having experienced such a childhood and witnessed the horrible lives that women lead, Chughtai became resolute about getting an education and having a career. Noticing that her parents' reticence might turn into a full-fledged bid to stop her from her pursuing her plans, she threatened to convert to Christianity. Her happiness and contentment at having gained financial independence is palpable: 'By God's grace, everything has changed. I am my own boss—free and independent. I drink tea lying in bed … I eat plenty of meat—well-cooked and soft. I can have as many eggs as I want. I laugh and enjoy myself as much as I want …' (Chughtai 2009, 56).

Despite the premium that the socialists pay to the cause of economic freedom, access to it would not solve the abject conditions of women's lives. Forbes mentions that despite the image of the housewife becoming the image of Indian womanhood, the reality was that thousands of women were part of the workshop as well, toiling away in factories and mines as well as unregulated sectors such as agriculture and domestic work. In the industrial spheres they were paid much less than their male counterparts and in the domestic sphere, they were, as has been discussed thus far, subjected to severe physical, mental and sexual abuse. Consequently, 'women were not emancipated by employment but rather became "beasts of burden"' (Forbes 2004, 187), a postulate that is echoed by Nirmala Banerjee who writes that women's economic position, irrespective of caste and class markers, was much better before the British colonial intervention and gradually worsened in colonial times owing to simultaneous factors: the waning of the traditional crafts and the lack of equal access in the modern professional arena. 'The occupations assigned to women in the traditional gender-wise division of labour proved to be especially vulnerable to obsoletion through modernization. Their participation in the modern sector, on the other hand, was constrained …' (Banerjee 1999, 283).

Conclusion

It is incumbent upon me to conclude by noting that despite its detailed ventures into the forms and workings of censorship in pre-Independence India, there are, regrettably, certain lacuna in this paper. For instance, the creation of the ideal Indian womanhood had a very specific, if not completely different, language for the Indian Muslim population; one that was dictated by various complex discourses surrounding Islamic law and its tussle and negotiations with the colonial government. Furthermore, the category of the Indian Muslim is not monolithic: it is divided along regional, linguistic, ideological, class and even caste lines. Additionally, the glaring lack of discourse surrounding caste in the Urdu literary milieu is a historical deficit that needs urgent and closer introspection. This paper has not discussed either of these elements. Intentions of looking into censorship as an epistemological category also prevented me from theorising the juxtaposition between the working woman versus the homemaker and the feminist implications of such a juxtaposition and its socio-cultural repercussions today. There are also important questions that need to be asked with regard to the notion of 'agency'. Chughtai notes her Dulhan Bhabhi's refusal to come out of purdah as an act of self-sabotage, self-censorship, calling it 'purdah of the mind'. Without glorifying the obviously suppressive elements of such a ritual, one is also called to analyse the defiance, the rebellion and the agency involved in this act, to try and understand the role of religion and piety in the forging of a revolutionary potential and how this 'potential' challenges and disassembles traditional structures of feminist thought. Furthermore, looking into the different treatments of death as a literary tool in the works produced by the PWA is also an important exercise. From the decay that ate away at Azim Beg Chughtai before culminating in his death in '*Dozhakhi*' to the sudden yet nonchalant death in 'Mishtake' to the death that is visible but blithely unacknowledged in Jeelani Bano's 'Tamasha', the ending of a being forms the vehicle that carries crucial understandings of society, physicality and the violence of life.

As a young woman and scholar, Chughtai represents to me a treasure trove when it comes scholarly endeavours. However, it is also prudent to note that she occupies an affective space in my life: teaching constantly and inspiring resilience. Therefore, it is only fair that I conclude by quoting

Chughtai's own words against censorship.

> If Manto was a giant, Krishan [Chander] was a ghoul, Sardar Jafri a demon, Josh Sahib a hobgoblin, Jigar Sahib (Jigar Muradabadi) a phantom. No, sir, we are all human beings. Very lovable, very sensitive. We carry the pain of the whole world in our hearts. . . Manto. . . dipped into filth not because he loved it but because he had a very strong sense of smell. He wanted to awaken those whose sense of smell had been deadened. . . Finally, I'd like to say that if you find some of things I have dashed off disturbing, please analyze them, don't just heap blame on me.
>
> Sincerely,
>
> Ismat (2001, 96–7)

Notes

1. Letter by Lytton, 15 March 1878, S. Gopal, *British Policy in India, 1858–1905* quoted in Chatterjee, *Nation and its Fragments.*
2. Quoted in Nicolas Dirks, *Castes of Mind: Colonialism and the Making of Modern India.*
3. Medinah (from Bijnor) 13 February 1933 report titled *Angarey: Ek Fahash aur Malhadanah Kitab*, quoted in Jalil, *Liking Progress, Loving Change.*
4. See, for example, entries titled "Affendi", "Communist Panth" and "Thaker" in Jones, *Censorship.*
5. An observation also made by Ismat Chughtai in *A Life.*
6. Veronika Bennholdt Thomsen, Subsistence Reproduction and Extended Reproduction, *The Hague*, mimeo, 5 quoted in Menon, "Women."

References

Ahmad, Aijaz. 1992. In *Theory: Classes, Nations, Literatures.* London: Verso.

———. "Jameson's Rhetoric of Otherness and the 'National Allegory'." *Social Text*, no. 17, (Autumn 1987): 3–25.

Ali, Ahmed. 2014. "The Clouds Aren't Coming." *Angaaray* translated by Snehal Singhavi. Gurgaon: Penguin Books.

Baltussen, Hans and Peter J. Davis. 2015. "Parrhesia, Free Speech, and Self-Censorship." In *The Art of Veiled Speech: Self-Censorship from Aristophanes to Hobbes,* edited by Hans Baltussen and Peter J. Davis. Philadelphia: U of Pennsylvania P.

Banerjee, Nirmala. 1999. “Working Women in Colonial Bengal: Modernization and Marginalisation.” In *Recasting Women: Essays in Indian Colonial History*, edited by Kumkum Sangari and Sudesh Vaid. New Brunswick: Rutgers UP.

Barrier, N. Gerald. 1974. *Banned: Controversial Literature and Political Control in British India. 1907–1947*. Columbus: U of Missouri P.

Bar-Tal, Daniel. “Self-Censorship as a Socio-Political-Psychological Phenomenon: Conception and Research.” *Advances in Political Psychology* 38, suppl. 1, (2017): 37–65. doi: 10.1111/pops.1239.

Bentick, Lord William. 2004. “Bentick’s Minute on Sati, 8 November 1829.” In *Archives of Empire: Volume I. From The East India Company to the Suez Canal*, edited by Barbara Harlow and Mia Carter. New York: Duke UP.

Besant, Annie. 1908. *Annie Besant: An Autobiography*. Adyar, Madras: Theosophical Publishing House.

Bhattacharya, Sanjoy. 2001. “India: 1900–47.” In *Censorship: A World Encyclopedia Volume 1–4*. Edited by Derek Jones. New York: Routledge.

Chakravarti, Uma. 1989. “Whatever Happened to the Vedic Dasi? Orientalism, Nationalism and a Script for the Past.” In *Recasting Women*, edited by Kumkum Sangari and Suresh Vaid. New Delhi: Zubaan Books.

Chatterjee, Partha. 1993a. *Nationalist Thought and the Colonial World*. New Delhi: Oxford University Press.

———. 1993b. *The Nation and Its Fragments: Colonial and Post-Colonial Histories*. New Jersey: Princeton UP.

Chughtai, Ismat. 2001. *My Friend, My Enemy: Essays, Reminiscences, Portraits*. Translated by Tahira Naqvi. New Delhi: Kali for Women.

———. 2009. *Lifting the Veil*. Translated by M. Asaduddin. Gurgaon: Penguin Books.

———. 2012. *A Life in Words: Memoirs*. Translated by M. Asaduddin. Gurgaon: Penguin Books.

Cohn, Bernard. 1995. *Colonialism and It’s Forms of Knowledge*. Princeton: Princeton UP.

Coulson, Margaret, Branka Magas and Hilary Wainwright. “The Housewife and her Labour under Capitalism—A Critique.” *New Left Review*, I/89, (1975): 59–72. https://newleftreview.org/issues/i89/articles/margaret-coulson-branka-magas-hilary-wainwright-the-housewife-and-her-labour-under-capitalism-a-critique.

Dirks, Nicholas. 2001. *Castes of Mind: Colonialism and the Making of Modern India*. Princeton: Princeton UP.

Eagleton, Terry. "Nationalism: Irony and Commitment." In *Nationalism, Colonialism, and Literature*, edited by Seamus Deane. Minneapolis: U of Minnesota P.

Forbes, Geraldine. 2004. *The New Cambridge History of India IV. 2 Women in Modern India*. Cambridge: Cambridge UP.

Freshwater, Helen. 2003. "Towards a Redefinition of Censorship." In *Critical Studies*. https://www.researchgate.net/publication/233702233_Towards_a_Redefinition_of_Censorship.

Gandhi, M.K. 1970. *Collected Works of Mahatma* Gandhi, *Vol 16*. New Delhi: Publications Division.

Gardiner, Jean. "Women's Domestic Labour." *New Left Review* I/89, (1975): 47–58. https://newleftreview.org/issues/i89/articles/jean-gardiner-women-s-domestic-labour.

Gramsci, Antonio. 1971. *Selections from the Prison Notebooks*. Translated by Q. Hoare and G. Norwell Smith. New York: International Publishers.

Gopal, Priyamvada. 2005. *Literary Radicalism in India: Gender, Nation and the Transition to Independence*. New York: Routledge.

Jalil, Rakhshanda. 2014. *Liking Progress, Loving Change: A Literary History of the Progressive Writers' Movement in Urdu*. New Delhi: Oxford UP.

Jones, Derek. 2001. "Colonial India: 18th and 19th centuries." In *Censorship: A World Encyclopedia Volume 1–4*. Edited by Derek Jones. New York: Routledge.

———. 2001. "Editor's Note." In *Censorship: A World Encyclopedia*. Edited by Derek Jones. New York: Routledge.

Kaur, Raminder and William Mazzarella (eds). 2009. "Between Sedition and Seduction: Thinking Censorship in South Asia." In *Censorship in South Asia: Cultural Regulation from Sedition to Seduction*. Bloomington: Indiana UP.

Malik, Hafeez. "The Marxist Literary Movement in India and Pakistan." *The Journal of Asian Studies* 26, No. 4, (1967): 649–64. https://www.jstor.org/stable/2051241?seq=1#metadata_info_tab_contents.

Mani, Lata. 1999. "Contentious Traditions: The Debate on Sati in Colonial India." In *Recasting Women: Essays in Indian Colonial History*. Eds. Kumkum Sangari and Sudesh Vaid. New Brunswick, NJ: Rutgers UP.

Menon, Usha. "Women and Household Labour." *Social Scientist* 10, No. 7, (1982): 30–42. https://www.jstor.org/stable/3516936.

Minault, Gail. 1998. *Secluded Scholars: Women's Education and Muslim Social Reform in Colonial India.* Delhi: Oxford UP.

Mir, Raza and Ali Husain Mir. 2006. *Anthems of Resistance: A Celebration of Progressive Urdu Poetry.* New Delhi: Roli Books.

Naqvi, Tahira. 2004. "Introduction." In *A Chughtai Collection: The Quilt and Other Stories, The Heart Breaks Free, The Wild One.* translated by Tahira Naqvi and Syeda S. Hamid. New Delhi: Kali For Women.

Norvel, Lyn. "Gandhi and the Indian Women's Movement." *The British Library Journal* 23, No. 1, (1997): 12–27.

Parkin, Jonathan. 2015. "Thomas Hobbes and the Problem of Self-Censorship." In *The Art of Veiled Speech: Self-Censorship from Aristophanes to Hobbes,* edited by Hans Baltussen and Peter J. Davis. Philadelphia: U of Pennsylvania P.

Premchand. M. "The Nature and Purpose of Literature." *Indian Literature* 29, No. 6, (1986): 184–191. https://www.jstor.org/stable/24159090?seq=1#metadata_info_tab_contents.

Rae, Noel. 2018. "How Christian Slaveholders Used the Bible to Justify Slavery." *Time,* February 2018. https://time.com/5171819/christianity-slavery-book-excerpt/.

Ross, Simon. 2001. "Britain: British Empire." In *Censorship: A World Encyclopedia Volume 1–4.* Edited by Derek Jones. New York: Routledge.

Said, Edward. 1979. *Orientalism.* New York: Vintage Books.

Segal, Alan. "Censorship, Social Control and Socialization." *The British Journal of Sociology* 21, No. 1, (1970): 63–74. https://www.jstor.org/stable/588272.

Taussig, Michael. 1999. *Defacement: Public Secrecy and the Labor of the Negative.* Stanford: Stanford UP.

Tharu, Susie and K. Lalitha, eds. 1993. *Women Writing in India 600 BC To The Present. Volume II: The Twentieth Century.* New York: The Feminist Press.

Young, Kimball. 1930. *Social Psychology: An Analysis of Social Behavior.* New York: Alfred A. Knopf.

9

The Possibilities of a Genre

Reading the Life Writings of Ismat Chughtai and Amrita Pritam

Krishnendu Pal

Ismat Chughtai (1911–91), raised quite a tumult in the literary horizons of twentieth century India through her powerful writings, films, and scathing critique of conventions. She largely tried to illuminate the oppressive circumstances that women in South Asia lived in, reiterated, and resisted. Her works are still significant sources to understand feminist praxis in South Asian literature and this anthology instantiates her ongoing relevance in today's world. In addition to her fictional works, Chughtai, has written extensively about her life in the form of essays and memoirs. This essay examines her memoir *Kaghazi Hai Pairahan* (A Life in Words/*KHP*, 1980) along with the autobiographical work of one of her renowned contemporaries—*Raseedi Ticket* (Revenue Stamp/*RT*, 1977) by Amrita Pritam (1919–2005), to understand how the generic understandings, theoretical premises and limitations concerning autobiographical/life writings manifest in their works. Pritam, like Chughtai, was a poet/author who created a furore in the male-dominated literary circuit of northern India by her 'unconventional' ways of life, and uncompromising candour in the literature that she wrote. This essay proceeds towards an understanding of the possibilities of the genre of women's life writing in late twentieth century South Asia by alluding to different theoretical and literary positions which have dealt with the idea of life writing, women's life writing and women's life circumstances that enable life writing.

Who Gets to Talk and How: Browsing Histories

Though talking about one's personal life was historically understood as a female practice, the genres of the autobiography and life writing, in the

Eurocentric context emerged as the prerogative of the man (Jelinek 1980, 26–28). The genre of the autobiography was attributed to the western enlightened man who would speak of a unique selfhood (Olney 1972, 22–23). These were the 'worthy lives' that required verbose and elaborate articulations so that designs of survival and acquired knowledge of one's life could be transmitted to the next generation (Gusdorf 1980, 29). The confessional writing on the other hand, as practiced by the likes of Saint Augustine, used the life of a man as a prop to glorify the unquestionable and all-encompassing divine-design (Felski 1998, 87). The autobiography/life writing was attributed to the man because the man spoke of the public—the sphere men have deemed themselves the champions of. Women, because of their systematic exclusion from the public sphere historically, were thought to not possess 'stories worth telling' as they were preoccupied with their experiences of the domestic and the mundane. Domna Stanton observes that women's writings were accused of being caught up in the quagmire of the personal, the sentimental, and the relational (Stanton 1998, 131–44). But Joan Scott instructs us that instead of privileging this idea of 'experience' as an ontological/unquestionable category of knowledge, one ought to understand the ideological overtures that make a certain kind of experiencing possible. So, if the experience of the individual is what makes their lives 'worth' narrating, interrogating the causality and possibility of that experience establishes how the hierarchy between the superior and mundane lives are created (Scott 1998, 57–71). The fact that women, at one point of time, spoke, or rather, were suspected to speak of the 'private', that is their experiences at home, is an indication of the historic specificity of their discourse that was positioned by men to be contained in the four walls of the house.

There is no coherent, unified, autobiographical self before the moment of self-narrating (Smith 1998, 108). Though the autobiography, and other forms of life writing, are considered more gripping because of the tone of immediacy/spontaneity characteristic of it, the conscious effort that goes into writing that 'spontaneous self' inaugurates the moment of split from that very spontaneous self (Felski 1998, 89). The author in order to furnish a certain coherence about the events of their life and accommodate a sense of immediacy, takes an external position which imposes an aesthetic/structural design on their narrative self. Sidonie Smith opines that the author's interiority that manifests in the autobiography is an act of 'performing' of that coherent self (1998, 18–110). It is difficult for a woman to experience herself as an 'entirely unique entity' because she is always aware of how she is being defined as a woman (Friedman 1998, 75). When women write about themselves confessionally, there is a risk of constant self-abnegation because, owing to the extraneous manifestation of the inner self, the woman might interpret her life choices in pertinence to the roles that have been stipulated (Felski 1988, 86). But as scholars like Friedman and Sheila Rowbotham observe, alienating oneself from these historic assigned roles enable 'creative' writing (Friedman 1998, 76). If cultural prescriptions actually limit the imaginations of women, they also enable the scope of challenging those prescriptions and talking about newer experiences and emergence of newer consciousnesses (Rowbotham 1973, 26–46). The autobiography/life writing enables women to render visible their opinions about these cultural stipulations, and their experiences of adhering to and resisting them. Given this approximate summative understanding of autobiographic/life writing as a genre in western academia, this essay now turns to South Asian understandings of autobiographical/life writing. South Asia, contrastingly, has had a collective method of storytelling which involved embedding the collective consciousness in the act of telling one's life story. In South Asian life writing, especially Islamic, the writer does not emphasise on maintaining a chronology of events in order to deal with the issue of character development. The character is often a centrally pre-embedded concrete presence and it is not always necessary to arrange events chronologically to foreground a convincing build up to the person that the writer is (Metcalf 2004, 120–21). Anecdotes from their lives, often thematically arranged, could establish the motivations and perceptions of the characters. Both Chughtai's and Pritam's life writings arguably chime with this idea because they also do not follow a strict chronological route in order to tell their life stories. They begin with the stories of their childhood, but constantly go back and forth as and when it is deemed necessary for them. There are chapters that are thematically arranged with headers like 'In the name of those married woman', 'Hell' (Chughtai 2012), 'Resurrecting Time', 'The Phoenix dynasty' etc. (Pritam and Gorowara 2012). Rajeshwari Sunder Rajan writes that editors are often of the idea that the 'aesthetic and the political are separate cognitive structures' (Rajan 1993, 2), and from this arises the unease of accommodating life writing within the domain of literature. This makes life writing, owing to its added allegiance towards spontaneity and veracity, a little ill-equipped in terms of the 'literary' quotient. (Felski 1998, 86). This is the first generic expectation that the texts by Pritam and Chughtai contest as they foreground unique 'literary' values of their own, which this essay argues. Chughtai, while reminiscing of her experiences in different stages of her life, equipped with her quirks, comics, and sardonic narration, makes reading the autobiography a very enjoyable experience. It also posits the possibility to be read as a book where a girl garrulously chats about her life that was characterised by the often-comical idiosyncrasies of her family members, the unserious fights with her siblings, and the occasional chiding of her mother. The elaborate descriptions of fun-filled times with her family that were punctuated with different comical situations provide the reader with an idyllic semblance of the extended joint family structure of Islamic north India. Chughtai's KHP was published in the Urdu Magazine *Aaj Kal* from March 1979 to May 1980 and the fact that it ran for quite a while, (Chughtai 2012, x) speaks of the capacity of the text to hold onto a dynamic readership that patiently waited to read all the instalments. This stands testament to the popularity that the narrative garnered.

A significant aspect that differentiates Pritam's autobiography from that of Chughtai's, is that the former is not very tentative or elaborate about real life occurrences unlike the latter. Pritam accords maximum importance to the articulation of a contemplative self where she picks up situational triggers from her life by briefly mentioning them and then philosophises on them. By adhering to this template, she talks about supernatural occurrences, dreams, and her perspectives towards life. Chughtai meticulously narrates the incidents from her life and punctuates them with contemplation, but the urge to communicate the psychological complexities in their entirety, that befuddle one's mind, is far more intense in Pritam. The latter also crosses genre boundaries and often introduces tracts of poetry, diary and journal entries amidst the prose. She shifts lucidly between genres, choosing the one that befits the literary urge that she has at that point of time. By challenging the phallogocentric[1] premise of elevated prose stifled by generic requirements, both these authors reclaim the 'literary' in their very unique ways.

In the South Asian context, where stereotypical gendered ideas of living are systematically inculcated into women, there is often an apparent voluntary obsession to prioritise domestic responsibilities, the *stri-dharma* (the duties of a woman) over one's aspirations and well-being. As Tanika Sarkar observes in her study of the first woman's autobiography Rasasundari Dasi's *Amar Jiban,* the woman could only chalk out very little time for herself in order to read and write, as executing endless domestic chores throughout the day took up most of her time (1999, 15–31). This time-consuming processes of contemplation, choice and elaboration can only be undertaken by women who, as some scholars say, have a 'luxury of remembrance' (Burton 2003,16–17).[2] Pritam and Chughtai have this 'luxury of remembrance' but one should also highlight another premise that probably guides their life writings—a conscious choice to articulate. The choice of life writing for both of them arguably is a conscious choice as there is a very emphatic demand to introduce into the horizon of the people the trials, tribulations, resistances, and success stories of two women writers of the country, who did not lead a very 'genteel' and comfortable life, adhering to the stipulations of a patriarchal order. We have to remember that both Chughtai and Pritam were literary personalities and they already had quite a readership. They had constructed this readership over time and hence it will not be unfair to state that their readers would want to know about their lives, families, and personal motivations that helped them craft their stories. Moreover, 'controversies' were regular occurrences that manifested in the lives of Chughtai and Pritam. The court trial about '*Lihaaf*' had generated significant negative traction with respect to Chughtai's image and she belligerently complains in her memoirs that she does not wish to be remembered as the writer of '*Lihaaf*'—she has other important stories to her name (2012, 40).

Pritam's life was marred by controversies mostly concerning her relationships with men like Imroz, Sahir Ludhianvi and Sajjad Haider. These controversies that illuminated their lives, definitely intrigued the curious Indian reader, who turned to the writer's autobiographies/memoirs. Scholars of women's life writings have figured a tendency in women writers to efface themselves from the narrative and chronicle the whereabouts of their relations and events that are collectively participated in the public (Stanton 1998, 131–132). Stanton observes that women are expected to ask self-transcending questions because that is the phallogocentric function of autobiography that has been transmitted to them (1998, 132). Talking too much about oneself might risk the possibility of self-aggrandisement or challenge the respectability of the social and filial units that they belong to (Vatuk 2015, 36–47). Effacing the personal would also resist the flaring up of sentimentality—a virtue considered unnecessary and unworthy of the autobiographical genre (Stanton 1998, 133). This self-concealment has been a part of South Asian life writing by women like Mahadevi Verma, who Francesca Orsini also refers to as the 'reticent autobiographer'. Orsini observes that Verma experiments with autobiographical writing by de-centering the subject and talking about different relations/people in her vicinity who have touched her life deeply and tangentially (Orsini 2004, 55–60). She augments and concretises her general understandings, perspectives, and philosophies of life by sketching these characters and ensuring that she resists 'the potential exposure' which 'poetic subjectivity' often entails (Orsini 2004, 60).

Chughtai and Pritam tend to subvert this practice of self-effacement and censoring of confidential information about their families. Their life writings are emphatically about them, their motivations, and comprehensions highlighted over the quagmire of experiences of other people that they mention. Pritam makes a point about women's praxis in literature and the struggles of a successful women litterateur by referring to her life—the fights that she had to put up with condescending and powerful men, when her texts were put in an anthology for the university without her consent (Pritam and Gorowara 1977, 59), or for a literature prize that was rightfully hers (73). Pritam referenced a delicately intimate story of her son gently asking her of his paternity (if he was Sahir Ludhianvi's child) (96), to subtly register the information to the public that curiosity and censure of people towards a woman, who is not shy about her sexual agency, affected her innocent children and her relationship with them. Chughtai, without expending much thought about protecting the respectability of the Chughtai-Mirza clan, exposes a handsy, sexually perverted, elderly cousin, Mazhar bhai (the son of Chughtai's maternal uncle Zafar Hussain), who 'would pass no chance to grab girls, he would grope even small tiny girls' (Chughtai 2012, 164). She also exposes the lecherous and sexist character of her venerated Bade Mamu, Zafar Hussain, who actually exterminated the last vestiges of happiness from the life of her Phupi (paternal aunt, Bachchu Phupi/Badshashi Phupi Khanum) owing to his maddening lust and desire to possess her daughters. She talks in detail of this character Phupi, and even allocates two chapters titled 'Conflict' and 'Incomplete woman' on her in order to disparage the perceptions of her family who dismissed her as a bitter, jealous, old woman who only heaped curses that bore the sting of a *bichchu* (scorpion) on her brothers and their family. Chughtai tries to provide the context that compelled her aunt to present such a bitter and harsh countenance so that her readers could develop a sympathetic niche for her. Bachchu Phupi's life had been engulfed with incessant tragedies that included the corrosive presence of a coward-yet-infidel husband, the death of a healthy daughter to a horrible ailment, and the disastrous marriage of another daughter that was executed hastily to protect her from the marauding lust of her son-in-law Zafar Hussain. Phupi's rage towards Zafar Hussain (Chughtai's uncle) extended to Chughtai's parents, because they did not protest against the misdeeds of their relative (Chughtai 2012, 61–94) Chughtai could relate to the frustrations and gnawing sense of loss of a woman whose family (brother and sister-in-law) stood by the powerful man who preyed upon her daughters and hence the narration of the tribulations of Phupi's life becomes instrumental in the foregrounding of Chughtai's 'selfhood' that possesses a great amount of empathy for women irredeemably wronged by powerful men. But here, the will to foreground the self/selfhood, instead of effacing it, is not a continuation of the idea of the individual unique selfhood that characterised male life-writings of the west (Gusdorf 1980, 29, Olney 1972, 22–3). Women's writing often tends to construct a selfhood by taking cognisance of the significant impressions that important relations from their vicinity have on them (Stanton 1998, 138–40). Like Bachchu Phuphi, Chughtai's relationship with her mother is accorded a lengthy space because Chughtai's interactions with her mother had contributed immensely to the making of the person that she is—a vocal critic of the purdah (practice of screening women from the men folk) and other kinds of oppression that has been inflicted on women by *sharif* (respectable) families in the name of tradition and socialisation. Chughtai's relationship with her mother was not difficult in any unique way because it posited the common hostility that is generated when a mother is concerned about transgressions that a daughter commits in not adhering to traditional codes of behaviour. Chughtai's mother would flare up instantly and chide her for not wearing a burqa, or replying too sharply, or not adhering to the norms of purdah in the presence of a male relative. Chughtai narrates that her mother was also dead against sending her for higher education and even volubly lamented when she managed to clear her matriculation exams but her brother Shamim could not: "She could have failed, for all I care" (Chughtai and Asaduddin 2012, 159). Chughtai also narrates that she was empathetic towards her mother whose entire life was consumed in giving birth to and raising children, and keeping up with the whims of her husband. It is evident in her writings that she does not wish to turn out like her mother and, in cognition with Adrienne Rich's understanding, refuses to carry forth the degrading, debased existence of womanhood that mothers transmit to their daughters (Rich 1986, 235). In order to posit herself as someone who creates a break from this debased existence and the motivations that compelled her to do so, Chughtai arguably had to necessitate the elaborate chronicling of her experiences with her mother that characterised reprimands, beatings, hurling of the shoe, and even agreeing to the demands of an obstinate daughter. But it would be reductionist to say that women's viewing of their lives is, by default, in relation to that of others. Instead, while reading these texts, one should try to assess the intensity of the significance that these relations have had in the protagonist's life—legitimately convincing them to accord textual space to them in one of their most special and personal creations. In addition to this, Chughtai, especially while talking about the women in her house like her mother, her aunt (Bachchu Phupi), and other elderly female acquaintances, ensures that she enlivens these characters by making them speak the *begumati zubaan*. Gail Minault refers to the begumati zubaan as an 'earthy, colourful, graphic' way of speaking that women living in purdah concocted for themselves; it was mutually intelligible but definitely different from the way men spoke. Since women lived in the restricted domain of the purdah there is a possibility that they were not exposed to the aesthetics and polite phrases of persianised Urdu that was spoken by the men and hence their speech would often be 'coarse' (Minault 2009, 117–19). The bewilderment of Chughtai's sister's prospective mother-in-law, on seeing the former coming close to speak to her, could only be expressed with an exclamation like '*chaati pe chadhi chali ati ho*!' (oh—you are climbing onto my chest!); and Chughtai does not filter that experience (Chughtai 2004, 230).[3] So, for Chughtai it was not just about talking superfluously about her significant relations but also enlivening them through her literary prowess.

Of Success, Confessions and Accountability

Pritam, in a very matter of fact way, quite emphatically establishes that she was recognised and celebrated as a litterateur. She does not shy away from elaborating her experiences in foreign lands where she was sent as a representative poet to several significant conferences for poets in Russia, Yugoslavia, and Bulgaria among others. She also refers quite elaborately to the praise and appreciation that she received on these foreign visits from celebrated poets. She provides a tentative list of languages from different parts of the world into which her works were translated (Pritam and Gorowara 1977, 62). In mentioning her casual camaraderie with the first woman Prime Minister of India, Indira Gandhi, while she was assigned the task of writing the screenplay for a film on the latter's life, Pritam also lets the readers be aware of her acquaintance with one of the most important persons of India. It is difficult to speculate if these were things that she casually mentioned while talking about her life, but nonetheless, they foreground the image of a very 'successful' woman. Lyn S. Bloom points out that an element that has often come up in the autobiographies of women in the twentieth century, is that these writers have had the need to manifest a 'self-fulfilling' image that is embellished with positives, so much so that, depressing episodes were mentioned in passing as they might often hinder the manifestation of the self-fulfilling image (Bloom 1978, 325–30). It is tedious to unpack all the ramifications of a term like 'positive' for an individual, but achievements that embellish one's career can inarguably be considered one of them. But it is not that *RT* lacks reflection on Pritam's very personal life. She does not go into the details, but speaks about the agonies she underwent when her relationships ended or underwent a rough patch. She also very candidly speaks of a very intimate moment with Sahir Ludhianvi, where she dabs Vicks (balm for colds) on his chest and confesses that she could have engaged in this act for eternity (Pritam and Gorowara 1977, 23). She fondly remembers how she used to smoke the cigarette butts left by Ludhianvi on her ashtray—a strategy for comforting oneself amid the bodily absence of a loved one (96). She is also quite candid in terms of talking about personal moments with Imroz or Sajjad Haider. This readily chimes with Helene Cixous's primary inflections about *lecriture feminine* (feminine writing) where she gives a clarion call to women to write unhesitatingly about their sexualities and tactile emotions without letting phallogocentric filters of morality shun them into silence (Cixous, Cohen, and Cohen 1976, 875–93). Pritam here breaks the chains of 'culturally inbred modesty' (Bloom 1978, 327) that have aggravated the habit of self-censure or self-erasure in women. Chughtai, on the other hand, refers to her relationship with Shadab Latif quite minimally and the tension that characterised their relationship is not a very prominent thematic presence in *KHP*. The only time she mentions her husband is when she talks about how perplexed and infuriated he was with her when the *Lihaaf* trials were on (Chughtai and Asaduddin 2012, 21–42). The 'private' life that Chughtai was more occupied with was the life that she spent with her family, growing up with her brothers and sisters, under the strict watch of her parents. She does not list her professional achievements and *KHP* does not talk about her life at a ripe age, but her referencing of her travails as a teacher, a principal of a girls' school, and a writer who actually had charges of obscenity levelled at her that required her to attend court hearings in a different country, definitely lay emphasis on her mettle as a successful working woman/writer.

Kathleen Dehler in her studies on 'confessional writing' by women, observes that there is often a harping need for certain women writers to let the readership know of the motivations that had convinced them to partake in events that have the potential to be misconstrued as reprehensible by a large number of people (Dehler 1978, 342). According to Rita Felski, women are constantly looking for a semblance of validation from the readership, who will 'understand, sympathise, and identify' (Felski 1998, 90). Structuring their motivations for their actions also hints towards the writer's hankering need for 'absolution'. This idea can be utilised to interpret certain incidents that Chughtai mentions in her memoir because they bear the risk of soiling her reputation as an empathetic person. One such 'incriminating' incident is Chughtai's attitude towards her dying hostel room-mate, Rasool Fatima. Chughtai writes that she was physically repelled by Rasool's sickly presence. But the fact that she did not call anybody when she saw that Fatima was lethally sick and went on to give her exams, only to find out that Fatima had expired—is a sin that she could not forgive herself for. The death of Fatima comes as a shock to the readers because Chughtai initially sketches her as an annoying, clingy roommate who had questionable hygiene: 'When she talked strings of saliva would make a web between her teeth and lips, and I would almost throw up' (Chughtai and Asaduddin 2012, 127). The delineating of Fatima's character has the possibility of triggering apathy/revulsion on the part of the reader. By evoking this shared revulsion Chughtai brings the reader to her side and creates, though not ethically justified, grounds for validating her misdemeanour towards Rasool Fatima. Chughtai provides the causality of her actions, albeit apprehensive, that passively contributes to Fatima's death and yields a certain amount of absolution from her readership. Another such event that comes up in *KHP* is Chughtai leaving behind two little nephews, Chabba and Tajju, in the estate of the Nawab in Jawra and fleeing to her sister's house in Bareilly. Her brother Azim Begh Chughtai, who was working for the Nawab, had to be taken to a health centre for his ailments and Chughtai was assigned the responsibility of taking care of their children. During her brother's absence, it was revealed to her that the Nawab intended to get her wedded to his son and since they were all the subjects of the Nawab, it was within his jurisdiction to do so. Chughtai fled to her sister's place taking only the youngest and eldest of her brother's children and leaving the other two behind. This abominable act of leaving two children behind is justified by her as an immediate 'flight' response to an impending danger. She validates the act of flight as a survival strategy that she had to employ in order to escape the throes of an early marriage into royalty that bore the possibility of annihilating her dreams of establishing herself as an independent woman. Dehler posits that these writings help women establish new moralities of personal honesty.

For Pritam, this need of absolution/accountability operates on a unique plane. Anshu Malhotra observes that it is the mythological memory that creates a template on which the self is fabricated at times. In South Asia, this template has been used by a number of writers (arguably having strong religious affiliations) to express their own stories. This act enables a divine validation, rather, corroboration to their lives and establishes a strong message that whatever one has done in the mortal world is basically the execution of a divine will. In the South Asian context, where religiosity is an integral component of the cultural ethos, alluding to a metaphysical occurrence or a divine template to tell one's story often absolves the narrator/the autobiographer of worldly accountability for their actions. Siobhan Lambert-Hurley observed in the memoirs of Rachana Tyabji that she often rationalises her amorous dalliances by referring to them as her attempt at replicating her love for Krishna (Lambert-Hurley 2015). While writing on one's life, the narrator has to stand outside the text in order to narrativise the events of their life in line with an aesthetic or 'textual principal', and for South Asian life writing this principle is often religious influence (Sarkar 1999, 10–11).[4] Scholars refer to this as the expanded sense of reality , which has the possibility of incorporating the miraculous (1999, 246).[5] Pritam's autobiography is rich in such miraculous referencing and description of events. She even interprets her birth to be a divine ordinance that came to fruition only because two young students of her father prayed to the Almighty that a girl would be born in the house of their teacher, instead of a boy (Pritam and Gorowara 1977, 1–2). She also draws a parallel between her relationship with her son to that of Mata Trupta and Guru Nanak. She relates the intensity of her love for her son to the mental state of Mata Trupta when she was carrying Nanak, and has written a long poem on the subject, claiming to have cerebrally inhabited that moment of divine union (52–53). She writes, 'The moment had walked me five dark centuries back to that worthy woman who had conceived Guru Nanak. In the density of that darkness there was yet a soft glow…' (53). Does this establish Pritam in the tradition of South Asian writers who are heavily reliant on their religious moorings, so much so, that they require it mandatorily to articulate their stories? In an interview with Rama Jha on being asked of her knack of making religious allusions in her works in spite of not being visibly religious (Rama remarks, 'I did not know you were so religious'), Pritam says, 'Yes; may be my cigarette smoking and cut hair. But who sees the suffering of the mind and the agony of the heart' (Pritam and Jha 1982, 194–95). This statement posits the contrast that Pritam's subjectivity bore; as somebody who, in spite of being popularly viewed as the woman who transgresses—a role that she vociferously agrees to—has certain indispensable cultural moorings that are often very organically expressed in her works, including her autobiography.

Of Historical Events and Individual Routes

The autobiography is not merely a text chronicling the momentous events in the life of an individual; it also accords the opportunity to study the ramifications of the historical circumstances/events in the lives of the people that influence their private spaces of inhabitation. Pritam's text has passing references to historical events of which the Partition is most important. To comment on the atrocities that were perpetrated on women during the Partition, she wrote the 'Aaj Aakhan Waris Shah Nu' (Today, I Say Unto Waris Shah) and she speaks of the empathetic response that she got from people from the both sides of the border (Pritam and Gorowara 1977, 21–22). But instead of focusing on a particular historical moment, Pritam's autobiography, by talking largely about her struggles as a woman writer, a divorced mother, makes the reader grasp holistic and historically replicated social perspectives about women who dare to subvert the ideals of domestic femininity. Chughtai's *KHP*, on the other hand, focuses quite meticulously and elaborately on significant historical junctures. She gives us the opportunity to understand the life circumstances of the Muslim woman from 'sharif' (that approximately translates to respectable) families at the cusp of Indian 'modernity' that confronted a quandary in terms of negotiating between conservatism and reform. Minault has written extensively on the history and processes of socialisation of the Muslim/sharif woman in northern India. She observes that the zeal and the motivation to 'emancipate' Muslim women from their 'depraved' situations were similar to that of the rest of the country, especially eastern India, which rigorously sought to emancipate the 'upper-caste/upper class' Hindu woman (Chatterjee 1990).[6] It was the marker of 'sharafat'(respectability) that characterised the new reformist policies sought for women belonging to these Muslim families. The women were expected to emulate certain refined ways of living and educate themselves so that they emerge as better homemakers who would be able to raise better families. This pre-decided limit of emancipation entailed women to mitigate the stringency of the purdah and step out to a new found freedom. But it was only for the purpose of benefitting the household (Minault 2009, 194–212). Minault observes that the schools, especially the one started by Shaikh Abdullah where Chughtai studied, ensured that the subjects like 'embroidery, needlework, calligraphy', and religious/moral instruction were taught in addition to the humanities and sciences so that women were equipped with the skill sets to supervise a family (206). The school also ensured purdah and this feature of the school was heavily publicised by Shaikh Abdullah, so that more respectable Muslim families would send their daughters over to Aligarh (208–18). Such schools aimed to 'reinforce role socialisation and establish a continuity between the family and the school' (Chanana 1998, 11). The emancipation of these women in the house was facilitated by the desire of male-members of the family, preferably a father or a brother, who were the ones influenced by this reformist surge. This historical factoid is evident in Chughtai's life because it was through the perseverance of her father and brother, in the face of social approbation, that she got the opportunity to educate herself. Her father was accused by his relatives of being hell bent on 'making his daughters Christian' (Chughtai and Asaduddin 2012, 72) because he was sending her to the boarding school for girls at Aligarh. But Chughtai did not wholly adhere to either of the two cultural scripts of social behaviour that were at her disposal, because the reformist one, in the garb of emancipation, ensured that the crux of the conservative script was retained (that is surveillance of women by according them limited mobility). As Chughtai was repelled by the difficult lives that her mother and aunts lived within the purdah, acclimatising to the whims of a patriarchal order, she was also perplexed with the school that prescribed purdah and gendered education for women who were expected to emerge from the institution as befitting wives. She was disillusioned with the fact that her erudite cousin Naier, who also studied in the same school, instead of concentrating on her career, looked forward woefully to marriage (Chughtai and Asaduddin 2012, 126). She is palpably angry when, as the principal of a girls' school, she was reprimanded by people for teaching 'boys' games' to girls (227). Felicity Nussbaum observes that the subject is created in a discursive space where different ideologies operate that interpellate individuals to their positions in the social order. It is within these interstitial spaces between different subject positions that resistance is often charted out by the individual (1998, 164), and Chughtai's actions echo this situation. These resistances are often just about articulating one's abhorrence towards mandates that were passed on as normative and voluntarily accepted by individuals. In *KHP*, Chughtai has often vehemently spoken about her aversion towards the practice of purdah, or wearing the burqa. She was often at loggerheads with her mother as the latter insisted her that she wore one. In her typical sarcastic yet funny tone, Chughtai narrates an incident on a train where she purposefully hid the head cap of her burqa in an entangled mass of luggage and bedding, when she was forced to wear the same by her mother (Chughtai and Asaduddin 2012, 52). It is also a significant example of a survival strategy that she sought for herself, to slip out of the burqa in a convincing silent way without vocal protest, because the burqa for her was a regressive blind that restrained her free existence. She writes, 'I had to wear a burqa for the first time, and I cannot put in words the sense of humiliation I had to suffer. So intense was the feeling of debasement.' Similarly in one of her essays, she talks about meeting a group of girls who were sitting in purdah at the PWA Bhopal meeting and were infuriated when some unshaven men grossly caricatured women in a play they staged (Chughtai and Asaduddin 2012). Chughtai chastises them by saying, 'Go sit behind the purdah a little more! And let people create your ghosts and scare each other!' In another essay she confesses that it is necessary for her to write about girls in her fiction who challenged these traditional modes of living because it is one of the plausible ways to actually manifest a change, and in hindsight, inspire women to register their resistance to the patriarchal order.

In order to trivialise the scope and content of women's autobiographical/life writing, their habit of according importance and textual space to the events at home (the private) has been highlighted. Antoinette Burton states that since the 'home' has always been precluded from the domain of serious history, it is part of the feminist endeavour to unearth the histories of the home because they are archives that 'document the relationship between domesticity and nationalist politics'. The home, in the South Asian context, had undergone changes that often replicated the political and cultural complexities of the world and since it was a domain that was historically specified to be inhabited by women, their experience and memories of the home are often indispensable in terms of locating histories that have been relegated to the margins by official discourses. Chughtai's autobiography largely deals with her experiences in her homes in Aligarh, Sambar and Bareilly. Pritam's references to her home, on the other hand, are quite scanty in comparison. But nonetheless, the stories that they tell of their childhoods often project certain intricate functioning of social decorum of that time. Pritam writes that she was flabbergasted when she saw that separate utensils were kept in the kitchen for her father's Muslim friends by her beloved grandmother. Though Pritam resolutely ends this practice by protesting against it, this simple incident in the kitchen of a small Punjabi house in Pakistan speaks of the intensity of the practices of purity and pollution then—a practice so intense and entrenched in the lives of the people that even a liberal household like that of Pritam's was not spared (Pritam and Gorowara 1977, 4–5). This delicate issue of purity-pollution, also recurs in Chughtai's reminiscences of her childhood where she recalls that she barely escaped a beating at the hands of her Hindu neighbours after she tried to cradle the Krishna idol at their house on Janmashtami (The auspicious day of Krishna's birth) (Chughtai and Asaduddin 2012, 7). She also recalls an incident of closure of this humiliating calamity when her friend Sushi, a resident of that house, in order to convince her that she was not a practitioner of orthodoxy devours the same sweet of which Chughtai had taken a bite (19). Chughtai and Pritam, thus speak of social histories, by not predicating on any official document, but on their lives and homes.

Conclusion

Chughtai and Pritam manoeuver through the genre of life writing through actively subverting the cultural script of modesty by delineating intimate details of their lives and by registering their protests against sexist practices that render women immobile in the name of tradition. They confidently delineate their stories of success and failure that are potent enough to serve as an inspiration for younger writers. By alluding to the lives of other people while telling their own stories, the writers not just highlight the importance of the collective in South Asian narrative praxis, but also posit the importance of these social/filial relations in making them who they are. In the west, one of the primary motivations, as well as requirements, to write a 'memoir' was to inscribe oneself into the course of history by drawing public implications/meanings from events of the personal. This again echoes the notion of a 'worthy' life that befits documentation. In Chughtai and Pritam, the efforts to actually inscribe oneself onto the course of history do not strike the reader to be inorganic or externally forced. Through vivacious, vivid and lucid narrations of their life circumstances, families, and careers, they have inevitably contributed to a historical archive that stores not just the experiences of transgressive women who try to eke out a career as successful working women (writers), but also their enquiries/assessments regarding the causality and manifestation of those experiences. These life writings remain intriguing sites that contain the elusive yet palpable intersections between literature and history.

Glossary

Amar (Bangla):	Mine
Bade Mamu:	Elder brother of the mother
Bichchu:	Scorpion
Jiban (Bangla):	Life
Dharma:	Duty/Religion
Purdah:	Practice of screening/segregating women from the men folk who are not from the family in certain cultures.
Sharif:	respectable/aristocratic
Stri:	Adult Women

Notes

1. The term is inspired from Helene Cixous.
2. See, Antoinette Burton, *Dwelling In The Archive: Women Writing House, Home, And History In Late Colonial India.* Burton refers to Janet Frame's idea of the luxury of remembrance where she observes how propertied women belonging to a certain class could actually develop an intellectual vantage to talk about their lives.
3. Ismat Chughtai, *Kaghazi Hai Pairahan* (Hindi). Translated from Hindi by the author of this essay.
4. Sarkar refers to M. Bakhtin's understanding of autobiographical writing.
5. Lambert-Hurley cites Metcalf "What happened in Mecca", who points out that this expanded sense of reality is a characteristic trait of the Urdu-Persianate tradition of life writing which was very much present in Pritam's horizon.
6. See Partha Chatterjee. "The Nationalist Resolution of the Women's question", in Kumkum Sangari and Sudesh Vaid eds. *Recasting Women: Essays in Indian Colonial History.* Chatterjee here talks about nineteenth century Bengal, that tried to emulate certain life-style changes in the inner quarters of the house (the *ghar*) inhabited by women.

References

Bloom, Lynn Z. 1978. "Promises Fulfilled: Positive Images Of Women In Twentieth Century Autobiography." In *Feminist Criticism: Essays On Theory, Criticism And Prose*, edited by Cheryl L. Brown and Karen Olson. Metuchen, NJ and London: The Scarecrow Press.

Burton, Antoinette. 2003. *Dwelling In The Archive: Women Writing House, Home, And History In Late Colonial India*. Oxford, New York: Oxford UP.

Chanana, Karuna. 1998. "Introduction." In *Socialisation, Education And Women*, edited by Karuna Chanana. New Delhi: Orient Longman.

Chatterjee, Partha. 1990."The Nationalist Resolution of the Women's question". In *Recasting Women: Essays in Indian Colonial History*, edited by Kumkum Sangari and Sudesh Vaid. New Brunswick, NJ: Rutgers UP.

Chughtai, Ismat. 2004. *Kaghazi Hai Pairahan*. (Transcribed into Hindi by Iftikhar Anjum). New Delhi: Rajkamal Prakashan.

Chughtai, Ismat, and M Asaduddin. 2012. *A Life In Words: Memoirs* (Translated from Urdu *Kaghazi Hai Pairahan*). New Delhi: Penguin Books.

Chughtai, Ismat, and Meenakshi Bharat. 2000. "From Bombay To Bhopal." In *Ismat: Her Life Her Times* edited by Sukrita Paul Kumar and Sadique. New Delhi: Katha.

Chughtai, Ismat and Krishna Paul. 2000. "Progressive Literature and I." In *Ismat: Her Life Her Times*, edited by Sukrita Paul Kumar and Sadique. New Delhi: Katha.

Cixous, Hélène, Keith Cohen, and Paula Cohen. "The Laugh Of The Medusa." *Signs: Journal Of Women In Culture And Society* 1, No. 4, (1976): 875–93. doi:10.1086/493306.

Dehler, Kathleen. 1978. "The Need To Tell All: A Comparison Of Historical And Modern Feminist "Confessional" Writing." In *Feminist Criticism: Essays On Theory, Poetry And Prose*, edited by Cheryl L. Brown and Karen Olson. Metuchen, NJ and London: The Scarecrow Press.

Eakin, Paul John. 2020. *Writing Life Writing: Narrative, History, Autobiography*. Oxford and New York: Routledge.

Felski, Rita. 1998. "On Confession." In *Women, Autobiography, Theory: A Reader*, edited by Sidonie Smith and Julia Watson. Madison, Wisconsin: U of Wisconsin P.

Friedman, Susan Stanford. 1998. "Women's Autobiographical Selves: Theory And Practice." In *Women, Autobiography, Theory: A Reader*, edited by Sidonie Smith and Julia Watson. Wisconsin Madison: The U of Wisconsin P.

Gusdorf, Georges. 1980. "Conditions And Limits Of Autobiography." In *Autobiography: Essays Theoretical And Critical*, edited by James Olney. Princeton, NJ: Princeton UP.

Jelinek, Estelle C. 1980. "Introduction: Women's Autobiography And The Male Tradition." In *Women's Autobiography: Essays In Criticism*, edited by Estelle C. Jelinek. Bloomington: Indiana UP.

Lambert-Hurley, Siobhan. 2015. "The Heart of a Gopi: Raihana Tyabji's Bhakti Devotionalism and Self-representation." In *Speaking Of The Self: Gender, Performance, And Autobiography In South Asia*, edited by Anshu Malhotra and Siobhan Lambert-Hurley. Durham and London: Duke UP.

Malhotra Anshu, and Siobhan Lambert Hurley. 2015. "Introduction: Gender, Performance, and Autobiography in South Asia." In *Speaking Of The Self: Gender, Performance, And Autobiography In South Asia*, edited by Anshu Malhotra and Siobhan Lambert-Hurley. Durham and London: Duke UP.

Metcalf, Barbara D. 2004. "The Past In The Present: Instruction, Pleasure, And Blessing In Maulana Muhammad Zakariyya's *Aap Biitii*." In *Telling Lives In India: Biography, Autobiography And Life History* edited by David Arnold and Stuart Blackburn. Bloomington: Indiana UP.

Minault, Gail. 2009. *Gender, Language And Learning: Essays In Indo-Muslim Cultural History*. Ranikhet: Permanent Black.

Nussbaum, Felicity A. 1998. "The Politics of Subjectivity and the Ideology of Genre." In *Women, Autobiography, Theory: A Reader*, edited by Sidonie Smith and Julia Watson. Madison, Wisconsin: U of Wisconsin P.

Olney, James. 1972. *Metaphors Of Self: The Meaning Of Autobiography*. Princeton: Princeton UP.

Orsini, Francesca. 2004. "The Reticent Autobiographer: Mahadevi Verma's Writings." In *Telling Lives In India: Biography, Autobiography, And Life History*, edited by David Arnold and Stuart Blackburn. Bloomington and Indianapolis: Indiana UP.

Pritam, Amrita, and Krishna Gorowara. 1977. Reprint. *The Revenue Stamp: An Autobiography*. New Delhi: Vikas Publishing House.

Pritam, Amrita and Rama Jha. "An Interview with Amrita Pritam." *Indian Literature* 25, no. 5, (1982):194–95. http://www.jstor.org/stable/23331122.

Rich, Adrienne. 1986. *Of Woman Born: Motherhood as Experience and Institution*. London. New York: W.W Norton Company.

Rowbotham, Sheila. 1973. *Woman's Consciousness, Man's World.* London: Penguin.

Sarkar, Tanika. 1999. Reprint. *Words To Win: The Making Of Amar Jiban A Modern Autobiography*. Reprint, New Delhi: Kali for Women.

Scott, Joan W. 1998. "Experience". In *Women, Autobiography, Theory: A Reader*, edited by Sidonie Smith and Julia Watson. Wisconsin Madison: U of Wisconsin P.

Smith, Sidonie. 1998. "Performativity, Autobiographical Practice, Resistance." In *Women, Autobiography, Theory: A Reader*, edited by Sidonie Smith and Julia Watson. Wisconsin Madison: The U of Wisconsin P.

Stanton, Domna. 1998. "Autogynography: Is The Subject Different?" In *Women, Autobiography, Theory: A Reader*, edited by Sidonie Smith and Julia Watson. Madison Wisconsin: U of Wisconsin P.

Sunder Rajan, Rajeshwari. 1993. Reprint. *Real And Imagined Women: Gender, Culture And Postcolonialism*. London and New York: Routledge.

Vatuk, Sylvia. 2015. "A Passion For Reading: The Role Of Early Twentieth-Century Urdu Novels In The Construction Of An Individual Female Identity In 1930's Hyderabad." In *Speaking Of The Self: Gender, Performance, And Autobiography In South Asia* Edited by Anshu Malhotra and Siobhan Lambert-Hurley. Durham and London: Duke UP.

Editors and Contributors

Debashree Dattaray is Professor in Comparative Literature and Deputy Coordinator, Centre for Canadian Studies at Jadavpur University, Kolkata, India. She has been the recipient of a Fulbright Alumni Award 2019, the Shastri Mobility Programme at McGill University, CICOPS Fellowship at University of Pavia, Italy, a Fulbright-Nehru Visiting Lecturer Fellowship at UC Berkeley, the Erasmus Mundus Europe Asia Fellowship at the University of Amsterdam and Fulbright Doctoral Fellowship at State University of New York, Stony Brook. She is author of *Oral Traditions of the North East: A Case Study of Karbi Oral Traditions* (2015) and has co-edited *At the Crossroads of Literature and Culture* (2016), *Following Forkhead Paths: Discussions on the Narrative* (2017), *Ecocriticism and Environment: Rethinking Literature and Culture* (2017), *Literature and the Other Arts* (2023) and has been Issue Editor for a special volume on Indigenous Studies for *Littcrit: An Indian Response to Literature* (December 2017).

Debjani Chakrabarty is a doctoral student at the Department of History in the State University of New York—Stonybrook. Her research interests include post-colonial studies, legal history, criminality and subaltern studies.

Epsita Halder is Professor at the Department of Comparative Literature, Jadavpur University. Her monograph *Reclaiming Karbala: Nation, Islam and Literature of the Bengali Muslims* (Routledge, 2023) is on the cultural nationalism and literary modernity of the Bengali Muslims. She has been researching on the sonic and visual piety around the Muharram-complex in West Bengal, parts of which were supported by grants and fellowship of the India Foundation for the Arts, Bangalore and Sarai-CSDS Social media Fellowship, Delhi. She was the visiting fellow at the Max Weber Kolleg, University of Erfurt and School of Oriental and African Studies, University of London. She has edited and co-translated an anthology of short stories by Abul Bashar (Seagull, 2021). She has also edited an anthology of short stories by Bengali Muslim authors translated to English, *Stayed Back, Stayed On* (Orient BlackSwan, 2025).

Fatima Rizvi is Professor in the Department of English and Modern European languages, University of Lucknow. Her areas of academic interest include Urdu studies, Urdu Literature in translation and Translation studies. Her research papers have been published in journals of national and international repute and anthologies of critical essays. She has published *Beyond the stars and Other Stories* (2021, Women Unlimited), a translation of Qurratulain Hyder's *Sitaron se Aage* (1947). Currently she is co-editing *Deglobalizing Disability: Text and Context*, a collection of academic essays on disability. She is also translating stories and essays for an anthology, *Summer Medley: A Qurratulain Hyder Miscellany*. She was awarded the Meenakshi Mukherjee Memorial Prize for excellence in academic research (2018), and the Jawad Memorial Prize (2019), for Urdu–English translation.

Kakul Hai is Assistant Professor at Amity University, Uttar Pradesh. She teaches courses in Social Psychology, Counselling Psychology, Positive Psychology and Gender Psychology. Earlier, she has taught Psychology at undergraduate and graduate levels at Jamia Millia Islamia University, New Delhi, and Manipal University, Jaipur. She has published research studies in national and international journals; she has also written pieces for magazines. She has a PhD in Psychology from Amity University, Uttar Pradesh, MA in Psychology from San Diego State University, California, USA, and an MA in Anthropology from University of California San Diego, USA. She has worked as Manager of Advocacy at a Delhi-based NGO called Udayan Care where she managed an academic journal published by Sage. Recently she was inducted into the Board of Directors of Mijwan Welfare Society, Mumbai, where she was earlier involved in volunteer work. She is also involved in volunteer work with Sanatkada in Lucknow.

Kiran Keshavamurthy is Assistant Professor of English at the Department of Humanities and Social Sciences, IIT Guwahati. He completed his PhD in South and Southeast Asian Studies from University of California, Berkeley. His research interests include gender and sexuality studies, caste studies and modern Indian literatures. His first book, published in 2016 by Oxford University Press, India, is titled *Beyond Desire: Sexuality in Modern Tamil Literature.*

Krishnendu Pal is a Senior Research Fellow and doctoral candidate at the Department of Comparative Literature, Jadavpur University. He has completed his BA and MA from the same department. He also has an MA in South Asian Area Studies, from the School of Oriental and African Studies (SOAS), University of London. His areas of interest are South Asia, gender, labour, marginalised communities and queer literary criticism.

Kunal Chattopadhyay is Professor of Comparative Literature, Jadavpur University. His current research interest focuses on the multiple ways in which Socialist Realism was received and transformed in the many languages of Indian literature. He was a faculty of the Department of History, Jadavpur University during 1984–2009, before joining the Department of Comparative Literature. His publications include five books, ten edited/co-edited books and three edited translations, as well as around 80 papers and book chapters/encyclopedia articles. Major works include *The Marxism of Leon Trotsky*, *Prachin Greecer Samaj O Sanskriti* (co-authored).

Madhuja Mukherjee is Professor of Film Studies, Jadavpur University, Kolkata, India. She extends her research into art-practice, curatorial-work and filmmaking. Madhuja's recent publications are *Popular Cinema in Bengal* (2020) and *Industrial Networks and Cinemas of India* (2021). She is the writer of *Ekti Tarar Khonje* (2010), *Qissa* (2013), and director of *Carnival* (2012). She has been principal investigator of Foundation Project, Archives and Museums Programme, at the India Foundation for the Arts, Bangalore & Victoria Memorial Hall, Kolkata, 2021–22; and artistic-director of *TENT Biennale*, Kolkata.

Manas Ghosh teaches Film Studies in Jadavpur University, Kolkata. The area of his research is Contemporary East Asian Cinema. He also works in the area of alternative Indian Cinema and is now editing a book dedicated to Ritwik Ghatak's *Subarnarekha.*

Sucheta Bhattacharya is Professor in the Department of Comparative Literature at Jadavpur University, Kolkata, India. Previously she taught

English in Serampore College, University of Calcutta. Dr Bhattacharya's specialization is in the literature of mid-nineteenth and the long nineteenth century and she has published essays in her research area in several anthologies and peer-reviewed journals. She is also interested in border studies and has carried out fieldwork on the cultural expressions of Indo-Bangladesh border and is preparing a manuscript on her findings. Dr Bhattacharya also teaches Latin American Literature. She has a keen interest in translation and has contributed translated pieces to different anthologies. Some of her publications are 'What is the Kid Doing at the Border? Some Thoughts on Representations of Children in Indian and Latin American Border-themed Cinema' in *Centering Borders in Latin American and South Asian Contexts: Aesthetics and Politics of Cultural Production*, Routledge; 'The form in theatre' in *Critical Discourse in Bangla* in the series 'Critical Discourses in South Asia', Routledge; 'In Defence of Intersemiotic Translation', in *Jadavpur Journal of Comparative Literature*, no 47; 'City-Sketchers: Hootum and Boz' in *Essays and Studies, The Dickens World: Post-Imperial Readings,* no 28–29, Journal of the Department of English, Jadavpur University; 'G. W. M. Reynolds: Re-written in Nineteenth Century Bengal' in *G W M Reynolds: Fiction, Politics and the Press,* Routledge.

Urmi Sengupta is Assistant Professor in the Department of English, ICFAI University, Tripura. She received her BA, MA and PhD degrees in Comparative Literature from Jadavpur University. Her areas of research and publication include Canadian Studies, Ecocriticism, Indigenous Studies, Hindi Literature, Gender and Translation Studies.